UNIT SINGLES

THE COMPLETE STORY

INCLUDING THE TRIUMPH DERIVATIVES

Other Titles in the Crowood MotoClassics Series

UNIT SINGLES

THE COMPLETE STORY

INCLUDING THE TRIUMPH DERIVATIVES

MATTHEW VALE

THE CROWOOD PRESS

First published in 2006 by
The Crowood Press Ltd
Ramsbury, Marlborough
Wiltshire SN8 2HR

www.crowood.com

British Library Cataloguing-in-Publication Data
A catalogue record for this book is available from the British Library.

ISBN 1 86126 843 2
EAN 978 1 86126 843 3

Acknowledgements
This is my second book, and I would like to thank all those involved in its preparation. These include my wife Julia and daughter Lizzie, who have put up with me disappearing into the garage to work on the C15T or into the study to write the book. Many thanks are due to Mick Walker, for providing me with photos. Chris Burrell gave me invaluable information on B50s and access to his bikes for photos. Simon Cheney gave me some valuable insights into the competition scene from the 1960s to the present day, and pictures and anecdotes on the successful Cheney bikes. The Automobile Association archivist and the REME Museum also supplied pictures. Last but by no means least, thanks to my old school friends Peter Isted and Tony Sumner, who helped to revive some memories of our epic trips to Wales and supplied some photos from that era.

Designed and typeset by Focus Publishing, Sevenoaks, Kent

Printed and bound in Great Britain by The Cromwell Press, Trowbridge

Contents

Introduction

The BSA range of unit construction singles was in production for over fifteen years, spanning the time of BSA's peak of success to the eventual failure of the company. In its time, the range provided BSA with its basic 'bread and butter' machines, gave thousands of learners an introduction to motorcycling they will never forget (not necessarily for the right reasons!), and provided increased performance models for the new 'youth' market. The range also won BSA many national and world championship wins in the off-road arena, mobilized the British Army's Despatch Riders and gave trail riders the world over the means to further their hobby.

The range kicked off with the 250cc ohv single-cylinder C15 Star in 1958, a roadster to replace the obsolete C10 and C12 range. The engine was based on Triumph's 200cc Tiger Cub model, itself a bored-out version of the 150cc Triumph T15 Terrier. The model range also effectively replaced the 350cc BSA heavyweight single, the B31, and was quickly expanded (in early 1959) to include two off-road models aimed at competition use in trials and scrambles (motocross). The model range was further expanded in 1960 when the roadster C15's 250cc unit was bored out and lightly developed to give 350cc and was introduced as the B40 range. This new mid-range single finally replaced the BSA 500cc heavyweight single, the B33.

The off-road competition potential of the range, based on the trials and scrambles models (C15T and C15S), was recognized early on by BSA. The competition shop took and modified the C15 and competed on the trials and motocross tracks of the UK and Europe, culminating in winning the world motocross championships with unit singles in 1964 and 1965. The developments made to the works bikes to improve performance, handling and reliability were reflected in the range as the 1960s progressed.

Derived from the works scramblers, the road and trail 441cc Victor models (B44) appeared in 1967, with new competition-derived frames and engines. Alongside the B44, the 250cc range was revamped, with the new frame and heavily redesigned engines resulting in the Barracuda and Starfire models (C25 and B25). These models were 'badge-engineered' as the Triumph Trophy model (TR25W) in late 1967 – which ironically replaced the T20 Tiger Cub in the Triumph range. The final fling came with the 500cc B50 and 250cc B25 models of 1971, which sported a new oil-bearing frame, along with the new corporate running gear of Ceriani style forks and conical hub wheels. The B50 and B25 were available in road (B50SS and B25SS) and trail (B50T and B25T) versions. Badge-engineered 250cc Triumph variants (T25SS and T25T) were also produced as road and trail versions. In line with BSA's competition heritage, a 'ready to race' motocross model, the B50MX, was also produced. In 1972, the range was reduced to the B50 model only, in road, trail and competition guises. The street and trail models were deleted from the range for 1973, leaving only the B50MX competition model to soldier on alone. The final batch of B50MXs was produced in 1974, with the last bikes being badged as the Triumph TR5MX Avenger, as by then the BSA name had disappeared. A version of the B50 frame and running gear was also used on the Triumph Trophy Trail/Adventurer (TR5T), which was powered by a 500cc Triumph 'C' range twin engine. However, the model was short-lived, being introduced for the 1973 model year, and was dropped very early in the 1974 model year – production of the 1974 model only occurring during July 1973.

In its fifteen-year life, the BSA unit single range saw the fall of BSA from its position as the world's largest producer of motorcycles and a massive industrial conglomerate to a failed company. In some ways, the range mirrored the problems that the company experienced – difficulty in coming to terms with the competition and underdevelopment of the product range. Both of these problems can be attributed to increasingly poor management decision-making, which was focused on short-term gains for the shareholders rather than ensuring the long-term viability of the company for the benefit of shareholders, employees and customers alike. This issue was recognized in the early to mid 1960s, but the company had by then lost too much ground to the competition to regain its once-dominant position. At the end of its life, the BSA range of motorcycles was outdated, killed off by the Japanese competition and by its own lack of sophistication in the face of an increasingly demanding customer base.

1 Prelude and Overview

A Brief History of BSA

In 1958, the year that the unit construction singles made their appearance, BSA had been in existence in various guises for just under one hundred years. In that time, it had produced many thousands of motorbikes in all capacity ranges. The company was a huge engineering conglomerate, with interests in motorcycles, car bodies and machine tools. Its roots can be traced back to 1692, when Sir Richard Newdegate secured a contract for five Birmingham gunsmiths to build muskets for the Crown. This alliance of gunsmiths continued to produce hand-built guns for the government and private sporting market through to the middle of the nineteenth century. However, with the outbreak of the Crimean War in 1854, the demand for all types of weaponry increased enormously. To meet this demand, mechanization was required, which necessitated the adoption of precision machinery to supersede the skills of the craftsmen.

At the start of the war, therefore, fourteen of the Birmingham gunsmiths came together and set up an association, the Birmingham Small Arms Trade, to formalize the old alliance. The association recognized that to survive the alliance would have to adopt the techniques of mass-production. To achieve this end, the Birmingham Small Arms Co. Ltd was set up in 1861, with the specific remit to manufacture guns by machinery. The company bought a 25-acre greenfield site, on which the now famous Small Heath Works was constructed, and the company entered the world of government arms contracts – an unstable market with periods of furious activity to meet urgent contracts, followed by no further work for months on end. The peaks and troughs of the market led to the closure of the Small Heath factory for a year in 1878–9, and on reopening to service another government contract, the directors at last recognized the need to diversify from the company's original remit.

This change of policy led to the production of the Dicycle, designed by E. C. F. Otto, which was a two-wheeled device with the wheels on each side of the rider. Bicycle production

The BSA production facility at Small Heath, Birmingham, was massive. Note the test track to the right. The cross shows where singles were produced up to 1969 and the white square shows where the post-1970 production track was positioned.

9

An early C15, with dual-tone seat and painted wheel hubs.

and design then continued with the design and production of the world's first rear-wheel-driven 'safety' bicycle, which set the scene for the standard bicycle design still produced today. The company then started to produce many pedal cycle components, such as the wheel hubs, chain wheels and bottom brackets that were supplied to the numerous companies engaged in assembling cycles in the Birmingham area and further afield. In 1908, BSA started to take a close look at the motorized cycles that were becoming practical forms of transport. This led to the first BSA-powered two-wheeler, a single-cylinder 3½ horsepower model that was produced in 1911.

After the 1914–18 War, BSA went on to produce a range of motorcycles and in 1924 the company introduced what would become one of its most famous models, the 250cc Model B, also known as the 'Round Tank'. This machine defined the 250cc market of the time, being light, simple, reliable and possessing a good performance – all factors that BSA wanted to achieve with the C15.

The Second World War saw BSA producing the workhorse of the armed forces, the M20, a side valve 500cc machine, which, while reliable, was not the fastest nor the best-handling machine. Post-war, BSA quickly introduced a vertical twin, the 500cc A7, which sat alongside its single-cylinder 250cc, 350cc and 500cc models. The two-stroke 125cc Bantam, a design 'liberated' from DKW as war reparations, fitted the bill for a commuter. With the introduction of the 650cc A10 in 1949, BSA had most sectors of the market covered during the 1950s. The company was about to enter the 1960s with a glorious history that would give no indication of the troubles ahead.

Prelude to the C15

While the 250cc market had been one of the cornerstones of the BSA range throughout the 1920s and 1930s, the market waned in the immediate post-war years, when the 250cc class was somewhat overlooked by the buying public. The class fell between that of the cheap utility lightweights of 100cc to 200cc, mainly the preserve of the smaller manufacturers such as James, DMW and Francis-Barnett, and the more substantial 350cc and 500cc four-stroke singles marketed by the larger manufacturers such as Ariel, BSA, Norton, AJS, Matchless and Royal Enfield.

The smaller manufacturers produced a myriad small utility models, which were mainly powered by two-stroke engines from Villiers. Exceptions to this rule included BSA and Royal Enfield, which used their own make of two-stroke engines to power the BSA 125cc Bantam and the Royal Enfield 150cc Ensign and Prince models. Triumph was the only British manufacturer with a four-stroke bike in the utility market, the 150cc Terrier introduced in 1953, which was rapidly upgraded to become the 200cc Tiger Cub in 1954. However, Triumph did market the Terrier and Cub as being a cut above the other 150 and 200cc machines, placing it as a real Triumph, only smaller. This stance was justified as it did offer more refinement and performance than the Villiers-powered bikes, and it was styled to

The Triumph Tiger Cub was a 200cc lightweight four-stroke that formed the basis for the design of the C15. Pictured is a 1957 model.

resemble the larger, more glamorous bikes in the range that hopefully the small bike rider would aspire to own next.

Most of these bikes offered adequate performance (especially the Cub) for riding to

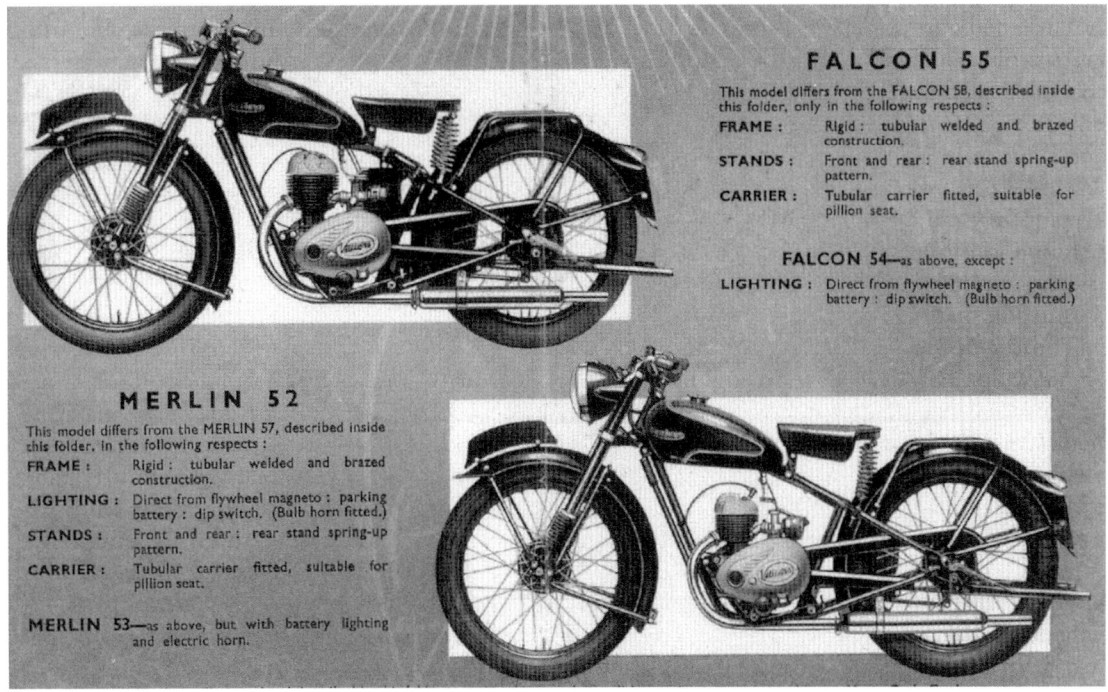

One of many makes, Francis-Barnett made lightweight motorbikes powered by Villiers engines. Illustrated are the Falcon 55 and the Merlin 52 from the 1950s.

11

The other BSA Unit Singles – The Bantam, Dandy and Beagle

BSA's unit singles did not start and end with the models addressed in this book. There were other models which used single-cylinder motors that were contemporary to the C15 and B40 models, albeit in smaller capacities than the C15s 250cc. These included the 35cc two-stroke 'Winged Wheel' cycle attachment and three 'proper' motorcycles – the ubiquitous Bantam, the Dandy and the Beagle.

The Bantam

The Bantam is probably the most famous of the three, with generations of riders (including the author) cut-

ting their teeth on the model. The Bantam has a two-stroke engine of 125, 150 or 175cc, the design of which was based on the German DKW RT125 of 1939, which was given to BSA as part of the war reparations after World War II.

The main change to the engine made by BSA was to make it as a mirror image to the original to get the gear lever on the right-hand (or foot) side. Despite this pre-war ancestry, the engine was reliable, light, relatively powerful and able to be stretched in capacity. The model was produced by BSA from 1948 (for export only) through to almost the very end, still being listed in the 1971 range. It was the small workhorse of the

The BSA Bantam D1 was a simple runabout powered by a 125cc two-stroke engine. Based on a DKW design, the bike was economical and reliable.

The Bantam grew to 175cc, gaining a swinging-arm frame and four-speed gearbox. But it just was not modern enough to compete with the Japanese in the late 1960s and its last year was 1971. The model shown is a D14/4 from 1968.

BSA range and was aimed at the ride-to-work market rather than the enthusiast. For all that, it was a faithful and reliable model and was steadily developed, from the original 125cc three-speed rigid framed models to a 175cc model with four speeds and a swinging-arm frame. However, by the end of the line the model was hopelessly uncompetitive against the Japanese opposition, both in terms of performance and sophistication. Its showroom appeal was limited when compared with the Japanese, with its need to pre-mix the oil with the petrol, no electric start or indicators and poor electrics and switchgear. Inevitably, sales suffered. While its death was mourned by many, it had reached the end of its useful life.

The Dandy

The Dandy, in contrast to the Bantam, was not a sales success. Introduced to the public at the Earls Court show in 1955, it was described as a 'Light Scooter'. The market got it in late 1956 for the 1957 model year. It adopted all of the current thinking of what was modern in motorcycling, with a step-through pressed-steel frame, leading link front forks, again in pressed steel, and a two-stroke 75cc motor with a rearwards facing cylinder fitted to the right-hand side of the swinging arm.

A fully enclosed chain drove the rear wheel on the left-hand side of the machine through a two-speed gearbox operated from a twist grip on the left-hand handlebar. The bike sported leg shields, which gave good weather protection, and had extras listed such as a rear carrier and panniers to increase its utility. But while it was not dissimilar in design to the Honda Cub,

The Dandy was one of BSA's famous mistakes. Unreliable and not stylish, it failed in the face of the Honda 50.

it did not enjoy the same degree of popularity. After disappointing sales, it was dropped from the range during 1962.

The Beagle

The BSA Beagle was introduced late in 1963 for the 1964 model year, and was the replacement for the 125cc Bantam, which was discontinued in 1963. In contrast to the Dandy, dropped the previous year, the Beagle was a 'proper' motorcycle with a spine frame and 19in diameter wheels. The bike featured a 75cc four-stroke engine that in appearance looked like a shrunken Tiger Cub engine, which was not too surprising as it had substantial design input from Edward Turner, Triumph's Managing Director and head designer. It could be argued that this design heritage gives the model a slight family link to the C15. The engine had a four-speed gearbox, with a gear-driven primary drive.

continued overleaf

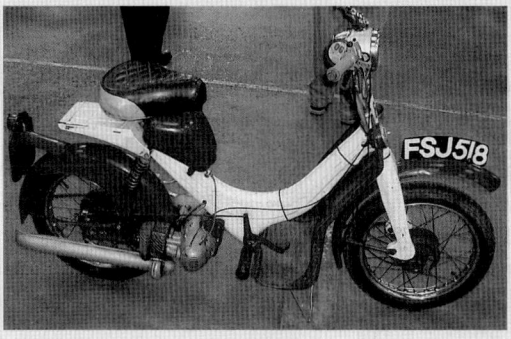

There are still some Dandys in captivity. This one was seen in 2004.

The other BSA Unit Singles – The Bantam, Dandy and Beagle *continued*

The oil system utilized a wet sump, with shared oil for the engine, gearbox and primary drive, and no external tank or oil lines. The crankcases were vertically split and featured a large sump bolted onto the bottom of the engine to hold the oil. The top end followed the design of the Tiger Cub, with two pushrod-operated valves with rocker gear mounted in the head casting.

The frame was a pressed-steel, 'T'-shaped spine type unit, with swinging-arm rear suspension and short leading link front forks. The bike had a stylish petrol tank, similarly shaped to that used on the Bantam Super of 1965 onwards, but with a painted finish and no detents for tank badges. Rather than having BSA on the tank, a scripted 'Beagle' was written on the fuel tank sides. A dual seat and passenger footrests finished off the plot. Interestingly, the bike did have a lot in common with, and looked similar to, the lightweights coming out of Japan that were starting to dominate the market sector. BSA described the bike as having: 'a first-rate performance with phenomenally low petrol consumption. Well sprung, well braked, it is light and easy to handle and completely dependable'

A last fling to generate sales was tried in 1964, with the introduction in the US Market of the 'Red Flash 75'. This was a Beagle with a metallic paint job, pin-striping on the mudguards and a chrome panel Bantam tank with proper plastic BSA tank badges. The bike was described by BSA's US publicity as a: 'New Sensation in Ultra-Lightweight Class! A real motorcycle now further developed and with sparkling new metallic

The BSA Beagle had a 75cc four-stroke engine that was similar in external appearance to the Tiger Cub's. The bike was not a success.

finish to give you the best in lightweight motorcycle pleasure.'

Despite this no-holds-barred publicity assault on the US market, the sales did not materialize and the production run was ended in August 1965 after just two seasons.

With the exception of the Bantam, all of BSA's efforts in the lightweight market during the early 1960s floundered in the wake of the competition, which consisted mainly of the lightweights introduced worldwide by the Japanese, especially Honda. BSA should have learned from this lesson, but didn't; the next target for the opposition would be the 250–500cc middle-weights.

The Red Flash was BSA's name for the Beagle in the USA. I wonder how many were sold?

work, were cheap to buy and run, were light and easy to handle and could get the owner out and about at the weekend – in effect, taking over the market that had belonged to the 250cc machines in the 1930s. The availability of these sub-250cc capacity machines, which provided performance broadly equal to a pre-war 250cc four-stroke, must have had a detrimental effect on the whole 250cc market of the early post-war years, especially for BSA, which offered at the time the C10, C11 and C12 models. These were essentially pre-WWII designs; they were of pre-unit construction with separate engine and gearbox, were relatively heavy and consequently had limited performance (especially the side valve C10). BSA's 1956 brochure gave the weight of the plunger framed C10 as 256lb (116kg) and the swinging-arm framed C12 as 312lb (141kg) – and these were dry weights, some 50–100lb (23–45kg) heavier than the smaller utility mounts. On the plus side, the bikes were robust and reliable and by the mid 1950s they were fairly modern, with battery and coil ignition, four-speed gearboxes and, in the C12's case, a swinging-arm frame. However, the use of battery and coil ignition rather than a 'proper' magneto was seen by many as an economy measure, which indeed it was.

BSA's Chief Engineer in 1953, Bert Hopwood, had recognized the need for a replacement for the company's 250 range; indeed, he had such a model under development that year. This had a single-cylinder four-stroke engine which was based on the A7 500cc twin. It was able to use many of the well-proven components from the twin and was equipped with a separate four-speed gearbox. The rolling chassis was fully up to date, with swinging-arm suspension and telescopic front forks. In his book, *Whatever Happened to the British Motorcycle Industry?* (Haynes Publications, *see* Bibliography), Hopwood indicates that three prototypes were produced and tested extensively, with good results in both reliability and performance. This testing included an endurance run at the Montlhéry track in France, where the bike lapped the course regularly at over 90mph (145km/h). However, the BSA board refused to put the machine into production, with the justification that the current C10/C11/C12 range was still 'holding its own in the market'.

The need for a replacement for the C10 and C12 ranges became more acute when, in 1956, Royal Enfield introduced a replacement for its pre-unit 250cc Clipper model, the Crusader. This was a unit construction 250cc four-stroke

By 1956, BSA's top of the range 250cc bike was the C12. Obviously a development of the C10, the C12 did feature overhead valves and swinging-arm rear suspension.

15

Announced to the world in 1956, the Royal Enfield Crusader set the design parameters for the 'new' 250cc class. These included unit construction, swinging-arm rear suspension and sleek, appealing styling.

In July 1958, Ariel (a BSA subsidiary) launched the Leader, a 250cc twin-cylinder two-stroke. It was an innovative design, with a pressed-steel frame, fully enclosed mechanics and excellent weather protection, as emphasized by the adverts!

single, which showed the way forward for the class by redefining the specification to which a modern 250cc motorcycle should conform.

The specification included unit construction, four-speed gearbox, alternator AC electrics, coil ignition, clean and tidy lines and a performance that was as good, if not better, than an average 350 of the time. Royal Enfield also produced a range of accessories for the model, including soft panniers and fairings, enhancing the model's appeal.

In addition, plans at Ariel were afoot to replace its entire range of four strokes with a 250cc two-stroke twin, the Leader. This model was designed to appeal to the mature, all-year-round 'sensible' rider, with full weather protection, clean appearance and an overall integrated scooter-like approach to motorcycle design as standard – which probably meant that it would take sales from the traditional C10/C11/C12 buyers. BSA did own Ariel at the time and must have been aware of Ariel's plans.

So, with the planned A7-based replacement for the C12 cancelled, BSA had a big problem in the mid to late 1950s. The existing 250cc pre-unit range was both expensive to make and was increasingly old-fashioned, factors that were making it uncompetitive against the emerging opposition.

Another issue was the looming prospect of legislation in the UK limiting learner motorcyclists to bikes of up to 250cc capacity. This law was due to be enacted in 1962. BSA obviously recognized that this would change the 250cc class overnight – most young men getting their first bike would want one that was as large as the law would allow and with as high a performance as possible. So the need for a competitive model in the 250cc market was becoming more urgent. The solution was found by looking to BSA's partner company, Triumph, and Edward Turner. The plan was to base a new 250cc model on Triumph's lightweight Tiger Cub. The Triumph Tiger Cub

The Royal Enfield Crusader engine of 1956 was an exceptionally clean and sleek design for the time.

was a 200cc overhead valve unit construction single, available in both commuting and sports models, and styled to match the other models in Triumph's range. It was light (around 220lb [100kg]) and despite its lack of capacity was substantially faster (on paper) than the then current BSA 250s in both acceleration and top speed – important factors in the increasingly youth-oriented marketplace. So the go-ahead was given for the development of the C15, the layout of which was based on the Cub. The development was carried out swiftly, being completed in 1958. The result was the C15, the first of the BSA unit singles, and it was a good, if not an outstanding, machine.

It had a unit construction engine, modern, clean styling, weighed 280lb (127kg) and had good performance, with a power output of about 15bhp. Top speed was just over 70mph (113km/h), with a comfortable cruising speed of 60mph (97km/h), quite respectable for the time. This basic model was destined to provide the starting point for a major programme of development, with capacity and power outputs eventually doubling. However, the path from the basic model was far from easy, with many

The C15 was a welcome addition to the BSA range. It was a modern design that at last gave BSA a model to compete in the 250cc market.

changes having to be made to correct faults and bring the product up to specification, rather than improving an already good product.

So the C15 had a hasty birth and a difficult upbringing. A typical example of this was the failure of the kick-starter pawls on the first bikes as a result of inadequate hardening – the whole of the initial production run had to have the faulty parts replaced. An apocryphal tale, which may well have a basis in truth, was that Bob Currie, a notable journalist of the time, had the dubious honour of discovering the fault as the kick-starter failed as he prepared to test the first bike off the line! The competition had hotted up as well, with Ariel introducing an unfaired sports version of the Leader, named the Arrow, at the end of 1959.

Different market issues drove the need for a replacement of BSA's offering in the 350cc class. While this segment of the market was viewed at the time as the sensible 'tourer' class, it was in decline in the UK, with the modern 250cc and larger 500cc machines taking its traditional customers. However, despite the declining numbers, the class still took significant numbers of machines and was worth pursuing, especially in the important USA market, where a 350cc machine was regarded

The Ariel Arrow was a naked version of the Leader. It was aimed at the emerging youth market, especially as the UK's new learner law was imminent, limiting learner riders to machines with a maximum capacity of 250cc.

18

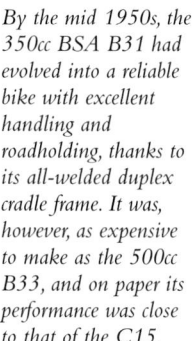

By the mid 1950s, the 350cc BSA B31 had evolved into a reliable bike with excellent handling and roadholding, thanks to its all-welded duplex cradle frame. It was, however, as expensive to make as the 500cc B33, and on paper its performance was close to that of the C15.

as an entry-level starter bike. BSA's offering in the 350cc class in 1958 was the pre–unit heavyweight B31, which was powered by an engine of pre-war ancestry.

This engine had started as a 350cc, then been stretched into a 500cc unit as well, but in contrast to the British bikes of the 1950s and 1960s, was built to take the stresses involved in the increase in capacity. The bike also had heavyweight running gear, which was common to the 500cc B33, and consequently carried a lot of weight. Along with the increasingly archaic pre-unit construction, it also had magneto ignition and dynamo electrics (although by 1958 it had coil ignition and a Lucas alternator, saving some cost and weight) and would have cost as much to make as its bigger brother, the B33. However, on the plus side it had an all-welded frame, modern swinging-arm suspension and a racing pedigree through the Gold Star range, with which it had many parts in common. While it was popular with the punters, being reliable with reasonable performance, its pre-WWII design left it heavy at 402lb (182kg), expensive to produce and it was becoming very old fashioned. While the competition was not as great as in the 250cc market, the B31 was obsolete by the end of the 1950s, with the new range of unit 250cc

bikes offering much the same performance with lower costs, albeit at the expense of reliability and robustness.

By the autumn of 1959, the 350cc B31 model had disappeared from the brochures, effectively replaced by the C15. It was not until mid 1960 that BSA's 350cc replacement model appeared. BSA followed the trend set by Royal Enfield of making a 350cc machine based on an enlarged 250cc, rather than basing the class on the current 500cc range. The result of this approach was the B40, which was the first major development of the C15 line. The new model was achieved at minimal development cost by increasing the C15's capacity to 350cc and making some modifications to the running gear, such as increasing the wheel size by 1in to 18in, and fitting a larger 7in diameter front brake. Thus BSA was able to produce a new 350cc model with a modern, clean, unit design, which, being based on the C15, was substantially cheaper to produce – and had minimal development costs. This approach went one step further when the B33 500cc single was dropped from the range completely in 1961, leaving the customer in the market for a 500cc machine with the option of the 350cc unit single with its similar performance to the 500cc B33, or the A7 500cc twin.

In a way, the unit single range reflected many of the reasons for the fall of the company. In conception, the design of the model was not new but based on a previous model – in this case, the Triumph Tiger Cub and Terrier range. The model was developed extensively but not always successfully to meet the increasing demands for performance and reliability that the market was demanding. This demand was driven in part by the increasing use of motorcycles as leisure vehicles and by the increasingly capable and affordable machines being imported from Japan. The model was developed in an evolutionary manner, with even virtually new designs showing a close relationship to the previous model, rather than reassessing what the markets really wanted and redesigning accordingly. By the mid 1960s, the customer base was abandoning the BSA offering in favour of the reliable, high-performance models being produced by the Japanese. Even the all-new Starfire/Barracuda in 1967, with its new frame and totally revamped engine, was still regarded by many as merely a development of the C15.

It is arguable that the engine design, with its one-piece forged crank and shell big end, was a retrograde step. The last C15 engine was closely based on the competition models with a roller big end and oil end feed crank, and was pretty much bulletproof, unlike the B25, which had a definite weakness in its big end. Despite this, when BSA eventually revamped its whole range in 1971, it ignored the maxim 'if it ain't broke, don't fix it', keeping the suspect motors but replacing the frames and running gear – exactly the opposite to what it should have done. No one had complained about the Starfire's handling; it was the engine that was compared unfavourably with the Japanese units, in terms of reliability, sophistication and performance. This sorry tale really sums up what was wrong with BSA – it had not moved with the times and possibly did not recognize that the opposition had raised the

The Automobile Association and the B40

The Automobile Association (AA) in the UK is a service provider to the motorist and one service it has provided since its early days is roadside breakdown assistance to members. During the 1950s the AA carried out Road Patrols along most trunk roads and other busy routes. The machines it chose to take on this task were the side-valve BSAs of firstly 500cc (the M20) and latterly 600cc (the M21), both equipped with a large box sidecar to carry tools, fuel and spares for the stranded customer. By the start of the 1960s the M series BSAs were obsolete and the ubiquitous Austin Mini Van had started to take their place in the AA's armoury. However, in 1963–4 the AA bought a small fleet of fifty BSA B40s to provide a replacement for the side valves and as cover for the holiday routes carrying heavy traffic.

Preceding this purchase was the appearance at the 1960 Earls Court show of a C15 equipped with an AA patrol box sidecar fitted with a Watsonian single point fixing chassis. Although the AA did not purchase any C15s thus equipped, the emergence of the B40 in late 1960 resulted in a bike that suited the AA's requirements better. These bikes were lightly modified from the standard specification, with fairings, single seats, panniers and provision for radio equipment.

The AA's B40s were well equipped with fairings and radio equipment. (Automobile Association (AA) Archive)

The intention of the AA was to use the bikes as solo (that is, without sidecars) to enable them to come to the assistance of members who broke down during busy periods such as bank holiday weekends, when the build-up of traffic could impede the progress of a combination.

However, the lightweight machines were not as reliable as the heavyweight side-valve singles they replaced. Problems appeared, with the rear suspension not being strong enough and the fuel tanks splitting. The rear suspension used the non-adjustable Girling units off the standard B40 and these were not up to handling the extra weight of the equipment carried, while the design of the tank top radio installation was also at fault.

Although introduced as solo machines, the AA's B40s were set up so that a sidecar could be swiftly attached should the need arise, for example in winter use when the extra stability of three wheels would be appreciated. The sidecar was the large fibreglass unit that had previously been used with the M21s, so it would be fair to assume that performance of the B40 with the sidecar fitted would not be brisk!

Overall, the use of the B40 was not considered to be a great success and the AA started to replace all of its motorcycles with the Austin Mini Van – the cheap, reliable, compact car that was blamed by many as the vehicle that killed the British motorcycle market. In the case of the AA's use of bikes they were right!

The radio speaker is prominent above the wider than standard handlebars. (Automobile Association (AA) Archive)

The sidecar from the old M20/21 outfits could be attached to the B40. (Automobile Association (AA) Archive)

stakes to such a level that BSA's current models just could not cut it in the new market. Misplaced and inadequate investment in the product and poor market sense had doomed BSA years before its eventual disappearance in the early 1970s.

Overview of the Unit Single Range

The BSA unit single range was introduced to the public in September 1958, with the announcement being reported in the United Kingdom's two weekly motorcycle papers, *The Motorcycle* and *Motorcycling*. BSA's policy during the post-war years was to introduce a new model range to the market by starting off with a 'cooking' model – invariably a softly tuned tourer/commuter model – and then increase the number of models in the range by introducing sportier and specialist models.

This was the case with the introduction of the C15 range in 1958 and the A50/A65 range in 1962. The new model was intended to replace the then current but obsolete C12 250cc model, the final overhead valve and swinging-arm frame derivative of the C10/C11/C12 range, whose ancestry could be traced back to before the Second World War. The new 'range' initially comprised a single model, called the C15 Star. As was to be expected, it was ideally suited to the touring and commuter role, with a softly tuned motor, heavily valanced mudguards, a decent capacity fuel tank and 'sit up and beg' riding position. A low saddle height was achieved by specifying 17in diameter wheels.

The C15 Star was light at 280lb (127kg) (some 30lb [13kg] lighter than the outgoing C12), handled well and, probably most important of all for BSA, was cheaper to produce than the outgoing range. The model range took on the then current trends for AC electrics and unit construction, whereby the engine and gearbox were contained in the same set of castings. This alone gave substantial savings in both cost and weight when compared with the earlier pre-unit ranges and enabled the use of a smaller and lighter frame to carry the engine unit, with no need for separate engine plates to join the engine and

This well-known BSA publicity shot shows Brian Martin, the Competition Shop Manager, on the new C15. An earlier BSA 250cc model is alongside for comparison.

gearbox, again saving weight. The substitution of a crankshaft-driven Lucas alternator and coil ignition meant that the dynamo and magneto of the older ranges could be discarded as well, although the outgoing C12 series had been equipped with AC electrics and coil ignition.

The range started with a single roadster model, the C15 Star, but was quickly expanded in 1959 to provide two specialist off-road bikes, the C15T (trials) and C15S (scrambler) models. For 1962, the SS80 was to provide a road sports version, with an implied top speed of 80mph (129km/h). In the US, the range soon featured on-/off-road 'Trials Enduro' models, based on the competition models that would be termed trail bikes today, as well as out and out off-road competition models. The C15 range was finally killed off in 1967, with the introduction of the B25/C25 Range.

The 350cc B40 Star was added to the range in 1960, effectively replacing the B31 in the BSA line-up. This was heavily based on the C15 and was very similar in appearance, but sported a 350cc motor and 18in wheels.

Overall weight went up to 300lb (136kg) and it had a 7in diameter front brake. The B40 Star stayed in production until 1965, although limited numbers were made up to 1967 in both on- and off-road models. An extensively modified version of the B40, the WD B40, was produced for the military market from 1967

The BSA production line in 1964–5, showing the final stages of assembly for B40s.

through to the early 1970s. It featured the B40 350cc motor, but the running gear was based on the competition-based frame used for the B25/B44 range. A 'civilianized' version, the B40 Rough Rider, was also produced and was aimed at the export market – with Australian sheep farmers being targeted by the publicity material.

The UK model C25 Barracuda and the US model B25 Starfire range were introduced in 1967. The UK Barracuda had a rapid name change, becoming the B25 Starfire for 1968. The bike was all new, but the engine shared the basic layout and dimensions of the C15 unit, while the frame was based on the C15S scram-

The BSA Rough Rider was a 'civilianized' WDB40. It was aimed at Commonwealth markets such as Australia and New Zealand, where there was a need for cross-country machines to round up livestock.

New for 1967, the US B25 Starfire was a radically styled replacement for the C15. This launch picture shows the steel fork shrouds that would be replaced the following year with rubber bellows.

bles item. The model was a high-performance road bike, set up for road use, although some late Starfires were configured for on-/off-road use with a high-level exhaust pipe.

There was a major problem with the bike, in that it was plagued by a weakness in the big end. This was a plain bearing that found it hard to cope with the combination of a 10:1 compression ratio, poor oil filtration and inexperienced young learner riders who could not resist the 9,000rpm capability of the engine! At this time, the B25 range also spawned a badge-engineered Triumph derivative aimed at the trail on-/off-road market, the

The Triumph TR25W Trophy was a replacement for the Tiger Cub. Introduced in 1968, the model was closely based on the B25 but with a styling makeover, as shown by this 1969 model.

The B44 was renamed Shooting Star in the US for 1968. This is a 1968 model – very similar in appearance to the Starfire.

The Victor Enduro was a true trail bike, designed for the American market. With its macho off-road looks, it sold well.

TR25W Trophy. This bike was listed for the 1968 model year and (somewhat ironically) replaced the Triumph Cub as Triumph's 'learner' or introductory model.

Parallel to the C15 being replaced by the B25, the B40 was replaced with the 441cc B44 range. This was made up of two models, the off-road Victor and the road-going Shooting Star (UK)/Victor Roadster (USA) in 1967.

Both models shared the frame and running gear of the B25, and the Shooting Star/Victor Roadster shared the Starfire's styling, with low-level exhaust, small fibreglass fuel tank and large side panels in the same material. The Victor was a true dual-purpose trail bike, with styling based on the racing scramblers. Its small rounded alloy tank, wide handlebars and up-swept exhaust was widely admired at the time.

The Isolastic B50

In 1974, NVT Ltd was casting around the remaining assets of the once-huge group to try to salvage something from the wreckage. One project among many was to investigate the feasibility of rubber-mounting the B50 engine using the Norton Commando Isolastic system. Denis Poore, the then boss of NVT, dictated that there were to be two versions of the bike developed in isolation, with two bikes being developed and built at the BSA (as was) Kitts Green Research and Development centre on the outskirts of Birmingham, and a third being developed by Alan Sargent at the Norton factory in Wolverhampton. The objective was to create a cheap, sporty road bike that could use existing components.

The two sites adopted a different approach to the project. The Kitts Green project, also known as Project P92, used the aborted BSA Fury/Triumph Bandit frame and running gear, with the isolastic mountings grafted on the front and rear of the engine. The engine canted forwards to create a sporty looking bike and to provide room for an electric starter in the future. The original prototype also had a one into two exhaust system, using Norton annular discharge silencers (the 'black cap' type), one on each side to cut down the noise. By all accounts, the Fury/Bandit frame, designed by Rob North (of BSA/Triumph Triple racers frame fame) handled very well. The Umberslade designed front forks and conical hub front 8in TLS brake also worked well in the package.

The prototype developed at Norton's Wolverhampton plant used a standard B50 frame but with lowered rear suspension, slightly shortened front forks and an

The P92 Isolastic B50 prototype certainly looked good. Sammy Miller's example wears Norton badges. The use of the Bandit/Fury frame is obvious due to the twin down tubes.

Drive-side shows the left-hand side gear change and the forward tilt of the engine in the frame.

The front engine mount was a large tube, designed to accommodate the rubber bushes.

AJS Stormer type swinging arm. The Stormer swinging arm was used as the rear isolastic mount precluded the use of the standard snail cam adjuster on the swinging-arm pivot. The engine was mounted upright in the frame and a front disc brake was used. A single cutdown Commando Mk 3 silencer was employed and the bike was ready for road testing.

When they were finished, the two types of bike were set head to head at the MIRA test venue, with tester Bob Manns doing the comparison. The result was that the Bandit/Fury framed bike was considered to be better on the road, while the B50 framed one was better off-road – all in all, not that surprising considering the ancestry of the two frames! However, the project was shelved as a result of the disintegration of the NVT empire and no further work was done on the concept.

Amazingly, all three prototypes survived, although one of the Kitts Green bikes was damaged in the fire at the UK's National Motorcycle Museum in September 2003. The Kitts Green bike pictured is from Sammy Miller's fine museum at New Milton, Hants, UK, while the B50-framed bike is, at the time of writing, with a private collector in the UK.

The revamped 1971 models were radically different to the previous range. The huge lozenge-shaped silencer with its stainless steel heat guard was certainly different.

The range included a works replica 441cc model, the Victor Grand Prix from 1965–7, which gave the clubman a competitive scrambler, in the spirit of the preceding C15S.

The final revamp of the range was in 1971, replacing all the existing B25, TR25 and B44 models. The range comprised 250cc road

The last unit single produced was the B50MX, albeit in Triumph colours as the TR5MX. The bike is Chris Burrell's 1971 B50MX.

and trail bikes from BSA and Triumph, as well as a 500cc in road, trail and competition trim from BSA. The engines were developments of the existing units, but the frame and running gear were all new, with a common frame that held the oil, the new corporate forks and conical hub wheels, and 'Street Scrambler' styling.

The final incarnation of the bikes caused some raised eyebrows in the motorcycling community due to the road versions (or Street Scramblers) of the BSA 250 and 500 being called the 'Gold Star'. Trail versions of the BSA were called 'Victor', the Triumph road bike (T25SS) was called the 'Blazer' and the trail bike (T25T) was the 'Trail Blazer'. The final bike in the range was the B50MX, a pure off-road competition machine. The 250cc bikes were discontinued at the start of the 1972 model year, with the B50SS being the only model offered in the UK in 1972, with the SS, T and MX still on sale in the US.

For 1973, the only BSA machine offered was the B50MX; finally, in 1974, the BSA B50MX was discontinued, with the final batch being badged as the Triumph TR5MX Avenger.

2 Model Development

Introduction

The BSA unit singles ranged in size from 250cc to 500cc and were in production from 1958–74. In that time there was a large number of different models produced, with many variants on the main models. The range expanded from the single 1958 C15 to a vast number of variants in the mid 1960s, then started to decline, with only one model still in production for 1974 – and that was badged as a Triumph. As this rise and fall occurred, it mirrored the fall of the BSA company itself.

The BSA model year needs an explanation as well. The factory worked a yearly cycle, from August through to July. During the production line's shut-down for the summer break, it was updated with the tooling and parts for the next year's range, with production then restarting after the holiday with the next year's models. Hence the model year followed this cycle, running from the August of the preceding year to the July of the 'current' year. So, in the case of the C15, the model was introduced in September 1958, which was just after the start of the 1959 model year. A machine built in the year 1959 will therefore be a '1959 model' if it was built between January and July 1959 or a '1960 model' if it was built between August and December 1959. In this book all dates relating to a specific model refer to the BSA model year, unless otherwise stated. Note that the date the machine was first put on the road may be later than the model year, as new bikes could sit around in dealers for a while. The only way to determine what model year a machine was made in is to check the engine and frame numbers and correlate them back to the factory records, a service that the BSA Owners Club provides.

The unit single range can be split into three distinct phases – the original C15 and B40 from 1958–66, the C25/B25/TR25 and B44 with their scrambles-derived running gear and heavily modified engines for 1967 through to 1970 and the final oil-in-frame models for 1971 through to the demise of BSA in 1973. The next sections of this chapter take each of these phases in turn, describing the various

BSAs were exported all over the world. Here is an early C15 in West Africa.

29

models BSA produced and the changes made to each model year on year. The following chapter then gives a technical description of the engines and running gear that were used to create the model range and provides a description of the development of the mechanical parts during the lifespan of the range.

The C15 250cc Models

The C15 Star 1959–67

1959 Models

The basic Star model was introduced towards the end of 1958 and hence came into being during the 1959 model range. From that date on the C15 Star formed the 'cooking' model of the range – the softly tuned, good all-rounder that was aimed at the ride-to-work rider who wanted reliability, dependability and

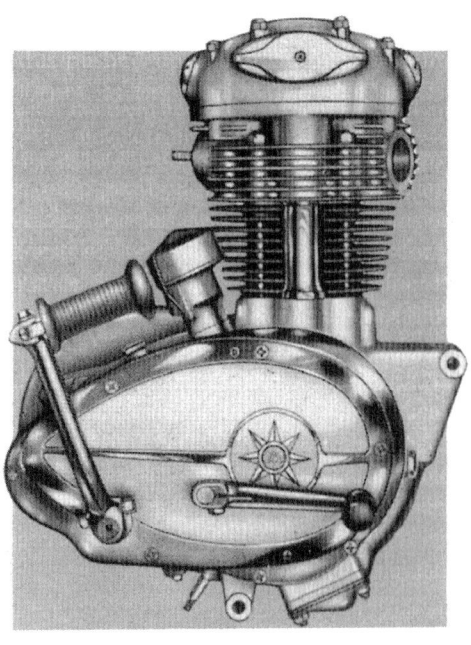

The C15 engine with its gearbox 'in unit' was a sleek design and very similar in appearance to the Triumph Tiger Cub unit. The vertical barrel was the main difference.

comfort rather than performance. In today's parlance it was a 'base' model, representing good value for money but little excitement.

The engine in the C15 Star was very similar in layout to the Triumph Tiger Cub, except that the cylinder was positioned vertically rather than leaning forwards as in the Cub. The unit was a single-cylinder 250cc unit with pushrod operated overhead valves (full details of the engine can be found in Chapter 3) and a four-speed gearbox. For this first incarnation of the Star the engine was softly tuned, with a 7.25:1 compression ratio and a claimed power output of around 15bhp at 7,000rpm. The crank was supported by a roller bearing on the drive side and a bush on the timing side. The big-end bearing was a bush; oil was fed to it under pressure through the timing-side bush. Primary drive made do without a tensioner, the justification for this being the closeness of the engine and gearbox centres at 5⅞in (149mm).

Carburetion was taken care of with an Amal Monobloc carburettor, type 375/34 with a ⅞in bore. A flat, round wire gauze air filter was fitted into the central fairing between the side panel and oil tank and was connected to the carburettor with a rubber hose.

The frame was made from steel tube and was of a hybrid construction that combined old and current technology, using both brazed lugs and welds to join the collection of tubes together. It was made in two halves, which were then bolted together and comprised a main loop and rear subframe. The main loop carried the engine, front forks, petrol and oil tanks and the swinging arm, while the rear subframe carried the rear suspension units and the seat. The main loop was brazed lug construction, where tubes were bent into shape and then joined together using cast-iron 'lugs' into which the tubes were pinned and then brazed. The rear subframe was of both welded and lugged construction and was bolted to the front loop at three points, the nose of the seat and at each end of the swinging-arm pivot. This gave a strong and reasonably rigid assembly, but at the cost of a relatively complex and labour-intensive production method. The construction method also resulted in a weight penalty over an all-welded frame and the bolted-on rear subframe was not as rigid as it would have been had it been welded on. The main loop also carried lugs for the centre stand and the (optional) side stand.

The pivot of the rear suspension's swinging arm fitted tightly into a cast lug at the bottom of the main loop's seat tube. It was braced by bolting the rear subframe arms' lower ends onto the ends of the swinging-arm pin. However, this probably did not impart much more rigidity into the design, as the relatively light subframe relied on the single front top bolt-up joint to resist twisting.

The electrics followed the trends set by the 'economy' model line of the time. It was a 6V system, with power supplied by a Lucas alternator fixed to the end of the crankshaft in the primary chain case. The alternator charged a 5amp hour battery, with a full wave rectifier converting the alternating current (AC) to direct current (DC). Ignition was by coil, with the contact breaker points housed in a 'distributor' mounted behind the barrel. All in all, the specification for the electrical system was much the same as for the preceding C12, but worked well enough.

The bike featured heavily valanced mudguards, painted the same colour as the fuel tank. The oil tank on the right and the side panel on the left were joined by a steel pressing under the seat nose, which carried the air cleaner and ignition switch. This arrangement made for a very tidy midriff, but had some issues of availability for the battery.

Fibreglass reinforced plastic leg shields were listed as an extra, at a cost of £5 19s 6d (£5.97 decimal); unusually for the time, they were illustrated in the main brochure for the

The 1958 C15 Star was an attractive and well-styled bike. Note the two-tone seat and ignition 'distributor' or points housing behind the barrel.

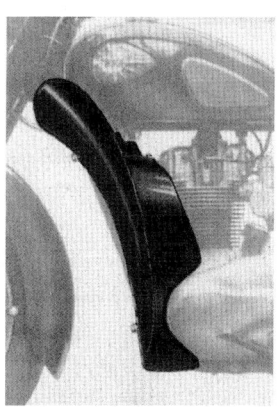

Leg shields were offered as one of a range of accessories.

Unit and Pre-Unit Construction

Up until the late 1950s the majority of British motor-cycles of 250cc and above were four-stroke singles or twins and virtually all had separate engines and gear-boxes. This reflected the industry of the time, with a number of specialist companies such as Albion and Burman producing gearboxes and supplying them to the motorcycle manufacturers. Interestingly, both BSA and Triumph were making their own gearboxes during the 1950s. Separate gearboxes provided manufacturers with flexibility and eased the design process, as the engine designer could just ask for a suitable gearbox in terms of strength and number of ratios. However, the use of a separate gearbox necessitated a method of moving the gearbox on its mountings to adjust the pri-mary chain, requiring a set of relatively complex mounting plates to allow this to happen, and a separate primary chain case, again with provision to allow movement between the engine and gearbox for chain adjustment. All this added weight and complexity to the

machines of the day and added to the possibility of oil leaks due to the number of adjoining components. An exception to this state was the New Imperial company, with the 3.50hp Unit-Plus Model 40 of the 1930s, a 346cc sporting single which featured unit construction.

As the 1950s progressed, there was a drive to cut down on the cost and complexity of the product and the use of a single casting to carry both the engine and the gearbox was one of the many measures adopted to achieve this aim. The use of such a cast-ing was described at the time as putting the engine and gearbox in a single unit – hence the term 'unit construction'. What had gone before was then termed 'pre-unit'; the author has been unable to find any reference to the term before the late 1950s/early 1960s in contemporary literature. While unit con-struction had been used for lightweights (notably in BSA's case in the Bantam, which was originally a

The old B31/B33 had complex engine plates to join the engine and gearbox together and allow the gearbox to move to adjust the primary chain.

TRIUMPH
The Best Motorcycle in the World

The Triumph 500cc 5TA was a development of the 21, the first unit construction 350cc twin.

The C15 was a very successful bike, especially in competition. A major contributor to its success was its unit construction.

DKW design, it had not been used for any mainstream middleweights or heavyweights before the 1950s. Royal Enfield produced what was probably the first modern 250cc unit construction motorcycle with its Crusader model in 1956, two years after the appearance of the Triumph Terrier/Cub 150cc/200cc line. The Triumph 21 350cc model, announced in 1957, was the first mainstream middleweight twin to adopt unit construction, followed by the BSA C15 unit single in 1958.

These unit construction bikes were lighter, less complex and hence cheaper to manufacture, as well as being easier for the owner to service and keep oil-tight. They also usually took advantage of knowledge gained in engine design to produce more power than the previous models. For example, the 1958 C12 weighed 312lb (142kg) and gave 11bhp, while the first C15, also of 1958, weighed 280lb (127kg) and gave 15bhp, giving it a clear advantage in the performance stakes.

However, although the use of unit construction by BSA and Triumph was a significant step forward from the pre-units that preceded them, it must be recognized that the step was evolutionary not revolutionary. While unit construction enabled the primary drive centres to be fixed, the basic architecture of the engines produced in Britain remained unchanged, with separate engine, primary drive and gearbox, each with their own individual compartments within the cases and all with vertically split covers – a primary cause of oil leaks. It was left to the Japanese and Italians to show the way forward with unit construction – horizontally split cases, with the engine, gearbox and primary drive all sharing the same engine oil. Such an engine configuration is the one most commonly used in motorcycles in the 2000s.

range. This helps to indicate the market at which BSA was aiming – the tourer/commuter.

Overall dimensions of the Star models were wheelbase 51¼in (1,300mm), ground clearance 5in (127mm), overall length 78in (1,980mm) and dry weight 280lb (127kg). The Star was introduced to the US market very early in its model year, for 1959. The original US model Star was very close in specification to the UK model, with the most noticeable difference being the high-rise 'Western' style handlebars, rather than the 'sensible' UK and general export low-rise bars!

1960 and 1961 Models
For the 1960 and 1961 model years there were few documented changes, the main one being a change of option colour from Turquoise Green to Almond Green. The other main change in the appearance of the model was the removal of the black painted finish on the brake plates and hub trims, leaving a rough natural alloy finish on the inner brake plates and dull chrome on the inner of the trim plates. The unpolished chrome finish was accurately described as silver sheen in the brochure and did look surprisingly good.

1962 and 1963 Models
For 1962–3 the major mechanical change was the adaptation of the slipper primary chain tensioner already seen on the SS80, which improved the life expectancy of the duplex primary chain and the chain cases. With a correctly tensioned primary, the quality of the gear change was also improved. The tensioner can be retrofitted to the earlier models and is a worthwhile modification. Midway through the 1962 model year the compression ratio was raised slightly to 7.5:1. The ignition switch, still mounted on the midriff shroud, gained a key, but did not offer a great deal of security as a screwdriver worked just as well! Colours available were now red, Nutley Blue or black.

1964 Model
The 1964 model year at last saw the adoption of the caged roller big-end bearing, which enabled the engine's compression ratio to be safely increased to 8:1, which, with the increase in 1962, is indicative of the gradual 'hotting up' of the range. The traditionally styled 3gal (13.6ltr) BSA chromed tank, with pear-shaped badges as used on the SS80, was also specified and the 'eyebrow' tank discontinued. Paint was Royal Red or Blue.

The C15 Star hit the US market for 1959. The main modification made to the UK model was the high 'Western' style handlebars.

The 1965 model C15 Star lost the distributor and the points moved to the end of the cam shaft, covered by a chrome plate. This made the engine look much more modern. (Mick Walker)

The final C15 Star model was built in 1967 for export only and was not listed in the UK. The model differed little in appearance from the original 1958 model, but featured extensive mechanical rework as a result of experience in competition.

1965 Model

The 1965 model year saw extensive engine changes, with the deletion of the mushroom type contact breaker points housing the 'distributor' and the relocation of the points into the timing cover. This gave a much more modern look to the motor, mimicking the works models and giving more precise ignition control as there was much less slack in the new mechanism. The clutch mechanism was modified to a rack and pinion arrangement, with the cable operating an external arm on the top of the timing cover, giving good access for cable changes. The gearbox was modified to give a toothed quadrant to operate the kick-starter, which required a longer main shaft. Standard paint was Royal Red with an option of black.

1966 and 1967 Models

The 1966 model year saw the C15 available only in Royal Red, but midway through the model year, the 'G' type engine (suffixed C15G), with its scrambles-derived bottom end with roller and ball-bearing main bearing, was introduced.

The final year that the C15 Star was listed was 1967 and only in the non-US export brochure – it was not listed in either the UK or US literature. The bike was basically

The 1962 SS80 sports a larger fuel tank with round badges and new transfers on the side panels. It retains the somewhat unsporting C15 Star mudguards. (Mick Walker)

identical to the 1966 model, still using the 'G' specification engine. By the 1968 model year, the bike had been quietly dropped from the range. The only major change for the 1967 year was the pattern of the fuel tank's paint scheme – the chromed sides forming a somewhat Triumph-like scallop above and below the tank badge, rather than being a large oval pattern as before. The top of the tank and the sides behind the badges were painted, along with the mudguards, oil tank and side panel, in Royal Red, Sapphire Blue or black.

The C15 SS80 and Sportsman 1961–6

Introduction – 1961 and 1962 Models
The C15 Sport Star, model 'C15SS 80', was introduced in the spring of 1961, halfway through the model year, with the first road tests appearing in the summer. This was the model that the youth of the time had been waiting for. It was aimed at the sports market and marked the start of the range's up-rating to meet the increasing competition from high-performance models from both home and foreign manufacturers. The basic bike was very

closely based on the C15 Star, but, with a tuned engine and some changes to the styling and finish, it came across as a model in its own right. The most significant difference from the C15 Star was a new 3gal (13.6ltr) fuel tank – which was the 'trademark' BSA design with chromed sides and round BSA Star badges, as seen on the B40. The tank retained both the styling strips across its top and the BSA central mounting. Other stylistic changes were optional chromed mudguards, although these were still the same heavily valanced design as on the C15 Star, and an all-black colour scheme. Decals, proclaiming 'Sports Star 80' adorned the side panel and oil tank; the dual seat was still in two-tone grey.

The engine was tuned, with larger diameter inlet valve (increased in diameter by $\frac{1}{16}$in), heavy duty valve springs and a 10:1 compression ratio and sports camshaft, taken from the scrambles model. The 10:1 compression ratio was quickly reduced to 8.75:1 by the factory only weeks after the launch and it is unclear if any 10:1 models were sold. The most significant change was the adoption of a roller-bearing big end, although the timing-side

Looking on the bright side – the heavily valanced mudguards could be chromed at extra cost on the SS80. This is another view of a 1962 SS80 with the optional chromed guards. (Mick Walker)

main bearing bush remained. The carburettor was increased in size to a 1 1/16in Amal Monobloc, to cope with the tuned state of the engine. The primary drive gained a slipper tensioner, and the four-speed gearbox gained a set of close-ratio gears.

The bike's performance was improved, with a surge of power between 3,000–4,000rpm and an output of approximately 20bhp at 7,000rpm. These improvements led to BSA claiming a top speed of 80mph (129km/h) – and contemporary road tests actually managed 83mph (134km/h), so the model lived up to its SS80 title. Despite this increase in performance, the brakes remained the same 6in units as fitted to the C15 Star. The bike continued largely unchanged into the 1962 model year.

C15 SS80 1963 and 1964 Models

For the 1963 model year, the engine was somewhat detuned, with the compression ratio dropping to a more manageable 8.75:1. The fuel tank badges changed to be pear-shaped, while the US models gained the legally required rear grab rail.

For the 1963 and 1964 model years the

finish was either as 1961 (all black), or there was an option of a bright blue (Flamboyant Blue) finish for the fuel tank, oil tank, side panel and central joining strip. The model at last gained some sportier slim mudguards for the 1963 model year, which lost the valances of the standard C15 Star and helped to differentiate the model as the sporting version of the C15 range. However, chrome plating was still an option for these mudguards.

C15 SS80 1965 Model

For the 1965 model year, the major changes was to delete the ignition tower and relocate the contact breakers into a new compartment in the timing case, driving them directly from the camshaft. A new mechanical advance/retard unit was fitted behind the points cover. The new mechanism was a lot more precise in operation than the previous ignition tower, with less complexity and backlash. It also used fewer parts and must have been significantly cheaper to produce.

By now, the US models were sporting the Lucas type 679 'tit' rear light, with its pointed round lens protruding from an 'n'-shaped

The evolution continued with the introduction of the points inside the 'F' motor in 1965.

For the US the SS80 was very similar to the UK model. High bars, separate headlamp and a different rear light are the main differences; mechanically, they were identical.

The C15 Sportsman replaced the SS80 for 1966, with a separate chromed headlamp. With the introduction of the 'G' motor with its end feed crank the final models were the ultimate C15. (Mick Walker).

reflector that was mounted on an attractive alloy carrier. As usual, the UK customers had to put up with the traditional pressed-steel combined rear number plate and Lucas 564 rectangular light.

C15 Sportsman 1966 Model

For the 1966 model year the SS80 was replaced by the '250 Sportsman', which was a lightly updated SS80, sporting a BSA corporate 'humped back' black vinyl dual seat, a separate chromed headlamp which still carried the small 3in speedometer and a chrome-plated top yoke cover. The SS80's close ratio gearbox was discarded for a set of standard ratios and the overall gearing was lowered to preserve the snappy acceleration of the sports model. A new transfer was placed on the side panel and oil tank to read 'BSA Sportsman', with a picture of a rider clutching a trophy. The most significant change was introduced midway through the model year, with the adoption of the 'G' model engine with its Victor Enduro bottom end. Despite these significant improvements, the overall engine tune, including camshaft, compression ratio and carburettor size, remained unchanged from the previous year. The model was only listed for the 1966 model year.

Specifications of C15 Star, SS80 and Sportsman (1959–1967)			
	C15 Star (1959–67)	**C15 SS80** (1961–5)	**C15 Sportsman** (1966)
Engine			
Compression Ratio	7.5:1 8.0:1 from 1964	Initially 10:1, but rapidly reduced to 8.75:1	8.75:1
Bore & Stroke	67 × 70	67 × 70	67 × 70
Claimed Power	15 @ 7,000rpm	20 @ 7,250rpm	20 @ 7,250rpm
Timing-side main bearing	Copper/lead plain bush	Copper/lead plain bush	Copper/lead plain bush (ball race from May 1966)
Drive-side main bearing	Ball race	Ball race	Ball race (roller from May 1966)
Big end	Plain bush Roller from 1964	Plain bush Roller from 1962	Roller
Oil feed	Timing-side bush	Timing-side bush	End feed (from May 1966)
Camshaft	Standard	Sports	Sports
Carburettor			
Type (Amal)	Monobloc 375/34	Monobloc 376/270 (1962 on 376/281)	Monobloc 376/281
Size	⅞in	1in	1in
Gear ratios			
Top gear	5.98:1	5.98:1	6.36
Third gear	7.65:1	7.19:1	8.14
Second gear	10.54:1	9.91:1	11.19
First gear	15.96:1	12.63	16.98

continued overleaf

Specifications of C15 Star, SS80 and Sportsman (1959–1967) *continued*

	C15 Star (1959–67)	C15 SS80 (1961–5)	C15 Sportsman (1966)
Brakes			
Front (diameter)	6in (15.24cm)	6in (15.24cm)	6in (15.24cm)
Hub	Cast-iron full-width	Cast-iron full-width	Cast-iron full-width
Rear (diameter)	6in (15.24cm)	6in (15.24cm)	6in (15.24cm)
Hub	Cast-iron, bolt-on brake drum	Cast-iron, bolt-on brake drum	Cast-iron, bolt-on brake drum
Wheels and tyres			
Front rim width – diameter	WM2 – 17	WM2 – 17	WM2 – 17
Front tyre	3.25 × 17	3.25 × 17	3.25 × 17
Rear rim width – diameter	WM2 – 17	WM2 – 17	WM2 – 17
Rear tyre	3.25 × 17	3.25 × 17	3.25 × 17
Electrics			
Voltage	6V	6V	6V
Headlamp size	6in	6in	6in
Headlamp shell	Cowl	Cowl	Separate chromed
Battery	6V 12amp/hr	6V 13amp/hr	6V 13amp/hr
Ignition	Coil	Coil	Coil
Weight and capacities			
Fuel tank	2½gal (11.4ltr)	3gal (13.6ltr)	3gal (13.6ltr)
Oil tank	4pt (2.27ltr)	4pt (2.27ltr)	4pt (2.27ltr)
Seat height	30in (762mm)	30in (762mm)	30½in (775mm)
Length	78in (1,981mm)	78in (1,981mm)	78in (1,981mm)
Wheelbase	51¼in (1,302mm)	51¼in (1,302mm)	51¼in (1,302mm)
Ground clearance	5in (127mm)	5in (127mm)	5½in (140mm)
Dry weight	280lb (127kg)	280lb (127kg)	275lb (125kg)

The C15 Competition Models – C15T and C15S 1958–65

The C15-based 250cc production competition models were introduced early on. The initial two models were announced at the beginning of 1959 as the C15T (for Trials) and C15S (for Scrambles). There were two distinct phases, which concerned the type of frame used. The first models were produced from 1959–62 and were equipped with frames closely related to the roadster. From 1963 to the end of the 250cc competition models in 1965, the models adopted a one-piece all-welded construction frame closely resembling that of the works offerings.

The first models, introduced in late 1959, were based heavily on the roadsters, but did have significant differences. Their frames were similar to the roadster, with brazed lug construction and a bolt-on rear subframe. The engine was offset to the drive side in comparison to the roadster models to allow the use of a wider rear tyre. The front loop and engine cradle of the frame was similar in appearance to the roadsters, but had a number of significant differences. The two members making up the engine cradle were positioned at the same level, giving a boost to ground clearance, the run of the cradle was altered to enable the engine to be positioned further over to the left and the rear extensions to the engine cradle that carried the pillion footrests were not present. The front and rear engine mounting lugs were also changed to offset the engine.

The footrests were positioned much further back than those on the roadsters and were fixed in position using cut-outs on the frame lugs and a single long stud, rather than using the roadster's individual taper arrangement. This necessitated the use of a 'looped' kickstart pedal that swung under the footrest – a very rare and difficult to find part. The rear subframe was modified, with an exhaust mounting lug on the right-hand side tube and a shortened rear seat loop. An easy recognition point for a competition rear subframe is the positioning of the mudguard lugs on the rear loop, which are on the outside of the seat loop. The rear swinging arm was about ½in longer, to give room for a larger rear tyre, and the front forks had external springs and thicker stanchions (taken from the larger models in the BSA range), giving more strength. Ground clearance of both models was increased over the standard model to give 6½in, while the weight was reduced to 265lb (120kg) for the scrambles and 275lb (125kg) for the trials.

The trials and scrambles engines were both tuned to match the power characteristics required for the two very different types of off-road sport – the scrambles models having more top end, with the trials tune optimized for low-end torque. For the 1960 model year, the scrambles model had a high-compression piston, giving a compression ratio of 9:1, a 'scrambles type' camshaft (*see* below), a larger bore carburettor (1in Amal Monobloc Type 376) and a plain upswept exhaust pipe with no silencer. The trials model was in a softer state

of tune, with a 'medium' compression piston, giving a compression ratio of 7.5:1 (changing quickly to 6.4:1 by the time the September 1959 brochure was published), 'trials type' camshaft (*see* below), a standard sized carburettor (Amal Monobloc Type 375), and an upswept exhaust pipe with silencer. Gearbox ratios also differed from standard and from each other, with the trials version having a very wide set of ratios. For 1961, the scrambles compression ratio was raised to 10:1, while the trials remained at 6.4:1

Interestingly, while the June 1959 brochure quoted above makes reference to a scrambles type and a trials type camshaft, the relevant parts manual shows only a standard cam and a competition cam (40-0477) listed for the trials and scrambles models, both of which utilized the same cam followers. So there may

In Canberra, Australian police riders are trained in the use of their C15 competition models. Note the single-sided front brakes, all-painted tanks and crash bars. (Mick Walker)

have been a bit of marketing speak going on from BSA! The parts manual specifies the use of a valve lifter on the competition type motor, which was not fitted as standard to the C15 roadster unit.

The running gear of the first competition models again borrowed heavily from the road-sters. Wheel rims were chrome-plated steel. The hubs were based on standard roadster items and both models used the standard road-ster full-width front hub, but laced to a 20in rim with a 3.00 section tyre. The rear wheel on both models had a modified brake drum which had a separate bolt-on rear drive sprocket, enabling easy changes to the final drive ratio. The rear wheel on the trials version had a wide rear rim to accommodate a 4.00 section 18in diameter tyre. In contrast, the scrambler had a 19in rear rim, with a 3.50 sec-tion tyre – which gives a similar rolling diam-eter to the trials model. Both models had rear tyre security bolts fitted as standard. Handle-bars were wide but relatively low-bend chromed items on both models, and while the scrambler was specified with safety oriented ball-ended steel levers, the trials model made do with ordinary levers – obviously BSA decided trials were safer than scrambles!

The tinware comprised steel painted mud-

guards, with chrome-plated items listed as an extra (priced in August 1959 at £3 0s 5d). The fuel tank was a special 2gal (9ltr) capacity steel item, with chrome-plated sides, BSA pear-shaped badges and no knee grips, which was unique to the competition models. While still using a centre bolt fixing, it had a single cen-tral seam and was not dissimilar in styling to the D7 Bantam tank. The roadster style central bolt fixing was retained, with the tank sitting on rubber bushes on the frame. The oil tank and side-panel were similar-looking to the standard models, but had different fixings and a thinner central joining plate that enabled them to be tucked in closer to the centre line of the bike. A new air filter was housed under the left-hand side panel and there was no pro-vision for a battery. Paint was Sapphire Blue for the tank and mudguards, with black enamel used on the oil tank, side panel and frame.

Electrics were simple. Ignition was supplied by the Lucas energy transfer system, which powered the ignition coil directly from the alternator and meant that there was no need for a battery. However, the system did need precise setting of the timing if it was to be a reliable starter or runner and it also could only provide a limited ignition advance range. While it seemed to work well in this applica-tion, any wear in the contact breaker drive or advance retard unit could cause starting or running problems.

The trials version could be supplied with lights as an optional extra; these were powered directly from the alternator so ran on AC cur-rent, with no need for a battery. Bikes so equipped had the rotary light switch (Lucas

LEFT: *The 1960 C15S Scrambler looks purposeful. Note the lack of any silencing!*

OPPOSITE: *David Lane on his 250cc C15S Scrambler at the Keysley Chase Scramble, Boxing Day 1962, where he was the winner of the 250cc final. Note the use of a standard steel fuel tank and full-width hubs. (Mick Walker)*

For 1962 the C15S and T gained a roller-bearing big end and BSA offered as options a half-width front hub and alloy fuel tanks. This C15S has all the options!

STARFIRE SCRAMBLER
250cc o.h.v. single

STARFIRE ROADSTER
250cc o.h.v. single

For the US the competition models were offered as the Starfire Scrambler and the Starfire Roadster. These two are 1961 models.

type 31356) and a round 'push to change' dip/main switch (Lucas type 31620) set into the Lucas 6in headlamp shell. The horn switch joined the standard kill switch (both Lucas type 76204) on the handlebars. Rear light was the ubiquitous Lucas type 564, mounted at the top of a pressed-steel number plate carrier that was bolted to the rear mudguard.

The first major changes to the competition range occurred in early 1962, in parallel with the appearance of the C15 Sports Star. The revised C15T and C15S sported a modified engine with a roller-bearing big end replacing the previous bush. In addition, BSA initially offered as options a new half-width front hub housing a 7in brake, new fork bottoms to accommodate the push-in front wheel spindle and a smartly styled alloy tank. These had been standardized by May 1962 – presumably because most customers took them up.

Both the scrambler and trials bikes were marketed in the US from December 1959, where they were named the Starfire Scrambler and the Starfire Roadster.

The Starfire Scrambler was essentially the UK scrambles model but equipped with lights, while the Starfire Roadster was a trials model with revised gearing for on-/off-road use with lights as standard. For 1962, the range was extended to feature the Starfire Trials/Enduro model, which was a specially set up Starfire Roadster, with the roller-bearing big-end engine, separate rear sprocket (as opposed to one incorporated with the rear brake drum), full direct lighting equipment (so no battery), engine silencing and a wide ratio gearbox with an extra low bottom gear. The front loop of the frame was derived from the roadster models, evidenced by the retention of the rear footrest support tubes at the back of the engine cradle. A single seat and no pillion footrests were specified. The folding footrests were positioned further forward than the previous models, allowing the use of a standard kickstart lever. The forks were heavyweight type, with rubber gaiters, as used on the other Starfire models and the rear subframe was the competition type with the shortened rear seat loop. An upswept exhaust that curved in under the oil tank, but was routed outside of the rear subframe tube, terminated in a short Burgess type silencer. The finish of these bikes was almost identical to the UK model; all had the blue tank and black oil tank and side panel, but the metal mudguards were chrome plated as standard.

The 1962 US market Starfire Trials Enduro was probably one of the first trail bikes. It was intended for trials, endurance runs, woods and cross-country competition.

By the end of these 'first generation' of competition models that used the roadster-derived frame, there was also a third UK and general export model (that is, not for the US export market), the Trials Pastoral. This model was based on the US Starfire Trials/Enduro model, featuring the roadster-derived frame married to the competition rear subframe. Overall dimensions of the first generation of UK market competition models with the roadster-derived frames were wheelbase 51¼in (1,302mm), ground clearance 5in (127mm),

The 1963 competition models gained a new all-welded frame, although they retained the rest of the running gear from the previous year's model. (Mick Walker)

45

overall length 78in (1,981mm) and dry weight 280lb (127kg).

For the 1963 model year, a new frame was specified. This was based on the previous year's works model and was an all-welded affair. It had a single top and down tube and a duplex engine cradle from which two tubes swept up to join the top tube at the seat nose. A conventional tubular subframe was welded to the main frame loop, supporting the seat and rear shock mounts. A development of this frame went on to be used for the C25/B25/B44 family of bikes. The easiest recognition feature of the frame was the twin seat tubes, running from the back of the engine to the seat nose, which meant that the oil tank had to be redesigned, becoming smaller in profile and more triangular than the previous models. The side panels were modified to suit.

The rest of the running gear was carried over from the previous model and the model was still offered in trials and scrambles form, as a pure off-road competition bike in the UK and as the C15 Trials Pastoral model – still a derivative of the C15T, but equipped for on-/off-road use with lights. It was similar to the US market Trials Cat. The US took to the model and continued to offer it in three

guises – the Starfire Roadster, the Starfire Scrambles and the Starfire Trials Cat.

The Starfire Scrambles was built as a ready to race scrambler, with large inlet port, 10:1 compression, racing valve springs and camshaft and trials Universal tyres. The bike carried an alloy tank, upswept exhaust with megaphone and quickly detachable lights.

The Starfire Roadster was touted as a versatile, 'many purpose' motorcycle. It had the same state of tune as the scrambler, but had full road equipment including lights, exhaust silencer, road gearing and multi-purpose on-/off-road tyres.

The Starfire Trials Cat was broadly the same as the UK trials specification model and was sold as being ideal for cross-country or enduros. The machine had a low-compression engine with low-ratio, wide-spaced gears, full direct lighting equipment and an exhaust silencer. All the bikes in the 1963–5 model years had unpainted alloy fuel tanks, black frame, forks, side panels and oil tank, and chromed steel rims.

The final year for the C15 competition models was 1965, when six distinct models were offered across the home, export and US markets, the C15T, C15S, C15 Trials Cat, C15 Starfire Roadster, C15 Starfire Scrambler and the C15 Trials Pastoral. With the demise of these models, BSA had no representation in the important 250cc trials and scrambles clubman's competition market. However, time had moved on and BSA recognized that the four-stroke singes had in any case been rendered obsolete by 250cc two-stroke models from home and overseas competitors.

The Trials Cat was the third of the 1965 US competition models. With a low-compression motor it was aimed at the cross-country and enduro markets; otherwise it was almost identical to the Starfire Scrambler and Starfire Roadster models.

Specifications of C15 Competition Models (1959–1965)

	C15T (1959–62)	C15S (1959–62)	C15T (1962–5)	C15S (1962–5)
Engine				
Compression Ratio	7.5:1 1960: 6.4:1	9.0:1 1960:10.0:1	6.4:1	10.0:1
Bore & Stroke	67 × 70	67 × 70	67 × 70	67 × 70
Timing-side main bearing	Copper/lead plain bush	Copper/lead plain bush	Copper/lead plain bush	Copper/lead plain bush
Drive-side main bearing	Ball race	Ball race	Ball race	Ball race
Big end	Plain bush 1961 – roller	Plain bush 1961 – roller	Roller	Roller
Oil feed	Timing-side bush	Timing-side bush	Timing-side bush	Timing-side bush
Camshaft	Trials	Scrambles	Trials	Scrambles
Carburettor				
Type (Amal Monobloc)	375/34	376/222 1961: 376/258	1964: 375/51	1962: 376/295 1963: 376/304
Size	⅞in	1959: $^{15}/_{16}$in 1960: 1$^1/_{16}$in	⅞in	1$^1/_{16}$in
Gear Ratios				
Top gear	7.92:1	7.92:1	9.0:1	9.0:1
Third gear	10.13:1	12.9:1	14.67:1	11.8:1
Second gear	13.93:1	19.4:1	22.05:1	14.94:1
First gear	21.13:1	25:1	28.53:1	19.0:1
Frame				
Construction	Two-piece, brazed lug front, bolt-on rear subframe	Two-piece, brazed lug front, bolt on rear subframe	One-piece, all-welded	One-piece, all-welded
Brakes				
Front (diameter)	6in	6in	7in	7in
Hub	Cast-iron full-width	Cast-iron full-width	Half-width	Half-width
Rear (diameter)	6in	6in	6in	6in
Hub	Cast-iron, bolt-on brake drum	Cast-iron, bolt-on brake drum	Cast-iron, bolt-on brake drum	Cast-iron, bolt-on brake drum
Wheels and tyres				
Front rim width – diameter	WM1 – 20	WM1 – 20	WM1 – 20	WM1 – 20
Front tyre	3.00 × 20	3.00 × 20	3.00 × 20	3.00 × 20
Rear rim width – diameter	WM3 – 18	WM2 – 19	WM3 – 18	WM2 – 19 1965 – WM3 – 18
Rear tyre	4.00 × 18	3.50 × 19	4.00 × 18	3.50 × 19

continued overleaf

Specifications of C15 Competition Models (1959–1965) *continued*			
	C15T (1959–62)	C15S (1959–62)	C15T (1962–5)	C15S (1962–5)
Electrics				
Voltage	6V	6V	6V	6V
Lights	Direct lighting option	None	Direct lighting option	None
Ignition	Energy transfer coil ignition	Energy transfer coil ignition	Energy transfer coil ignition	Energy transfer coil ignition
Weight and capacities				
Fuel tank	2gal (9ltr)	2gal (9ltr)	2gal (9ltr)	2gal (9ltr)
Oil tank	4pt (2.3ltr)	4 pt (2.3ltr)	5pt (2.8ltr)	5pt (2.8ltr)
Length	81in (2,057mm)	81½in (2,070mm)	80½in (2,045mm)	80½in (2,045mm)
Wheelbase	51¹¹⁄₁₆in (1,313mm)	51⅛in (1,300mm)	50½in (1,283mm)	51¹¹⁄₁₆in (1,313mm)
Ground clearance	6½in (165mm)	6½in (165mm)	8in (203mm) 1963: 7⅛in (183mm)	7¾in (197mm) 1963: 7in (178mm)
Dry weight	275lb (125kg)	265lb (120kg)	280lb (127kg) 1963: 265lb (120kg) 1965: 270lb (123kg)	270lb (123kg) 1963: 265lb (120kg) 1965: 270lb (123kg)

The C25 and B25 Series 250cc Models 1967–70

The C25 Barracuda and the B25 Starfire

Introduction – 1967 Model

The C15 replacement, the C25, was introduced in 1967 as the Barracuda in the UK and the Starfire in the USA. In this latter market, the name provided a nod to the past by resurrecting the name used for the competition and off-road variants of the C15 in the USA. There was also a copyright problem, as the Plymouth owned the Barracuda name and used it on a car, thus precluding BSA using the name in the USA. The bike moved BSA further from the original C15 softly tuned 'ride to work' concept, reflecting the changing market in the UK towards performance rather than utility, which was following the trends set by the US markets. In addition,

although home-grown competition was virtually non-existent, the Japanese were making their presence felt, with two- and four-stroke sports 250cc twins with performance far in excess of that of the C15. The model was firmly aimed at the learner/youth market and was marketed as a high-performance road machine, with a highly tuned motor and robust running gear. The BSA off-road tradition was, perhaps strangely, carried by the similar Triumph TR25W for the 250cc class, with the B44 Victor Special ensuring a BSA presence in the off-road market. It should be noted that some 1969 US Starfires were equipped with high-level exhaust pipes for on-/off-road use. These mounted the exhaust pipe on the left-hand side, with a wire 'chip basket' heat shield to protect the rider and passengers legs.

The styling was a complete break with the past, with a heavily sculptured tank and flamboyantly styled fibreglass side panels divorcing the bike from what had gone before. While the bike was all new and the appearance was radically different from the outgoing C15, the frame was a development of the production competition frame used on the later C15T and S models and the engine was very similar in appearance and layout to the outgoing C15, so still gave an impression that it was a development of the old model. The competition-derived frame was made from steel tube and comprised a large diameter top tube with a single down tube, that split into a twin tube cradle to carry the engine and a tubular rear subframe to carry the seat.

The frame was in one piece and was of all-welded construction. Finished in black, it was slightly larger than the C15, with a seat height of 31in (787mm) and length of 82in (2,083mm), a small increase over the last C15 Star's 30½in (762mm) seat height and length of 78in (1,981mm). The dimensions gave the model a 'big bike' feel. The swinging arm was mounted on silent-bloc bushes and was well supported at its outer edges. The frame gave the model superlative handling and roadholding and was virtually identical to that used on the 441cc models. The centre stand was fitted

to lugs under the engine cradle, with provision being made for a side stand.

Front forks were the corporate heavyweight pattern, hydraulically damped with thicker stanchions than the outgoing C15. The front brake was also increased in size from the C15's to 7in in diameter and was housed in a half-width hub with a push-in wheel spindle. The front wheel was of 18in diameter and carried a 3.25 section tyre. Steel shrouds were fitted over the external fork springs. A speedometer was centrally mounted in a rubber cup on the top yoke. The new forks signalled the end of the BSA cowl. A 7in chrome headlamp was mounted on 'ears' incorporated into the spring shrouds and carried the rotary headlamp switch (off, pilot and headlight), a headlight main beam warning light to the left of the switch and ammeter. Above the headlamp, mounted in a large rubber cup on the top yoke was a 3½in diameter 125mph Smith's magnetic speedometer, which managed to obscure the main beam warning light from a normal sized rider. At long last, a proper ignition switch was fitted, using a key rather than a pressed-steel blade. The switch was positioned on the left-hand side of the bike, just

The Starfire was introduced in 1967 and sported steel shrouds over the fork springs and a half-width front hub. This US market model was almost identical to the UK model C25 Barracuda apart from the finish.

under the nose of the seat. While this sounds awkward, in practice the positioning of the switch is a fair compromise between accessibility and exposure.

Rear suspension was by swinging arm, with the ubiquitous Girling oil-damped rear shock absorbers. The rear wheel was 18in in diameter with a 3.50 section tyre and featured the standard BSA quickly detachable 'crinkle' hub, plus a 7in diameter, rod-operated rear brake. Side and centre stands were fitted. The rear light was the Lucas 'tit' type (type 679), mounted on an attractive slim alloy casing.

The fuel tank was made in fibreglass and was fixed to the frame using BSA's central bolt mounting. It was styled with deep scallops for the rider's knees in white, a quick-release chromed filler cap and pear-shaped cast alloy BSA star badges. The overall styling of the tank followed the style of the rather bulbous 5gal (22.7ltr) UK model A65 Spitfire tank, but had been successfully slimmed down to provide a slim and sporting profile. The colour was impregnated into the gel coat, giving a tough and deep scratch-resistant finish. Capacity was a victim of the styling at a meagre 1¾ UK gal, (2.0 US gal/9ltr). The bolted-on seat was the current 'Racing Dual Seat' corporate design,

The 1967 Starfire was a slim machine, with its small fibreglass fuel tank. Note the short-lived exhaust lifter on the left-hand bar.

with the humped rear with the BSA logo in large script on the back. The side panels were in fibreglass and were the same colour as the tank, again with the colour impregnated. Mudguards were made of steel, with a slim sporting profile, and were finished in chrome plate. Front and rear mudguard stays were in black, as was the frame.

Electrics were to the emerging British standard, with the Lucas alternator providing 12V and with voltage regulation by Zener diode mounted under the bottom yoke on a large alloy heat sink. A small selenium plate rectifier was positioned under the sea, and an online fuse was incorporated on the positive side of the battery.

The engine, while similar in appearance to the late C15 unit, was extensively revised, as described in Chapter 3. The bottom end lost the C15's built-up crank, with its roller (or earlier plain) big-end bearing, replacing it with a plain bearing running on a one-piece forged crank, with a light alloy split con rod.

The high-pressure oil feed to the big end was routed through the end of the crank on the timing side; the oil pump was modelled on those used in the larger BSA unit 500cc and 650cc twins. The top end comprised an alloy barrel with 'square' fins and a cast-in pushrod tunnel. The cylinder head was fixed to the barrel with four through studs around the bore and two additional studs outboard of the pushrod tunnel. A valve lifting mechanism was fitted to aid starting, with a trigger lever on the left-hand handlebar.

The gearbox retained the four speeds and featured the stronger gear teeth fitted to the last C15s. Change pattern was retained as one down, three up. BSA claimed 24bhp and the chain was enlarged to ⅝in by ¼in dimensions to help to cope. The engine did gain a reputation for bottom-end trouble quite quickly. A low-level chromed exhaust pipe swept down under the right-hand side of the engine and connected to a large, traditionally BSA styled

The UK market C25 Barracuda was decked out in a bright orange colour, in contrast to the US market's more restrained blue and white. The bike was renamed the B25 Starfire for the 1968 model year, with a change to the US model's colours.

chrome silencer with a short tail pipe. Handlebar controls were chromed pressed steel.

The UK C25 Barracuda models were finished in a bright Bushfire Orange and white for the tank and side panels, with a 'Barracuda' decal on the side panels. The US B25 Starfire model's fuel tank and side panels were finished in Sapphire Blue, with Ivory (off-white) knee inserts on the fuel tank. Side panels carried 'Starfire 250' decals. All models had a black frame and cycle parts and black plastic-covered seat. The mudguards, wheel rims and headlamp shell were chrome-plated; the frame and other ancillary parts were all in black. Some US models had black painted crankcases, although the brochures do not show this. The main difference between the US and UK models was the handlebars, with high bars for the US and lower, more conservative bars for the UK and general export markets.

1968 Model

For 1968 the main change to the UK model was to rename it the B25 Starfire. There is speculation that this was due to the bad reputation for engine reliability gained by the Barracuda, although there were no major changes to the engine components to support this view, with even the 10:1 compression ratio being retained. More likely, the change was made as part of BSA's ongoing programme of rationalization, which was aimed at cutting down the number of variants of particular models. In fact, the 1968 UK model was virtually identical to the US model. New pear-shaped cast alloy tank badges were fitted. The main difference between the two 1968 models was the fitment of a chromed rear grab rail on the US model. Other changes introduced for the year were a full-width front hub, still 7in in diameter.

The front forks needed new lower legs to incorporate clamp-on caps to retain the front spindle, rather than the push-through type, the yokes were widened slightly to accommodate the new hub, and the forks gained a more modern look with the introduction of rubber gaiters to cover the springs. The rotary light switch mounted on the headlamp shell was replaced with a toggle type, while the rear light carrier was changed to a larger alloy casting that carried red triangular reflectors on each side. These were

The 1969 UK market spec B25 had a new silencer and gained the excellent corporate 7in diameter TLS front brake.

fitted, along with amber reflectors under the nose of the fuel tank, to meet US regulations. The main mechanical change was the deletion of the valve lifter. The finish was a Sapphire Blue and Ivory fuel tank, with the Ivory colouring the knee grips and a stripe across the top. The side panels were Sapphire Blue and carried the 'Starfire 250' decals as used in 1967. The other cycle parts were finished in black or chrome, as in the previous year.

1969 Model

For 1969, there were further changes to the front end. The forks adopted the Triumph-developed two-way shuttle valve damping mechanism, resulting in 1in less movement but improved performance. In addition, the model adopted the new BSA/Triumph corporate twin leading shoe (TLS) front brake, albeit in 7in diameter form. The fuel tank was changed to steel construction to meet UK legislation and the opportunity was taken to increase capacity to a more useful 3¼UK gal (14.8ltr) and to provide two petrol taps.

The styling of the tank remained broadly similar, though its styling looked like a 'blown-up' version of the previous year's tank,

retaining the overall sculpted style with the scalloped knee grips, but becoming wider and more bulbous. The US models retained the 2gal (2.5US gal/9ltr) tank. The side panels were also produced in steel, rather than fibreglass, but retained the sculpted style of the previous year. The colour scheme for the year was Flamboyant Aircraft Blue for the tank and side panels, with black rubber knee pads. Tank badges were the large cast BSA type. The silencer design was changed to a cigar shape with no tail pipe, which lost the BSA corporate look but was quieter. Some export models had their engines painted black for better heat dissipation.

The engine also remained broadly similar to the previous year's, but the crankcase and primary chain case joints were increased in size by around 15 per cent to address oil tightness. The inner timing case was modified to enable the fitment of a mechanical tachometer drive, driven by the worm gear on the crankshaft that drove the oil pump.

1970 Model

There were only limited changes to the model for 1970, presumably as much of the engineer-

ing effort within the company was being direct-
ed to the major revamp of the whole range
scheduled for 1971. The main change was to
lose the side panel from the oil tank and having
the drive side cover reduced in size and restyled
to match. The fuel tank colour remained as in
1969, Flamboyant Aircraft Blue, but the oil tank
and new side panel were painted gloss black and
carried new transfers with 'Starfire' in the new
corporate typeface sitting above a larger '250'.
The engine's breathing system was revised to
assist with oil retention at high revs. Again for
the US market, some engine crankcases and the
inner timing case, barrel and head were painted
in heat-radiating black paint. The sides of the
fins on the barrel and head were polished.

An option on US specification models was
a high-level exhaust pipe that swept round the
front of the engine, running over the top of
the primary drive side of the engine. The standard long cigar-shaped silencer mated with
the pipe and the rider's and passenger's legs
were protected by a wire 'chip basket' heat
shield. This was mated to a Fleetstar styled
tank, finished in blue and white with no tank
badges. The side panel and oil tank were finished in white with a blue stripe.

B25 Fleetstar 1969–71

The Fleetstar was introduced in 1969. It was
based on the 1969 Starfire specification frame
and running gear but with a number of
changes to ensure it appealed to sensible 'corporate' buyers. Prior to this model, the C15
and B40 had been supplied to various 'fleet'
users. These were usually UK or foreign government organizations such as various police
forces and the UK's Home Office. The experience of building batches of bikes to a specific organization's requirements led BSA to provide an 'off the shelf' solution. The advantages
of this to BSA was ease of production and
potentially lower unit costs, as only one model
was made for many customers. The customers
got a well tried and tested machine with good
spares back-up and a competitive price.

To achieve these objectives BSA took the
Starfire as a basis, which was probably not the
best starting point, and carried out a number
of modifications to meet the collective needs
of the potential customers. The changes
included detuning of the engine, by reducing
the compression ratio to 8.5:1 (down from
10:1), giving 21bhp and a consequent
improvement in reliability. The gearing was

*The 1970 Starfire also lost
its fibreglass side panels,
giving it a cleaner appearance.*

changed, with a larger (52-tooth) rear sprocket giving a slightly lower overall ratio. The frame and suspension parts were based on the 1969 Starfire, but the mudguards were deeply valanced and the fuel tank was made in steel in a rounded style. The fuel tank was also used on the 1970 US market Starfire. The oil tank did not have a covering panel and the drive-side panel was in steel and styled to match the oil tank.

Finish was predominantly black, with chromed sides on the fuel tank, and a black oil tank and side panel. Stylized 'Fleetstar 250' decals were fixed to the oil tank and side panel. A range of accessories were listed, all from the BSA subsidiary, Motoplas. These included crash bars, panniers, leg shields, screens and handlebar fairings.

The model collected the minor engine breather modifications and new oil pump for 1970, but remained unchanged in appearance. The Fleetstar was listed into the 1971 model year, when it adopted the new Umberslade oil-in-frame running gear and was based on the B25SS 'Street Scrambler'. There were three main changes to the B25SS model's specifica-tion: the engine was fitted with a low compres-

LEFT: *The Fleetstar fuel tank was also used on some 1970 US market Starfires.*

BELOW: *This 1970 Fleetstar shows the heavily valanced front mudguard and the narrower section guard used on the rear. The 7in TLS brake was standard.*

sion piston, giving an 8.5:1 compression ratio rather than the standard 10:1; a larger and boxier 3gal (13.6ltr) steel fuel tank was fitted as standard (which was also standard on the B50SS for 1972) and the frame was painted black.

The B25SS and B25T

B25SS Gold Star 1971

The Gold Star 250SS was a radical revamp of the Starfire and was the road-oriented replacement for the Starfire. It featured completely new running gear, using the second of the new Umberslade Hall designed frames, which carried the oil and was based on, although not identical to, the works frame. The overall look of the bike was referred to as a 'Street Scrambler' – with its upswept exhaust, wide handlebars and slim fuel tank, it maintained the off-road looks. Interestingly, the bike was provided with a side stand but no centre stand as standard. Provision was made for a centre stand with lugs on the bottom frame and it is rumoured that a BSA/Triumph twin oil-in-frame stand will fit. The stand specified in the parts manual appears to be similar to the twin item, but has no lifting loop, which would help with cornering clearance but not ease of use!

The engine was very similar to the previous year's Starfire unit, although mysteriously the power output had gone down to 22.5bhp, despite being in the same state of tune. The main difference was the provision of a wider rear engine mounting plate to allow for the new frame's wide rear engine plates, further revisions to strengthen the con rod, and, probably most important of all, the full-flow paper element oil filter, similar to that fitted to the WD B40, and situated between the two rear engine plates.

Running gear for the UK market Gold Star was the same as the 650cc twins and 750cc triples in the BSA and Triumph ranges, with the new Ceriani type front forks, wide handlebars, and the infamous 'balance cable' 8 inch TLS front brake in a conical hub. This brake

The UK market B25 SS Gold Star sported the 8in TLS front brake, as featured on the larger bikes in the BSA and Triumph ranges.

TLS front brake in a conical hub. This brake was used throughout the range, but was considered by many to be worse than the previous 8in mechanical linkage TLS brake. While it can be argued that it did not perform adequately in stopping the 455lb (206kg) A75R Rocket III, it actually performed very well on the single. The front rim was 18in in diameter and carried a 3.25 × 18 road tyre. The rear wheel, with its conical hub, carried a rod-operated 7in brake and a 3.50 × 18 tyre. Dunlop K70 road tyres were fitted front and rear by the factory. A short unsprung painted steel mudguard was fitted to the fork lower legs and the rear was again in steel and was short and slim. Both mudguards were slated in the UK for not giving much weather protection.

The electrics were the new corporate standard, supplied by Lucas and included flashing direction indicators and a capacitor to enable the ignition to work without a battery. New corporate handlebar switches, again produced by Lucas, were fitted, with built-in lever pivots and attractive alloy handlebar levers at last replacing the cheap-looking chromed steel

With its braced handlebars and high-clearance front mudguards, the UK market B25T Victor looked the part.

items previously fitted to the range. The main electrical components, the coil, capacitor, rectifier, Zener diode and flasher unit, were fitted into an alloy box mounted under the nose of the fuel tank. A nine-pin plug positioned at the back of the electrics box allowed for the easy removal of the headlamp unit complete with the front indicators for off-road use.

Instrumentation was fairly basic, with three warning lights (main beam, oil and indicators) positioned in the headlamp, with a small 3in diameter, black-faced Smith's speedometer in a rubber cup attached to the right-hand side fork top nut using a chromed steel ring. A tachometer, driven from the front of the engine, was optional. The tachometer was a matching 3in Smith's instrument, fitted in an identical rubber cup on the other fork leg top nut. The horn was suspended from the electrical box's front mounting bracket. The bracket came in at least two designs, the distinguishing feature being the side on which the horn was mounted. There seems to be no definitive view on which bracket was fitted to which model.

The US market Gold Star 250SS was pushed as a dual-purpose on-/off-road bike.

The main difference from the UK specification was the use of the Victor's 6in single leading shoe (SLS) front brake rather than the 8in TLS unit on some bikes. The fuel tank was the same slim, 2½gal (11.4ltr) capacity steel unit as used on the UK model, with a twist-off chromed filler cap; it fitted in well with the overall styling. It was available in Red or Blue, and carried BSA decals on each side.

There were two striking and controversial styling features of the model range. First was the colour of the frame. It was painted in a very light grey (Dove Grey), with the official explanation of this finish being that it was supposed to look similar to the nickel-plated frames that were a feature of the motocross circuits of the time. Unfortunately, while the finish was quite striking, it managed to look dirty (even before it had been used) and so was not a practical finish in the UK. The rear shock absorbers were also finished in the colour. At least a black frame did not show so much dirt, as evidenced by the Triumph version of the model. The second striking feature was the upswept exhaust system's silencer. It was a large, black lozenge-shaped box that had a big stainless-steel heat shield and was radically different to anything that had gone before.

B25T Victor Trail 1971

The B25T Victor 250 (UK), or Victor Trail (US), was virtually identical to the 1971 B25SS Gold Star. Engines of both bikes were in identical states of tune. However, as its name suggested, this particular Victor was designed to be a trail bike and so had a number of changes made to the Gold Star's cycle parts.

The handlebars were braced motocross style, albeit with a very similar rise and width to those fitted to the SS model. The front mudguard was made from lightweight alloy and was mounted on a bracket attached to the lower fork yoke, so was sprung and gave ample clearance for the 20in front wheel. Dunlop Trials tyres were specified. The footrests were pivoted, to prevent them snagging in the undergrowth and to meet

US legislation. The most significant change was the use of a 6in (SLS) front brake in a smaller version of the conical hub.

The fuel tank was made from light alloy, and while styled the same as the roadster's steel tank, had slightly less capacity at 2gal (9ltr) and had a fixed quick release filler cap. It was left in natural alloy finish, with a broad dark blue/black cross superimposed on it, delineated with red pinstripes and carrying the BSA logo on each side. Somewhat bizarrely, the speedometer was a larger 3½ diameter unit, again mounted in the 'corporate' rubber cup and chrome bracket. This was the opposite to what would become the norm for road and trail bikes, with the smaller instrument being fitted to trail models where they would be less likely to be damaged in a spill and be cheaper to replace. The instrument did have a trip meter (which the smaller speedo did not) and this was probably why the instrument was fitted to the off-road bike, as a trip meter was considered essen-tial for enduro events. Just to be different, the speedometer was fitted under the left-hand fork top nut, on the opposite side to the SS roadster, and was the same as that fitted to the 650 twins in the range. The frame was painted Dove Grey, like the roadster, and showed the dirt just as much – if not even worse as it would be exposed to more on the rough!

The B25SS and B25T were well received by the press at the time, albeit with some justified reservations about the apparently unchanged engine. However, its running gear was built to a high standard and was easily capable of handling more power, plus the model's handling and roadholding both on- and off-road were considered to be excellent.

The B25SS and B25T models did not appear in the publicity literature for the 1972 model year, although the production records show that some were made in the 1972 model year. With the demise of the model, BSA and Triumph finally lost their toehold in the UK learner mar-

---

Specifications of C25/B25 Starfire, Gold Star and Victor Trail (1967–1971)

	B25 Barracuda/ Starfire (1967–70)	B25SS Gold Star (1971)	B25T Victor Trail (1971)
Engine			
Compression ratio	9.5	10:1	10:1
Bore & stroke	67 × 70	67 × 70	67 × 70
Claimed power	25 @ 8,000rpm 1969: 24	22.5 @ 8,250rpm	22.5 @ 8,250rpm
Timing-side main bearing	Ball	Ball	Ball
Drive-side main bearing	Roller	Roller	Roller
Big end	Plain	Plain	Plain
Oil feed	End feed	End feed	End feed
Camshaft	Sports	Sports	Sports
Carburettor			
Type (Amal)	Concentric R928/1 1969 R928/8	Concentric R928/20	Concentric R928/20
Size	28mm	28mm	28mm

continued overleaf

Specifications of C25/B25 Starfire, Gold Star and Victor Trail (1967–1971) *continued*			
	B25 Barracuda/ Starfire (1967–70)	**B25SS Gold Star (1971)**	**B25T Victor Trail (1971)**
Gear ratios			
Top gear	6.942:1	6.916:1	7.348:1
Third gear	8.613:1	8.603:1	9.141:1
Second gear	11.4:1	11.38:1	12.09:1
First gear	18.36:1	18.34:1	19.49:1
Brakes			
Front (diameter)	7in SLS 1969: 7in TLS	8in TLS	6in SLS
Hub	Half-width 1968: full-width	Conical	Conical
Rear (diameter)	7in	7in	7in
Hub	Half-width, QD	Conical	Conical
Wheels and tyres			
Front rim width – diameter	WM2 – 18	WM2 – 18	WM1 – 20
Front tyre	3.25 × 18	3.25 × 18	3.00 × 20
Rear rim width – diameter	WM2 – 18	WM2 – 18	WM3 – 18
Rear tyre	3.50 × 18	3.50 × 18	4.00 × 18
Electrics			
Voltage	12V	12V	12V
Headlamp size	7in	6in	6in
Headlamp shell	Chrome	Chrome	Chrome
Battery			
Ignition	Coil	Coil	Coil
Weight and capacities			
Fuel tank	1¾gal (8ltr) 1969: 3.25gal (14.7ltr)	2gal (9ltr)	2gal (9ltr)
Fuel tank material	Fibreglass 1969: Steel	Steel	Alloy
Oil tank	4pt (2.3ltr)	4pt (2.3ltr)	4pt (2.3ltr)
Seat height	31in (787mm)	32in (813mm)	32in (813mm)
Length	82in (2,083mm) 1969: 83in (???cm)	85in (2,159mm)	85in (2,159mm)
Wheelbase	52in (1,321mm) 1969: 53in (???cm)	54in (1,372mm)	54in (1,372mm)
Ground clearance	7.5in (191mm) 1969: 7in (18cm)	7in (178mm)	7in (178mm)
Dry weight	315lb (143kg) 1969: 302lb (137kg)	290lb (132kg)	290lb (132kg)

ket. The company was soon to meet with the same fate in the mid-range and top-end markets that they were concentrating on from 1972.

The 350cc B40

The B40 Star – 1960 to 1967

Introduction – 1961 Model Year
The 350cc B40 Star was introduced to the UK market in September 1960, reintroducing a 350cc model into the BSA range after the demise of the B31 range, which had been dropped from the range during 1959. The announcement of the B40 coincided with the dropping of the 500cc B33 from the range, leaving the B40 as the largest 'cooking' single in the BSA range, although the 500cc Gold Star model was listed for the US market into the 1962 model year. The layout of the model followed that of the C15 Star, with a similar, although not identical, single looped frame. The main changes were the provision of heavier duty forks than those on the C15 (but sim-

ilar to those used on the competition models) and the use of 18in wheels, carrying a 3.25 section tyre on the front and a 3.50 section on the rear. The forks looked similar to those fitted to the C15, but had its springs on the outside of the stanchions, which were covered by steel shrouds. This combination of larger diameter wheels, different forks and a larger section rear tyre increased the length of the machine over that of the C15 by 2in (51mm) to 80in (2,032mm), and gave a 2in boost to ground clearance to 7in (178mm). The new front wheel carried a 7in front brake, giving a welcome increase in braking performance. The bolt-on rear subframe was retained and the swinging-arm rear suspension continued to use non-adjustable Girling shock absorbers.

Overall, the new B40 Star weighed in at a claimed 300lb (136kg), adding just 20lb (9kg) in weight to that of the C15. Power output was claimed as 21bhp, as opposed to the C15's 15bhp, which resulted in an enhanced power to weight ratio and better performance than the C15.

The first B40 Star of 1961 was similar to the C15 Star, with the valanced mudguards. Subtle differences included larger 18in wheels and a bigger front brake, no pushrod tunnel and a different fuel tank with round badges.

The B40 engine unit was very similar in appearance to the C15 unit. The pushrod tunnel cast into the barrel, improving oil retention, is the most obvious difference, but the crankcases were strengthened.

The oil tank, side panel and central joining strip with ignition switch were similar to the C15, as were the heavily valanced touring mudguards and the headlamp cowl. The fuel tank was different from that on the C15, with chromed sides like the larger BSA twins, but with round rather than pear-shaped plastic BSA Star badges. The capacity of the fuel tank was raised to 3gal (13.6ltr), reflecting the B40's slightly increased fuel consumption and its greater touring potential. In the US the 'cooking' B40 was introduced in 1961 as the 350 Star Sportsman. Apart from the US 'Western' bars, the specification of the bike was the same as the UK's B40 Star.

The centre bolt fixing and the two chromed trim strips covering the welded joins on either side of the centre of the tank were retained.

The engine followed the layout of the C15, with a ball race and bush main bearings and a copper-lead bushed big end. However, it was beefed up to handle the increased capacity, with stronger crankcases. A further recognition point is the absence of the C15's chromed pushrod tunnel on the timing side of the barrel – the B40's pushrods were fully enclosed in a tunnel cast into the barrel itself, thus both simplifying the engine design and cutting out a potential source of oil leaks.

The main problem with the B40 was its lack of popularity in both home and export markets. There was little incentive for a youngster in Britain in the 1960s to move from a 250cc machine to a 350cc, as its performance increase was perceived to be negligible, while the more mature 'ride to work and tour at weekends' rider was moving to the BMC Mini. Barry Ryderson's book, *The Giants of Small Heath*, contained production figures for some years. From these figures, in the 1964 model year 573 B40 Stars were produced, as opposed to over 2,000 C15 Stars. The sports SS90 fared little better – during 1964 only 165 were produced as opposed to 664 SS80s.

1961–4 Models

The B40 Star received steady rather than spectacular development over its life. The first major change came for the 1962 model year, with the introduction of a roller-bearing big end. While the engine retained the timing-side bush and the oil was still fed to the big end through the bush, the big end was much more tolerant of low oil pressure and hence suffered less from a lack of maintenance. Alongside the introduction of the SS90 in 1962, the standard B40 fuel tank lost its round badges, which were replaced with the corporate plastic pear-shaped items.

For 1965 the B40 Star's engine received the points inside modification as per the C15, but still no significant changes to the appearance of the bike.

The sports B40 SS90 exploded onto the scene with more of a whimper than a bang. Styling-wise, it was almost identical to the B40 Star, even using the Star's touring mudguards.

1965 Model

For the 1965 model year, the B40 Star shared the improvements derived from the competition models. While the frame and running gear remained broadly unchanged, the engine lost its 'distributor' and had the contact breaker points relocated in the timing side, driven directly from the end of the camshaft.

The clutch mechanism was also modified to a rack and pinion mechanism in the outer timing case, with the clutch cable engaging in a pivoting arm on the top of the case, making cable replacement much easier. The tooth and pawl kick-starter mechanism was replaced with the quadrant mechanism; the gearbox layshaft and main shafts were modified to cater for these changes. The engine number was prefixed B40F to reflect these changes. Note that the engine did not, however, gain the ball bearing on timing side, retaining the bush, although this modification was made later.

During 1965 BSA supplied a number of B40s to the UK Home Office. These bikes were standard B40 Star models and should not be confused with the later WD B40 discussed below. These B40s were very close to the standard road bike; the main differences were the paint finish, a fetching Dark Green gloss

enamel, no chrome on the fuel tank and a set of pannier frames for the standard British canvas kitbags.

The B40 Star eventually disappeared from the BSA brochures at the start of the 1966 season, but small numbers were made in the 1966 and 1967 model years, using the B40F (timing-side bush) and B40G (timing-side roller-bearing) motors. The B40 did live on, in the UK Army model discussed later in this section, but was a radically changed model, with more in common with the B44 than the original B40.

The B40 SS90 1962–5

The B40 Sports Star SS90 was introduced in June 1962. It was the 350cc equivalent of the C15 SS80. Differences between the standard B40 and the SS90 were mainly in the engines' internals and external finish.

Engine-wise, the SS90 modifications were very similar to those inflicted on the standard C15 in order to produce the SS80. The SS90 received a high-compression piston, which pushed up the compression ratio from the standard B40's 7.0:1 to a heady 8.75:1 – a significant increase. The raised compression ratio was complemented by a larger diameter

The US got the SS90 in a slightly modified state, including rubber gaitered forks with a front mudguard from the competition models.

inlet valve, heavy duty valve springs and a sports camshaft, all contributing to better breathing for the engine. Finally, a larger bore carburettor was fitted, going up ⅟₁₆in to 1⅛in. All this pushed up power output to 24bhp at 7,000rpm, as opposed to the standard B40's 21bhp.

To capitalize on this increase in power, a close-ratio gearbox (based on that used in the scrambler model) was fitted. Contemporary road tests of the SS90 gave good marks for performance, with *The Motorcycle* in June 1962 getting a maximum one-way speed of 85mph (137km/h) in foul conditions and *Motorcycle Mechanics* in October 1963 achieving a one-way maximum of 92mph (148km/h) and an average of 89mph (143km/h). In the US, *Cycle World* did slightly less well, with a 'practical maximum speed' of 82mph (132km/h) achieved after a half-mile run, probably as a result of the high 'Western' style handlebars fitted to the US models.

In appearance, the 1962 SS90 was very similar to the standard B40, with the same valanced mudguards and cowled headlamp. The fuel tank was similar to that used on the standard B40 with chromed sides, but pear-shaped BSA badges replaced the round versions. The oil tank and side panel sported Sport Star 90 transfers and the mudguards were chrome-plated. Other than these differences, the SS90 shared the rest of the running gear with the standard B40. Introduced late in the 1962 model year, the SS90 remained largely unchanged through to the end of the 1963 model year.

For 1964, the SS90 was given a slightly sportier look with the introduction of blade mudguards, still chrome-plated, and a sleeker rear light and number plate carrier. However, it still looked very similar to the standard B40, which by this time had adopted the same fuel tank as the SS90. The 1964 US models, called the Sportsman SS90, had at last gained the heavy duty forks with rubber gaiters and a front mudguard derived from the competition variants with a single looped stay supporting the front and back blades of the guard fixed halfway up the fork sliders.

The headlamp was still in a cowl in the first models, but was later supported by ears mounted between the fork yokes, giving a much sportier look.

The 1965 SS90 model remained virtually identical, apart from slight changes to the SS90's gear ratios and the model slowly faded away that year, disappearing from the BSA brochures in 1966.

The B40 Enduro Star 1965
The B40 Enduro Star was introduced in the 1965 model year and was listed for that year only. It was the forerunner to the Victor series of dual-purpose on-/off-road oriented bikes of the following years. The bike was essentially a parts bin special, with the C15 competition type frame combined with the 350cc iron barrel B40 engine. It had the on-road equipment of the C15 Trials and C15 Starfire Roadster and hence was fully road legal, with lights, horn, stop light and silencer.

Specifications of B40 Star and SS90 (1960–1965)

	B40 Star (1960–5)	B40 SS90 (1962–5)
Engine		
Compression ratio	7.0:1	8.75:1
Bore & stroke	79 × 70	79 × 70
Claimed power	21 @ 7,000rpm	24 @ 7,000rpm
Timing-side main bearing	Copper/lead plain bush	Copper/lead plain bush
Drive-side main bearing	Ball race	Ball race
Big end	Plain bush From 1962 – Roller	Roller
Oil feed	Timing-side bush	Timing-side bush
Camshaft	Standard	Sports
Carburettor		
Type (Amal)	Monobloc 375/34	Monobloc 376/270 (1962 on: 376/281)
Size	⅞in	1in
Gear ratios		
Top gear	5.48:1	5.78:1
Third gear	7.0:1	6.93:1
Second gear	9.63:1	9.6:1
First gear	12.3:1	12.3:1
Brakes		
Front (diameter)	7in	7in
Hub	Cast-iron full-width	Cast-iron full-width
Rear (diameter)	6in	6in
Hub	Cast-iron, bolt-on brake drum	Cast-iron, bolt-on brake drum
Wheels and tyres		
Front rim width – diameter	WM2 – 18	WM2 – 18
Front tyre	3.25 × 18	3.25 × 18
Rear rim width – diameter	WM2 – 18	WM2 – 18
Rear tyre	3.50 × 18	3.50 × 18
Electrics		
Voltage	6V	6V
Headlamp size	6in	6in
Headlamp shell	Cowl	Cowl
Battery	6V 12amp/hrs	6V 13amp/hrs
Ignition	Coil	Coil

continued overleaf

Specifications of B40 Star and SS90 (1960–1965) *continued*		
	B40 Star (1960–5)	**B40 SS90 (1962–5)**
Weight and capacities		
Fuel tank	3gal (13.6ltr)	3gal (13.6ltr)
Oil tank	4pt (2.3ltr)	4 pint(2.3ltr)
Seat height	30in (762mm)	30in (762mm)
Length	80in (2,032mm)	80in (2,032mm)
Wheelbase	54in (1,372mm)	52in (1,321mm)
	1963: 52in (1,321mm)	
Ground clearance	7in (178mm)	7in (178mm)
Dry weight	300lb (136kg)	295lb (134kg)

The running gear comprised: a 4.00 × 18 rear tyre and a 3.25 × 19 front, both on chromed steel rims; the BSA heavyweight fork; a single seat with no pillion footrests; a 2.6 US gal (9.8ltr) alloy petrol tank with quick-release hinged fuel cap; and wide 'trials type' handlebars. The hubs and brakes used standard BSA components, following the path set by the smaller 250cc off-roaders. The front wheel hub was the half-width 7in model, as used on many previous BSA models and which was substantially lighter then the B40 full-width hub used on the roadster – this also meant that the front wheel had a push-fit spindle, making tyre changes easier. The rear hub and brake were still the same as the roadsters, with the standard 6in brake and the full-width cast-iron hub, with a bolt-on 6in diameter brake drum. The rear sprocket was bolted on, rather than being cast into the drum, enabling easy changes to the final gear ratio. Mudguards were chromed steel, while the rest of the colour scheme was mainly black or natural metal – with the only real splash of colour being provided by the BSA star transfer on the tank.

Electrics comprised full road equipment, albeit without a battery, and ignition was provided by the energy transfer system. The headlamp was a 6in diameter unit with the light switch and dipswitch fitted to the shell. Rear light and number plate were standard BSA items, with a Lucas type 679 'tit' unit. Basic instrumentation comprised a single Smith's 3½in diameter 120mph speedometer. There were no warning lights, ammeter or tachometer.

The black enamelled semi central oil tank, the small triangular affair, was fitted to the right–hand side of the frame and carried the

Enduro Star

A real go-anywhere motorcycle. Has trials-type engine with low compression pistons and special camshaft for maximum torque. Specification includes engine undershield, upswept "tucked-in" exhaust, extra high ground clearance and many other "Enduro" features. Finish — silver alloy tank, chrome fenders, black frame.

The 350cc B40 Enduro Star was only available for the 1965 model year. A development of the C15 competition models, it was the forerunner of the 441cc off-road models.

BSA piled arms logo. The left-hand side of the underseat area was left bare, with no side panel to cover the air cleaner.

This model was the link between the small capacity dual-purpose on-/off-road bikes produced to date and the large capacity, single-cylinder on-/off-road or trail bikes that BSA produced until 1972. As such, it is probably accurate to say that it was the precursor of the concept that was reinvented by the Japanese with the Yamaha XT500 of the mid 1970s. Although it was well received by its primarily US market customers, the model was only in production for one model year. Its successor was the 441cc Victor, introduced for the 1966 model year that was aimed at satisfying the US market's appetite for increased performance – there is no substitute for capacity!

The WD B40 1967–70

The BSA B40WD was produced as a result of BSA successfully tendering for the replacement despatch riders' bike for the British Army. By the mid 1960s the British Army's main despatch riders' bike was the Triumph TRW, a 500cc side valve twin. BSA was keen to regain this market from its arch rivals, entering into a long and protracted bid process with

the British Ministry of Defence (MoD). The MoD, through the Fighting Vehicles Research and Development Establishment (FVRDE), carried out extensive trials of prototype vehicles from BSA, Triumph, Royal Enfield and Matchless, working with the manufacturers to arrive at a specification for a bike that met as many of the MoD's requirements as possible. This was a long and time-consuming process, starting in 1962 with FVRDE assessing machines from BSA, Triumph, Matchless and Royal Enfield. When the contract for the supply of the bikes was awarded in late 1966 or early 1967, the tendering process for the procurement had taken so long that the B40 model was technically obsolete and no longer in production! However, the specification of the B40WD had been developed by BSA and MoD, and what was specified was what would be delivered.

The frame was the competition variant, developed from the pre-oil-in-frame competition models and the later C15S and T models. It was very similar to the B25 Starfire/B44 Shooting Star frame introduced in 1967 and was described in the brochures as a 'Cradle type competition frame'. The frame tubes were modified for extra strength and the frame car-

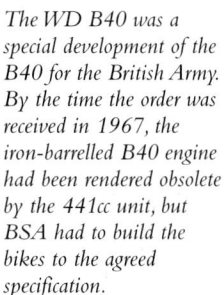

The WD B40 was a special development of the B40 for the British Army. By the time the order was received in 1967, the iron-barrelled B40 engine had been rendered obsolete by the 441cc unit, but BSA had to build the bikes to the agreed specification.

ried a crankcase 'bash plate'. The running gear featured a large paper air filter positioned in a steel box with a hinged lid on the left-hand side of the bike in the Vee of the seat tube and rear subframe tube, which mirrored the position of the triangular oil tank on the right-hand side. Ahead of the oil tank was a battery carrier, looking rather tacked on, and ahead of the air cleaner, sitting just below the carburettor, there was a canister for a cartridge type oil filter, again looking like a bit of an afterthought, but giving good access. The oil filter supplemented the standard B40 mesh filters in the oil tank and sump. The fuel tank was virtually identical to that used on the earlier pre-unit Gold Star models, with the exception of the depressions used to mount the Gold Star's round BSA badges.

Forks were again derived from the competition types, being heavyweight double damped items, with rubber gaiters over the springs and carrying a separate 7in Lucas headlamp mounted on brackets. The Smith's 3in speedometer, ignition switch and light switch were carried in the shell. The front wheel hub was a half-width with 7in diameter brake and push-in spindle. Rear suspension was by swinging arm with Girling dampers and a fully enclosed rear chain case was fitted. Pannier frames were fitted to carry the standard British canvas kitbags, as were fitted to the Home Office B40s of 1965. Wheels, complete with green painted rims, were 18in diameter front and rear and were fitted with a 3.25 section front and 4.00 section rear tyres.

The engine was virtually the final development of the B40 and retained the iron barrel. The points were positioned in the side of the timing chest. The crankshaft was particularly robust, with a roller bearing on the drive side and a ball bearing on the timing side. The big end used needle rollers and ran in a forged-steel 'H' section con rod. The compression ratio was modest at 7:1, while the power output was a claimed 18bhp at 6,000rpm. The gearbox was the standard competition type. The electrical system was 12V, with Zener diode regulating.

The carburettor used on the WD B40 deserves comment. The FVRDE engineers wanted the bike to be 'squaddie proof' – which entailed making the bike easy to ride, maintain

The armed forces didn't just use the WD B40 for despatch riding. Here, Marine White of 77 Coy, Royal Marines, is seen 'clearing the knife edge' at a services trial. (Courtesy of REME Museum)

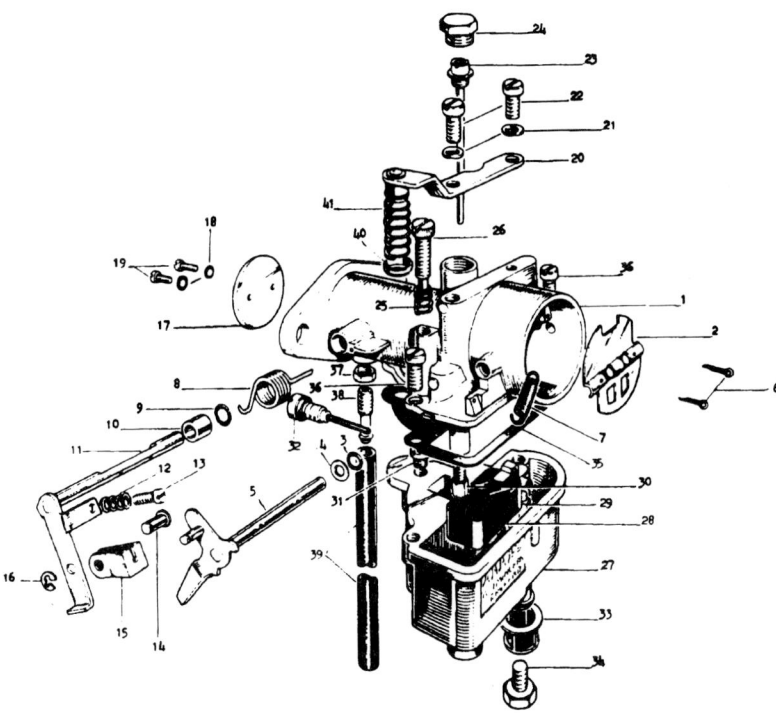

The Amal carburettor fitted to the WD B40. Its use of butterfly valves for the throttle and choke (items 2 and 17), rather than conventional slides, meant that it could be thoroughly dust- and waterproofed.

and fix. One stipulation was that the carburettor should have all external air passages protected against dust and water ingress. While the then current Amal Monobloc and soon to be introduced Concentric carburettors could be fitted with adequate air filters, FVRDE found that the use of a throttle slide with the cable coming in from the top of the carburettor body allowed in unacceptable levels of water and dust during testing. This led to throttles sticking and unacceptable wear to both the carburettor and the engine. In addition, replacing a broken throttle cable was not an easy, quick or squaddie-proof operation! The FVRDE specified that the carburettor must use a butterfly throttle valve which was well sealed against the elements and was operated by an outside linkage to enable easy cable changes. Up to 1964, the B40s under test had been fitted with Monoblocs, while the rival Triumphs were fitted with Solex butterfly

valve types. In the trials carried out to date, the FVRDE engineers had had a number of problems with the Monobloc, mainly caused by the ingress of water and dirt. This led to bad running and sticking throttle valves. BSA had not told Amal about these problems, but had switched to using a Solex similar to that used by Triumph, but were encountering some problems with the Solex, including fuel surge when running on rough ground and with the mounting flange being distorted, allowing air leaks. As it happened, Amal had got butterfly operated carburettors in its range, used mainly for stationary motors. One of these was modified to produce the prototype of the 26mm choke, type 398/6. This new model was successfully fitted to the B40 in time for the final set of trials in 1966, which resulted in the BSA being chosen.

The 398/6 carburettor was fitted to all of the B40s supplied to the British Army and to

The B40 Rough Rider was closely based on the WD B40. It used a conventional Amal Concentric carburettor rather than the butterfly valve 398/6 fitted to the military machines.

most of the armed forces that bought the model. The main exception was the Australian Army, which specified a 26mm Amal Concentric for its model L626/4. This carburettor was supplied with a plastic dust cap, which was a tight fit over the top cap, protecting against the ingress of dust and water from around the throttle cable. This model of carburettor gave a slight performance boost over the type 398/6 and can be used as a direct replacement for butterfly 398/6 and the 1 1/16 Monobloc fitted to 'civilian' B40s.

A letter from a BSA man, Norman Vanhouse, in *Classic Bike* (January 1995) indicated that the total number of bikes supplied to the British armed forces was 3,087, which included 141 for the RAF and 34 for the Royal Navy. A further order for an additional 235 machines was received by BSA in 1971, which the company was unable to fulfil due to its increasingly precarious state at the time.

As well as serving in the British Army, Royal Navy and Royal Air Force, the WD B40 was sold to the armies of Australia, Denmark, Jordan, Sudan, Jamaica and Zambia.

As an aside, the B40 was replaced by a Canadian-made Can-Am two-stroke bike in the early 1970s, which was in turn replaced by the Armstrong MT500, a machine that can trace connections to the CCM concern (*see* Chapter 4). Inspection of the frame of the MT500, especially the oil-bearing top tube, reveals that there are possibly some B50 genes in there!

The B40 Rough Rider 1968–70
Once the first tranche of the Army's order for the WD B40 had been produced, BSA started to sell the WD B40 to other armed forces and into the trail bike/working bike markets, mainly in BSA's traditional 'working' trail bike markets of Australia and New Zealand.

The WD B40 was lightly 'civilianized', producing the BSA Rough Rider model for the 1969 model year. The main change from the WD specification was the substitution of a 26mm Amal Concentric carburettor for the type 398/6 cable-operated model, the deletion of the rear chain case and the use of the full-width front hub to carry the 7in (SLS) front brake as used on the then current Starfire.

The use of this hub and brake meant that the wheel was held in the forks using bolt-on caps on the fork sliders rather than the push-in spindle. Front and rear wheels were 18in

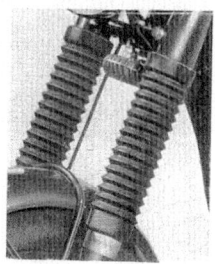

Air Filter
Air supply to carburetter is filtered through a large removable paper filter unit. The unit is fully enclosed behind the left-hand sidepanel and is internally vented.

Engine Unit
The low compression — high torque engine/gearbox unit, clean functional design makes for simplicity when routine maintenance is required. Crankcase is held in wrap-around frame tubes and a steel sump guard is fitted for extra protection, ground clearance is 7½ in.

Oil Filter
In addition to oil tank and sump filters a special cartridge type oil filter unit is located in the return oil line. The unit is compact and service or filter element replacement requires the removal of a single bolt.

Front Forks
Front suspension is by special two-way damped B.S.A. telescopic forks. Flexible rubber bellows are fitted for water and dust exclusion.

Rear Suspension
The rear suspension is swinging arm controlled by enclosed Girling units adjustable for load. Rearwheel is quickly detachable and sprocket is bolted direct to brake drum. Wheels are 18 in. diameter and rear tyre has 4.00 section.

The B40 Rough Rider featured an oil filter, decent front forks and a substantial air filter, all shared with the WD B40.

diameter, with a 3.25 × 18 Dunlop K70 tyre on the front and a 4.00 × 18 K70 on the rear. Other changes included a Smith's 3½in diameter speedometer carried in a rubber cap on the top yoke and a slim headlamp shell carrying a 7in Lucas light unit, with a Triumph style toggle light switch in the back of the shell, all features shared with the mainstream Starfire and Shooting Star models of the time. Overall finish was in Khaki, including the wheel rims.

The 441cc B44 Models 1966–70

The Victor and Victor Special 1967–70
The 441cc BSA Victor was initially a US market model that was a direct development of the B40 Enduro Star. It replaced the 350cc machine during 1966 and was in fact tested by the US magazine *Cycle World* during April 1966 at the start of the selling season for the 1966 model year. The bike confirmed

The 1967 Victor 441 Special improved on the 1966 model with a dual seat and new oil tank, giving a much tidier appearance. The engine still used the alloy 'round' barrel.

the popularity in the US of the format that BSA pioneered with the Enduro Star for what would become the trail bike. The frame and running gear remained largely unchanged from the Enduro Star, with the all-welded frame, separate small triangular oil tank, single seat and the 2gal (9ltr) alloy fuel tank.

It retained the general off-road look, with high-level exhaust, sump guard, folding footrests and high and wide handlebars. Utilizing BSA's competition experience, the engine was comprehensively revised, retaining the built-up crank with a roller-bearing big end, but had ball and roller main bearings and a roller-bearing big end. Oil was fed to the big end through drillings in the inner timing cover that fed the oil through the end of the crankshaft through a garter seal. The crankcases, although looking similar to the B40 unit had extensive internal strengthening, again applying the experience gained with the works motocross bikes. In its first year of production the 441 motor had a round finned cast alloy barrel and was in appearance very similar to the B40 unit it superseded. It also included an enclosed pushrod tunnel.

From the middle of the 1967 model year, the unit gained an alloy barrel with square finning on the head and barrel, making it look very similar to the new 250cc C25/B25 unit. The engine retained the decompressor as fitted to the B40, with an operating lever fitted alongside the clutch lever on the handlebars. The upswept exhaust system followed the factory line, sweeping over the timing side of the crankcases, before diving behind the two frame tubes to emerge above the swinging arm. The silencer was a short 'shotgun' type, but despite the bike having a dual seat and pillion footrests no heat shield was fitted. The frame was based on the pre-oil-in-frame scrambles frame and retained the separate oil tank on the right-hand side. It carried a dual seat, with BSA's trademark hump – described by BSA at the time as a 'Dual Racing' seat. The rear wheel was 18in in diameter and was quickly detachable using BSA's splined method. A 7in rod-operated rear brake was fitted and the rear shocks were semi-shrouded Girling units. The 19in diameter front wheel had a 7in diameter SLS brake in a half-width hub and push fit spindle. Standard fit tyres were Dunlop Gold Seal K70s, considered to be

For 1968 the Victor 441 Special gained a rear grab rail and the 'square' barrel.

The first B44 Victor Roadster was introduced to the UK and general export markets in 1967. This model was almost identical to the C25 Barracuda in appearing, but was finished in Ruby Red tank and side panels.

an on-/off-road tyre in the USA. Front forks were the BSA corporate heavyweight design, with external springs covered by steel shrouds. Electrics comprised direct lighting, running straight from the alternator and energy transfer ignition – described by BSA as A.C. Magneto. The 6in headlamp carried the light switch and dip switch and the rear light was the Lucas 679 unit in an attractive alloy casting. BSA claimed a weight of 288lb (131kg) for the bike. The bike's 2gal (9ltr) alloy fuel tank had the front half painted in bright BSA Racing Yellow, with the rear half in polished alloy, while the rear of the bike was in black, with chrome for the wheel rims, steel mudguards and fork seal holders.

For 1968 the appearance of the Victor was very similar, but a 'civilizing' process had started, taking the bike away from its role as an almost ready to race machine and orienting it towards the trail bike/dual-role market that was emerging. The model had already gained the square-finned barrel, giving better cooling, and gained battery ignition with 'normal' points and coil operation rather than the energy transfer system of the previous year. This meant easier starting and better ignition

advance characteristics, making the machine much more tractable and forgiving. The front wheel received the BSA 8in single side hub with the Gold Star-derived SLS front brake. The steel shrouds on the front forks were replaced with rubber gaiters.

Development of the model seemed to tail off from 1968, with the minor changes made in 1969 all appearing to address the legislation requirements of the US market. A larger silencer with a heat shield was fitted, which must have quietened down the bike a bit. The heat shield was very similar in appearance to that fitted to the 1968 TR25W, but the silencer was substantially shorter. The rear light carrier was changed to the BSA standard unit with red side reflectors and amber reflectors fitted under the fuel tank. For 1970 the model was identical to the 1969 model and the range was superseded by the B50T in 1971.

The Victor Roadster and Shooting Star 1967–70

Introduced for the 1967 model year, the 441cc road model was named the Victor Roadster or the Shooting Star depending on the market – for the UK it was the Victor Roadster and for the general export market it was the

The 1969 specification Shooting Star boasted an 8in diameter TLS front brake identical to those on the 650cc twins and the 750cc Rocket 3. (Mick Walker)

Shooting Star. The Victor Roadster name was dropped for 1968, with all markets getting the Shooting Star from then on.

While the Victor Roadster name reflected the current glory of the motocross championship wins, the Shooting Star was an 'old' BSA name that used to refer to a sporty version of the 500cc A7 pre-unit twin. Even the press at the time thought this introspection was a little strange, with the strength of the 'Victor' brand name. While confusion reigned over the name, the bike itself was very similar to the new 250cc Starfire/Barracuda models, sharing the same frame, running gear and styling. This meant that the 441cc model had the same scrambles-derived frame as used on the Victor Special, a small 2gal (9ltr) scallop sided fibreglass tank, large fibreglass side panels and chromed mudguards. The wheels were both 18in in diameter. The front wheel had the half-width 7in brake, with push-in spindle. The rear wheel was the standard BSA quickly detachable hub, again sporting a 7in diameter brake. Front forks were the standard BSA heavyweight design, with two-way damping. The fork springs were covered with metal shrouds, giving a clean but somewhat old-fashioned appearance, while the 7in chromed headlamp

was carried on ears attached to the shrouds. The main differences between the 250 and the 441 were in the colour, with the Shooting Star appearing with a Ruby Red tank and side panels and with transfers on the side panels that proclaimed the engine size and model name.

The 441cc motor was almost identical in appearance to the smaller unit, but reflected the motocross experience by keeping the built-up crank with a roller big end, rather than the 250cc unit's one-piece crank and shell bearing big end. The other main differences to the 250cc unit were the larger bore and stroke at 79mm × 90mm and the valve adjustment mechanism, which was by tappet and locknut bearing on the valve stems, rather than the 250cc motor's eccentric rocker shafts. This meant subtle changes in appearance of the rocker boxes and the cover on the right-hand side of the rocker box. The 441cc motor was in a softer state of tune than the 250cc unit, with a compression ratio of 9.4:1 and softer cams, which gave it a claimed 29hp at 5,750rpm, as opposed to the Starfire's 10:1 compression ratio and claimed 24bhp at 8,200rpm. This gave a performance on paper that was substantially better than that of the Starfire.

Contemporary road tests (*Motorcycle Mechanics* of November 1967) gave a top speed of 95mph (153km/h), standing-start ¼ mile of 15.8sec and 0–60mph time of 8.9sec for the Shooting Star, while a test in *Motorcycle Mechanics* in October 1968 of the Starfire gave a top speed of 83mph (134km/h), standing-start ¼ mile of 18.1sec and a 0–60mph time of 11.5sec. However, while the performance of the larger machine was better on paper, the larger capacity, softer state of tune and much higher gearing also gave a much more relaxed ride, plus the greater torque made it much more flexible – more of a plodder than a screamer. This also meant that the motor was subject to less wear, as it did not have to be revved to 8,000rpm to deliver respectable performance. Finish for the introductory year was Ruby Red fuel tank and side panels, with chromed mudguards and black frame.

For the 1968 model year, the fork yokes (or triple trees) were changed, becoming slightly wider to accommodate a Triumph type full-width 8in diameter front wheel hub, with increased braking area provided by the use of a spoke flange on the brake side, allowing the use of wider brake shoes. This enabled the fitting of an 8in SLS brake and at the same time rubber gaiters replaced the steel shrouds covering the springs, giving a more sporting and up to date appearance.

The engine was largely unchanged, but gearing was lowered by changing the gearbox and rear wheel sprockets. The larger 3¼ UK gal (14.7ltr) steel fuel tank was standardized on UK models, while the US still had the 2gal (9ltr) fibreglass unit. New cast alloy tank badges replaced the plastic ones. Finish was Cherokee Red with Ivory knee inserts on the fibreglass fuel tanks, or all Cherokee Red tanks with black rubber knee grips for the larger steel tank. All models had side panels painted to match the fuel tank in Cherokee Red, with large Shooting Star decals.

For 1969 the main change was the adoption of the corporate TLS front brake. The unit used was the 7in diameter model similar to that used on BSA's 650 twins. The 7in version of the brake was introduced a year after the original 8in TLS brake appeared in 1968. The original 8in design had problems with the length of cable, which led to a redesign that resulted in 'bell crank' operating levers being introduced in the 1969 unit, which gave a shorter, straighter cable pull than the initial 1968 model. The silencer design was also changed to a 'cigar' shaped unit rather than the 'Burgess' type fitted previously, to meet increasingly restrictive noise regulations. Colours for the 1969 Shooting Star were Peony Red for the fuel tank, with chrome mudguards and black side panels and frame.

The model carried on into the 1970 model year with few obvious changes, the most noteable being the loss of the fibreglass side panels. The oil tank was left exposed on the right-hand side, while a matching triangular steel side panel covered the battery on the left. Both oil tank and side panel were painted black and carried a '441 Shooting Star' transfer. The fuel tank was painted Flamboyant Red, while the frame remained black.

The model was superseded by the new range for the 1971 model year, when the B50SS Gold Star took over the big roadster single mantle.

A new seat cover, steel fuel tank and an exposed oil tank show that this is a 1970 model 441cc Shooting Star. (Mick Walker)

BSA Victor 441 Scrambles Model B44 GP 1965–7

In 1964 Jeff Smith won the motocross 500cc championship for BSA on his works 420cc single, with a staggering record of seven wins, six second places and third in one race out of the fourteen races that made up that year's series, and won again on a 441cc machine in 1965. BSA took the decision to capitalize on this victory by making a production replica for the public to buy.

The bike was called the BSA Victor. It was designated the B44 GP and was a true competition model, aimed at the serious clubman and private rider, with a focus on winning motocross meetings. It was claimed by BSA in the bike's publicity that it was an exact replica

The Victor GP had a round alloy barrel 441 cc motor. Note the oil pipe to the header tank on the left-hand side just below the carb. (Mick Walker)

of the bike used by Jeff Smith. In the BSA launch brochure Jeff Smith is quoted as saying: 'You can take it from me that BSA are not offering you just a 'hotted-up' version of a standard model. The VICTOR is a carbon copy of the machine that I rode on throughout the 1964 season, and on which I ultimately won the World Championship.'

The details of the bike confirm that the model was pretty special. The layout of the frame followed that of the previous production competition frame used on the C15T and C15S and was of all-welded construction. The main loop had a well-supported and braced headstock, with a large diameter top tube with a second strengthening tube under it. There was a single front down tube and a duplex engine cradle, which ran back up to the rear of the top tube, giving two seat tubes. The duplex cradle had a bracing tube on its base which also acted as the footrest mount, plus two further bracing tubes, one at the swinging-arm pivot and one a few inches higher. The swinging arm was attached to two substantial plates welded to the rear of each of the seat tubes. The all-tubular rear subframe supported the seat and rear shock absorber mounts. It comprised a loop attached to the rear of the top tube with two braces across its width and two straight tubes running from the rear shock absorber mounts to the swinging-arm pivot plates on the seat tubes, giving some additional bracing to this important area.

The most significant differences between this new frame and the previous production frame used on the C15 trials and scrambles models was that the new frame was made from top-quality Reynolds 531 tubing and the use of the frame tubes to carry the engine oil. The Reynolds tube was lighter and stronger than the usual tubing used in the production models and use of the frame to carry the oil, instead of a weighty and complex separate oil tank, led to significant savings in both weight and complexity. The top tube carried the oil filler cap

The Victor Grand Prix frame was closely based on the works models. It carried its oil in the tubes and had a 'header' tank positioned just above the swinging-arm pivot.

The oil filler was positioned just behind the headstock. The top yoke carried the handlebars on extensions behind the steering head.

just in front of the fuel tank and the oil was contained in the top two tubes, the front down tube and a flat oblong header tank sitting between the two seat tubes, which gave an oil capacity of 4¼pt (2.4ltr).

Front suspension was the standard BSA heavyweight type, with chrome molybdenum stanchions and hydraulic double damping (spring and return). Fork springs were external and covered, surprisingly, by steel shrouds rather than rubber gaiters. Handlebars were braced and were mounted on the top yoke with two clamps, which were extended back behind the steering tube. Rear suspension was by Girling dampers, with semi-exposed rear chrome springs and adjustable pre-loading.

The running gear followed the 'standard' BSA route, with a quickly detachable rear hub that carried a 7in rod-operated brake. The front wheel was a push-through spindle type, with a 7in brake in a single-sided hub. Both wheel rims were chrome-plated steel, with an 18in rear and 20in diameter front. Tyres were Dunlop Sports with a 4.00 section rear and 3.00 section front. The 1½gal (6.8ltr) fuel tank and mudguards were in lightweight alloy. Side

panels were fibreglass; the right-hand one covered a paper element air filter and both were styled to act as competition number plates. A front competition number plate was mounted on the front of the forks, between the yokes.

The frame, swinging arm, fork sliders and side panels were finished in black, while the front fork spring shrouds were in silver. The fuel tank was painted in Deep Ivory, a light yellow shade, with BSA transfers in red outlined in white on each side. The knee grip areas on each side of the tank were left unpainted, showing the polished alloy underneath. The alloy mudguards were polished and a single seat in black vinyl sat on the subframe.

The engine was the first 'production' (albeit limited) 441cc unit and differed substantially from the C15/B40 unit. The bore and stroke was 79 × 90mm and at a simplistic level was a stroked version of the B40. The barrel was round (rather than square like the later road and trail B44s) and was made from light alloy with a hard chrome-plated bore, rather than the 'normal' B44 alloy barrel with shrunk-in iron liner. The engine's compression ratio was a heady 11.4:1, which assisted in giving the

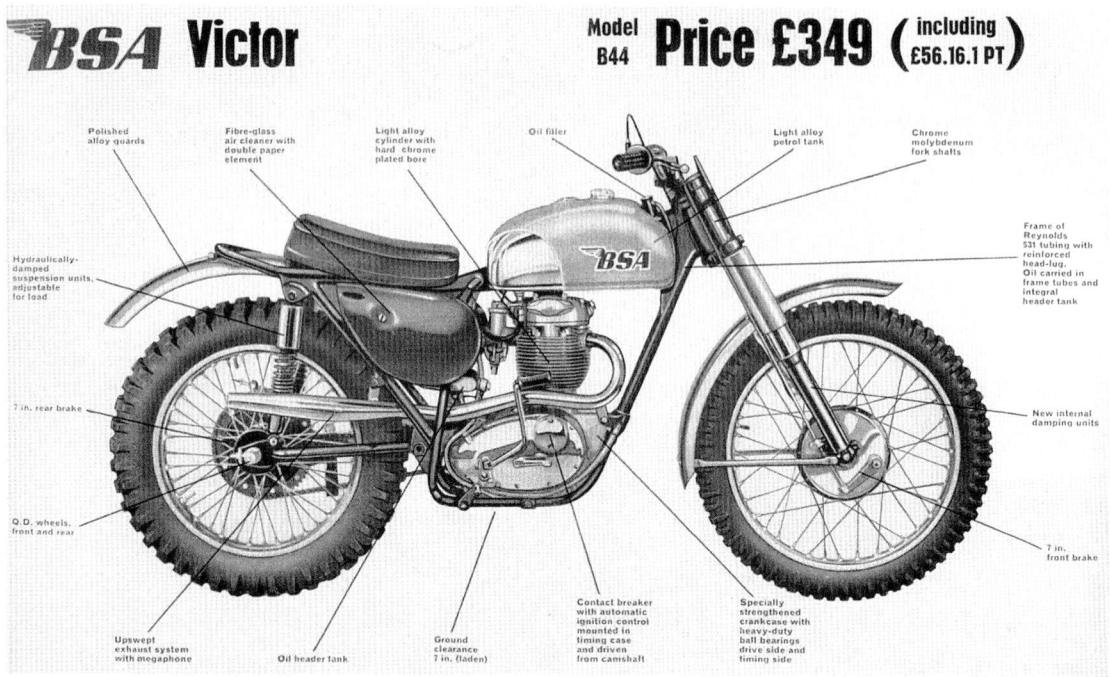

The Victor Grand Prix was a handsome bike which closely resembled the works bikes.

bike excellent performance. Unfortunately, BSA did not publicize the power figures from the engine.

The crankcases were strengthened from those of the B40, with ball-bearing main bearings and a roller-bearing big end, a great improvement on the plain bush used by the B40. Oil was fed to the roller big end through the end of the crank. A high-performance camshaft was fitted. The four-speed gearbox had motocross ratios of 6.97 (top), 8.65, 11.42 and 15.4 (bottom) and drove the rear wheel through a ½ × 0.305in rear chain. The upswept exhaust exited on the right-hand side, running over the top of the crankcases, tucked in behind the seat tube. Carburetion was taken care of with a 1⅜in Amal Monobloc and a large air cleaner lived behind the drive-side number plate.

The electrics comprised the ignition system only, with no provision for lights. The Lucas energy transfer system was employed to avoid the use of a battery; another weight and complexity saving. Contact breaker points were driven off the cam shaft and covered with a chrome cover on the timing case. All of the above combined to give a compact, competitive scrambles for the clubman. The bike boasted 7in (178mm) of ground clearance, a 32in (813mm) seat height, a wheelbase of 52¾in (1,340mm) and a length of 81½in (2,070mm), making for an easy to handle package. Finally, the weight control measures resulted in BSA claiming a weight of 255lb (116kg), substantially less than that of the road and trail B40 Enduro Star at 297lb (135kg).

The BSA Victor B44 GP model remained in production for the 1965 and 1966 model years, but was quietly dropped during the 1967 model year.

Specifications of B44 Shooting Star, Victor Roadster/Endure/Special and GP (1966–1970)

	B44 Shooting Star/ Victor Roadster (1966–70)	B44 Victor Enduro/ Victor Special (1966–70)	B44 GP (1965–7)
Engine			
Compression ratio	9.4:1	9.4:1	11.4:1
Bore & stroke	79 × 90	79 × 90	79 × 90
Claimed power	29 bhp @5,750rpm 1968: 28 bhp @ 6,500rpm	28 bhp @ 6,500rpm	n/a
Timing-side main bearing	Ball-bearing	Ball-bearing	Ball-bearing
Drive-side main bearing	Roller	Roller	Ball-bearing
Big end	Roller	Roller	Roller
Oil feed	End feed	End feed	End feed
Camshaft	Sports	Sports	High-performance
Carburettor			
Type (Amal)	Concentric 930/11 1969 930/38	Concentric 930/1 1969: 930/38	Monobloc 389/221
Size	30mm	30mm	1 5/32
Gear ratios			
Top gear	5.36:1	5.36:1	6.97:1
Third gear	6.70:1	6.70:1	8.65:1
Second gear	8.84:1	8.84:1	11.42:1
First gear	14.2:1	14.2:1	15.4:1
Brakes			
Front	7in 1968: 8in 1969: 7in (TLS)	7in 1968: 8in	7in
Hub	Half-width 1968: full-width	Half-width	Half-width
Rear (diameter)	7in	7in	7in
Hub	Half-width, QD	Half-width, QD	Half-width, QD
Wheels and tyres			
Front rim width – diameter	WM2 – 18	WM2 – 19	WM1 – 20
Front tyre	3.25 × 18	3.25 × 19	3.00 × 20
Rear rim width – diameter	WM2 – 18	WM3 – 18	WM3 – 18
Rear tyre	3.50 × 18	400 × 18	4.00 × 18
Electrics			
Voltage	12V	12V	6V
Headlamp size	7in	6in	n/a
Headlamp shell	Chrome	Black	n/a
Battery	8 amp/hr 1969: 10 amp/hr	8 amp/hr 1969: 10 amp/hr	n/a
Ignition	Coil	Coil	Energy transfer

continued overleaf

Specifications of B44 Shooting Star, Victor Roadster/Endure/Special and GP (1966–1970) *continued*

	B44 Shooting Star/ Victor Roadster (1966–70)	B44 Victor Enduro/ Victor Special (1966–70)	B44 GP (1965–7)
Weight and capacities			
Fuel tank	2gal (9ltr) 1969: 3¼gal (14 l)	1¾gal (8ltr)	1½gal (6.8ltr)
Fuel tank material	Fibreglass 1969: Steel	Steel	Alloy
Oil tank	4pt (2.3ltr)	5pt (2.8ltr)	4¼pt (2.4ltr)
Seat height	31in (787mm)	32in (813mm)	32in (813mm)
Length	82in (2,083mm) 1969 83⅛in (2,113mm)	82in (2,083mm)	81⅛in (2,070mm)
Wheelbase	52in (1,320mm) 1969: 53in (1,346mm)	53in (1,346mm) 1968: 52in (1,320mm)	52¾in (1,340mm)
Ground clearance	7½in (191mm)	8in (203mm)	7in (179mm)
Dry weight	320lb (145kg)	306lb (139kg)	255lb (116kg)

The 500cc B50 Models

The B50SS and T 1971–2

BSA's first production 500cc single since the Gold Star model of the early 1960s, the B50, continued the BSA tradition of building on competition experience. While the running gear of the machine was the same as the B25SS and B25T, with the group conical hubs, Ceriani type forks and oil in frame, the engine was a further development of the B44. With a bore and stroke of 84mm × 90mm the capacity came up to 499cc and the compression ratio was 10:1. To cope with the additional power (up from the B44's claimed 28hp to 34hp) the built-up crank ran on three main bearings, two on the drive side, one on the timing side.

The bike was still a bit of a revver rather than a plodder, with maximum power of 34bhp being developed at 6,200rpm, and in road trim it had excellent performance, handling and braking. The conical hub and TLS front brake was able to cope with the 90mph 145km/h) plus performance (*Cycle World* clocked up a best of 92.5mph [148.8km/h])

due to the relatively light weight of 310lb (141kg) dry.

The B50MX 1971–3

Carrying on the tradition set by the C15T, C15S and the Victor GP, the B50MX was the competition version of the B50. While it shared the oil-bearing frame of the road and trail models, it was an off-road competition motocross bike. It had several features that distinguished it from the road models, such as a slim 1gal (4.6ltr) alloy fuel tank, energy transfer ignition, no lights or indicators, a hot cam and a minimal exhaust system. The bike weighed a mere 240lb (109kg) and pushed out an extra 4bhp, giving a significant performance boost over the road models.

The Triumph Models

The TR25W 1968–70

The Triumph Tiger Cub was reaching the end of its life by 1967 and production of the model was, by then, carried out at the BSA works at

The B50T was a trail bike with a high front mudguard and small 6in front brake.

The BSA production competition tradition was carried forward into the 1970s with the B50MX.

Specifications of B50 Victor, Gold Star and MX (1971–1974)

	B50T Victor (1971–2)	B50SS Gold Star (1971–2)	B50MX (1971–4)
Engine			
Compression ratio	10:1	10:1	10:1
Bore & stroke	84 × 90	84 × 90	84 × 90
Claimed power (bhp)	34 @ 6,200rpm	34 @ 6,200rpm	38 @ 6,200rpm
Timing-side main bearing	Ball	Ball	Ball
Drive-side main bearing	Roller & ball	Roller & ball	Roller & ball
Big end	Roller	Roller	Roller
Oil feed	End feed	End feed	End feed
Camshaft	Sports	Sports	M×
Carburettor			
Type (Amal)	Concentric R930	Concentric R930	Concentric R932
Size	30mm	30mm	32mm
Gear ratios			
Top gear	6.438:1	6.036:1	6.898:1
Third gear	8.009:1	7.508:1	8.541:1
Second gear	10.60:1	9.935:1	11.35:1
First gear	17.07:1	16.01:1	15.06:1
Brakes			
Front (diameter)	6in SLS	8in TLS	6in SLS
Hub	Conical	Conical	Conical
Rear (diameter)	7in	7in	7in
Hub	Conical	Conical	Conical
Wheels and tyres			
Front rim width – diameter	WM1 – 20	WM2 – 18	WM1 – 20
Front tyre	3.00 × 20	3.25 × 18	3.00 × 20
Rear rim width – diameter	WM2 – 18	WM3 – 18	WM3 –18
Rear tyre	3.50 × 18	4.00 × 18	4.00 × 18
Electrics			
Voltage	12V	12V	12V
Headlamp size	6in	6in	N/A
Headlamp shell	Chrome	Chrome	N/A
Ignition	Coil	Coil	Energy transfer
Weight and capacities			
Fuel tank	2gal (9ltr)	2gal (9ltr)	1gal (4.6ltr)
Fuel tank material	Steel	Steel	Alloy
Oil tank	4pt (2.3ltr)	4pt (2.3ltr)	4pt (2.3ltr)
Seat height	32in (2,083mm)	32in (2,083mm)	32in (2,083mm)
Length	85in (2,057mm)	85in (2,057mm)	85in (2,057mm)
Wheelbase	54in (1,372mm)	54in (1,372mm)	54in (1,372mm)
Ground clearance	7.5in (191mm)	7in (178mm)	7.5in (191mm)
Dry weight	298lb (135kg)	310lb (141kg)	240lb (109kg)

Triumph's Tiger Cub replacement for 1968 was a modified Starfire, the TR25W. The bike sported a high-level exhaust system with a short silencer.

Small Heath to enable Triumph's Meriden plant to concentrate on producing the popular twin. The last versions of the Tiger Cub were using BSA Bantam running gear and were in urgent need of replacement with a 250cc model to maintain Triumph's presence in this market. In a reversal of 1958, the BSA Starfire provided the basis for Triumph's Cub replacement, the somewhat awkwardly titled Triumph TR25W Trophy. While the model was a re-badged version of the BSA machine it had a number of significant changes to the road-oriented BSA model.

The Triumph version was aimed directly at the on-/off-road market. It featured the BSA B25/B44 frame which was mated to Triumph's medium weight forks from the 350cc twin range. The engine was a B25 unit, but had a restyled primary chain case with a cast-in styling scallop and carried Triumph logos on the pushrod cover on the cylinder head and the rotor cover in the primary chain case. The bike employed a steel fuel tank, styled to keep the Triumph 'look', and carried a chromed Triumph 'eyebrow' tank badge to emphasize it's identity. Simple steel side panels, carrying a horizontal silver flash with a 'Trophy 250' logo, were fitted on both sides and helped to differentiate the model

from its BSA cousin with its heavily styled side covers. The exhaust pipe on the 1968 TR25W was upswept on the right-hand side (timing side) of the bike in the manner of the BSA Victor, going over the top of the timing cover before looping in behind the frame's seat tubes and emerging just above the swinging arm.

The exhaust pipe was terminated with a small Burgess-type silencer carried horizontally above the swinging arm (sometimes called a 'bullet silencer' due to its small size) and ended just after the rear wheel spindle, emphasizing the model's on-/off-road aspirations. The silencer was equipped with a chromed, sheet-steel heat shield with chevron-shaped perforations to protect the pillion's leg. Complementing the high-level exhaust, the model featured folding front footrests and a steel crankcase bash plate to give the bike some off-road credibility. Wheels were 19in front and 18in rear and the model was equipped with Dunlop K70 tyres, which in the US were considered to be dual-purpose on-/off-road tyres, in contrast to the UK where they were considered to be good road tyres. Brakes were 7in diameter, SLS front and rear. A small, 6in diameter headlamp was fitted, with a built-in push button dip switch and toggle light switch. A small 3in grey-faced speedometer with milometer but no trip meter was fitted to a bracket on the top yoke; this was the total of the model's instrumentation – there was no ammeter or rev counter. A Lucas 679 type rear light with triangular side reflectors sat on the rear mudguard, supported by a U-shaped subframe which also carried a passenger grab rail fitted to a bracket on the top rear suspension mounts. The colour scheme for the model was Hi-Fi Scarlet tank and mudguards, with gloss black side panels and frame and chromed wheel rims.

The TR25W continued into 1969 with few changes, the most significant being the exhaust system – which incidentally changed every year that the model was in production. The exhaust pipe still swept over the timing side of the motor, but now ran outside of the frame tubes. A much longer Burgess type silencer was fitted, still on the right-hand side of the machine, but extending all the way to the rear of the bike. This gave much better silencing when compared with the 1968 model's 'shorty' pipe, but did not improve the appearance of the bike. The silencer was equipped with a wire 'chip basket' leg protector that continued the chevron pattern seen in the previous year's model. The front brake was replaced with the corporate 7in TLS model, a significant improvement on the previous year's

Triumph T25 Trophy, Blazer and Trail Blazer Specifications (1968–1971)

	TR25W Trophy (1968–70)	T25SS Blazer (1971)	T25T Trail Blazer (1971)
Engine			
Compression ratio	10:1	10:1	10:1
Bore & stroke	67 × 70	67 × 70	67 × 70
Claimed power	24 @ 8,000rpm	22.5 @ 8,250rpm	22.5 @ 8,250rpm
Timing-side main bearing	Ball	Ball	Ball
Drive-side main bearing	Roller	Roller	Roller
Big end	Plain	Plain	Plain
Oil feed	End feed	End feed	End feed
Camshaft	Sports	Sports	Sports
Carburettor			
Type (Amal)	Concentric R928/4	Concentric R928/20	Concentric R928/20
Size	28mm	28mm	28mm
Gear ratios			
Top gear	7.82	6.916:1	7.348:1
Third gear	8.6:1	8.603:1	9.141:1
Second gear	11.4:1	11.38:1	12.09:1
First gear	18.3:1	18.34:1	19.49:1
Brakes			
Front (diameter)	7in SLS 1969: 7in (17.8 cm) TLS	8in TLS	6in SLS
Hub	Full-width	Conical	Conical
Rear (diameter)	7in	7in	7in
Hub	Half-width, QD	Conical	Conical

SLS unit. At the rear of the machine, the previous year's integrated pillion grab rail and rear mudguard support became separate, with the grab rail being bolted onto the seat base. The colour scheme remained the same as 1968.

For 1970 the exhaust system changed again, with the exhaust pipe now curving around the front of the engine and frame down tube to sweep back over the primary drive side of the motor. It ran outside of the rear frame tubes and ended with a long Burgess type silencer that again terminated behind the rear wheel. The side of the exhaust pipe and silencer was covered by a large fibreglass heat shield, in a garish metal-flake silver finish. This guard pro-

tected both the rider's and pillion's legs; it ran from just behind the cylinder to the rear suspension unit. Small gold transfers replaced the long silver logo on the side panels and a larger 3½in diameter speedometer with trip meter in a vibration-proof rubber cup was fitted to the fork top yoke. The bike's fuel tank and mudguards were finished in Trophy Red, with black and chrome being used elsewhere.

The T25SS and T25T 1971

While the TR25W paid some lip service to the different roles expected of the BSA and Triumph, the T25SS and T25T were very much re-badged versions of the B25SS and

	TR25W Trophy (1968–70)	T25SS Blazer (1971)	T25T Trail Blazer (1971)
Wheels and tyres			
Front rim width – diameter	WM2 – 19	WM2 – 18	WM1 – 20
Front Tyre	3.25 × 19	3.25 × 18	3.00 × 20
Rear rim width – diameter	WM3 – 18	WM2 – 18	WM3 –18
Rear tyre	4.00 × 18	3.50 × 18	4.00 × 18
Electrics			
Voltage	12V	12V	12V
Headlamp size	6in	6in	6in
Headlamp shell	Black	Chrome	Chrome
Battery	10amp/hr	10amp/hr	10amp/hr
Ignition	Coil	Coil	Coil
Weight and capacities			
Fuel tank	US: 2.5gal (11.25 l) UK: 3gal (13.5 l)	2gal (9 l)	2gal (9 l)
Fuel tank material	Steel	Steel	Alloy
Oil tank	4pt (2.3ltr)	4pt (2.3ltr)	4pt (2.3ltr)
Seat height	31½in (800mm)	32in (813mm)	32in (813mm)
Length	82in (2,083mm)	85in (2,159mm)	85in (2,159mm)
Wheelbase	52in (1,321mm)	54in (1,372mm)	54in (1,372mm)
Ground clearance	7½in (191mm)	7in (179mm)	7in (179mm)
Dry weight	285lb (129kg)	290lb (132kg)	290lb (132kg)

LEFT: *It was all change in 1971, with the adoption of the new oil-in-frame running gear. The UK T25SS Blazer had the 8in TLS front brake in the new conical hub.*

BELOW: *The final unit single was the Triumph TR5MX Avenger. Essentially, it was a re-badged B50MX and was aimed at the competition market.*

B25T, differing only in minor cosmetic details. The T25SS (named Blazer) and the T25T (named Trail Blazer) were the road and trail versions respectively. The T25T was equipped with a high-level front mudguard, alloy fuel tank and braced handlebars, while the T25SS had a low-level front mudguard, steel fuel tank and high but unbraced handlebars.

The T25T also had a 3½in black-faced speedometer with a trip meter, while the SS made do with a black-faced 3in unit with no trip facility. The T25SS could be specified with a rev counter. The most significant difference between the T25T and T25SS models was the front wheel – the T25T had a 20in diameter wheel and a small 6in SLS front brake in its conical alloy hub, while the T25SS for the UK market had an 18in wheel with an 8in TLS front brake. Overall finish of both models was an orangey red shade called Bloody Red, used on the tank and mudguards. There was a black stripe on the centre of the front mudguard and black scallops on the fuel tank above the 'Triumph' name transfers, pinstriped in white. The black side panels carried gold transfers, either 'Trail Blazer 250' or 'Blazer SS' according to the model. The frame was finished in black. The T25 was produced for 1971 only.

The Triumph 500cc TR5MX Avenger 1974

The Triumph TR5MX Avenger was part of the final gasps of the BSA/Triumph group. Introduced for the 1974 model year as a US market model, it was a B50MX with Triumph

The final B50MX and TR5MX models sported a new exhaust system to meet noise requirements. It comprised two megaphone type silencers, each with a US Forestry approved spark arrester in the end.

badges, built to fulfil a market that was rapidly disappearing. As a pure off-roader, it had few frills and the alloy tank carried a blue painted Triumph style scallop rather than the traditional BSA 'cross' pattern.

Some of the final models arrived in the US with a peculiar exhaust system comprising two megaphone type silencers branching from the single upswept exhaust pipe on the timing side of the machine, with built-in spark arresters to meet the USDA requirements for not setting fire to the scenery.

3 Technical Description and Development

Introduction

This chapter provides technical details of the various components that make up a BSA unit single. For the purposes of this book the range has been split into three distinct chronological ranges, based on the points at which major changes were made to the overall range. These ranges are 1958–67, which covers the introduction of the C15 and B40 ranges through to the final C15 models. The next range is 1967–70, which covers the 250cc C25/B25 and the 441cc B44 ranges. The final section covers the 'last gasp' of the range of 1971–4, covering the B25 and B50 ranges.

Each section starts with a description of the major components that were used at the inception of each of the model ranges and

The C15 timing side shows the gear oil pump and distributor, both driven from a shaft driven from the crank. The camshaft is driven directly from the crank by a pinion.

then describes the major changes that were introduced to each component as the range was developed and refined.

Stage 1: C15 and B40 1958–67

Engine Layout and Design

At its introduction in 1958, the C15 engine was not state of the art by any stretch of the imagination. Bearing in mind the circumstances of the development of the model it was no surprise that the engine design was based heavily on the Triumph Tiger Cub.

Both the BSA and Triumph engine were dry sump, single-cylinder four-stroke units, with pushrod operated overhead valves and a four-speed gearbox incorporated in unit with the main crankcase castings. The reader should bear in mind that in the 1950s overhead camshafts were the preserve of foreign exotica or homegrown racing machines and were virtually unheard of on the road – in contrast to the situation in the 1930s when several manufacturers offered ohc motors for road use. In line with most BSA (and Triumph) engines of the time, the primary drive was positioned on the left-hand side of the engine, while the camshaft and timing gear, oil pump and gear change mechanism were positioned on the right-hand side. There was a shaft driven from the crankshaft using a seven-start worm gear, which drove the oil pump that sat at the bottom of the shaft and the ignition distributor that sat at the top of the shaft.

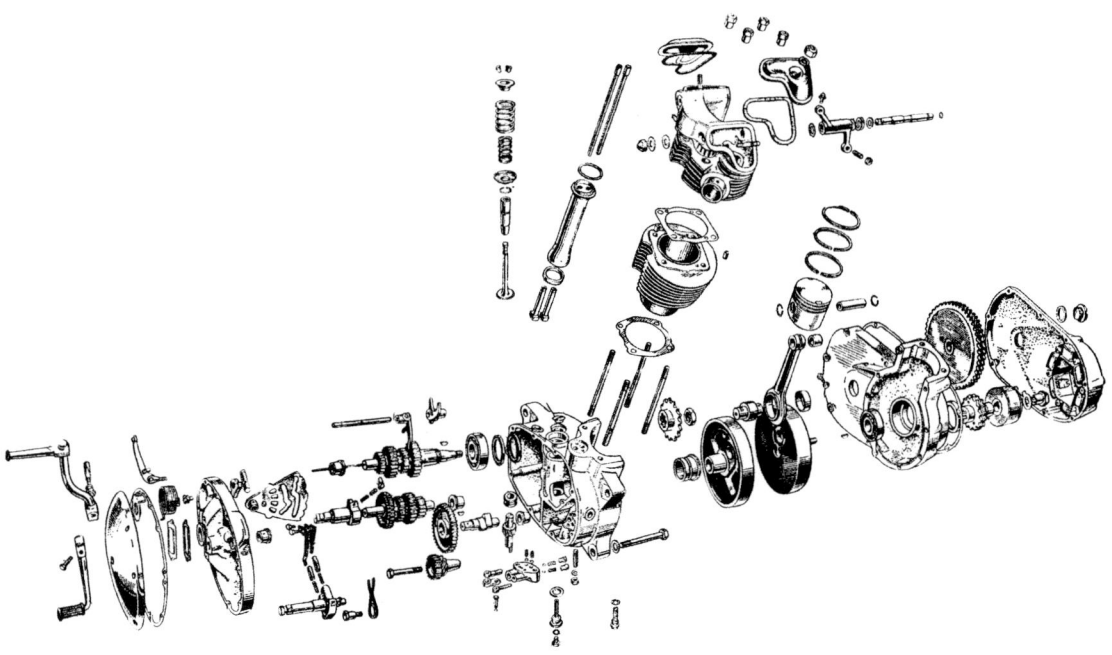

The C15 engine followed the overall layout of the Tiger Cub. This diagram shows a Cub engine.

The ignition points were housed in a sepa-rate housing behind the cylinder barrel, set back at about 15 degrees from the vertical. The housing carried both the ignition contact breaker points and a mechanical advance/retard unit, which used a bobweight and spring mechanism to advance the timing as the engine revs rose. While the unit is named as a distributor in the official BSA literature, it was not really a distributor in the commonly used sense of distributing a spark from a single coil to two or more cylinders; rather, it was in function simply an ignition points housing. However, for consistency this book will refer to it as a distributor!

At the other end of the drive shaft the oil pump used standard BSA technology and was a gear unit with both the feed and the scavenge functions contained in one alloy body. The pump was bolted onto the crankcases at the lower end of the shaft and the scavenge tube

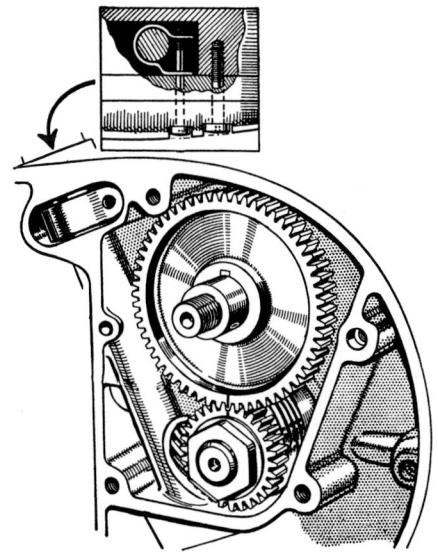

The shaft driving the oil pump and distributor was driven from a worm gear on the crank. The distributor body was locked in place with a clamp.

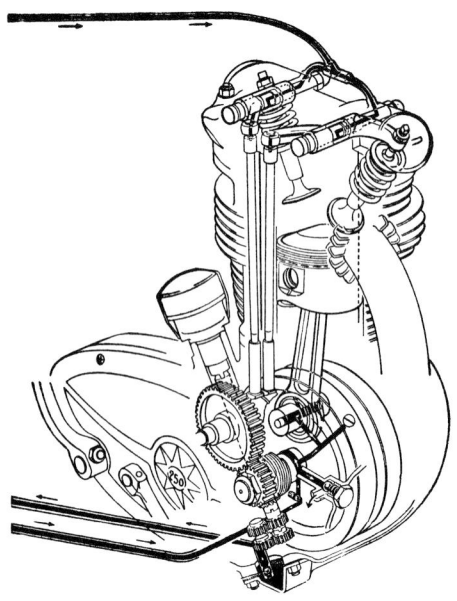

The oil pump sucked oil from the tank and pumped it to the big end. Oil dropping into the sump was returned to the oil tank.

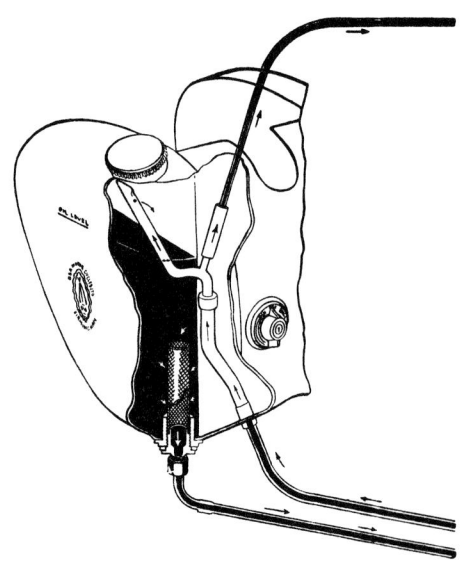

The oil tank carried a gauze filter in its base to filter the oil being pumped to the engine. The return side had a take-off to lubricate the top end.

protruded downwards into the sump. This was in contrast to the Cub, which had a traditional Triumph twin plunger unit that was driven using a sliding block connected to an eccentric drive from the bottom of the distributor drive.

The scavenge side pulled used oil from the sump in the bottom of the crankcase, which was covered by a square steel sump plate that incorporated a gauze oil filter, then returned it to the oil tank. Oil feed to and from the separate oil tank used flexible rubber hoses and the oil feed to the rockers was taken from the scavenge side return via a fitting on the oil tank. There was a second steel gauze oil filter incorporated in the main feed from the bottom of the oil tank.

The oil feed to the rockers followed Triumph practice with a dual union copper pipe feed to each of the rocker spindles, fixed to the spindles using domed nuts with copper washers. Outboard of the oil pump/distributor drive shaft's worm drive was the pinion that drove the camshaft, which was positioned directly above the crank and was supported by bushes in the crankcase and the inner timing cover.

Inboard of the worm drive was the timing-side main bush, a copper/lead plain bearing that was drilled to act as the main oil feed from the pump to the big end. The bush was fitted into a steel sleeve that was a tight fit in the crankcases and was set in position by two flats machined into the cases which lined up with two slots on the bush housing. This ensured that the oil way drillings in the crankcases and the bush lined up. The bush ran on a hard steel sleeve that was a tight fit on the timing-side main shaft, so the crankshaft was protected from wear in the main bearing. Four holes were drilled in the sleeve in order to allow the oil fed to the bush to be fed through a groove in the inside edge of the sleeve into the oil way in the main shaft that led to the big-end bearing.

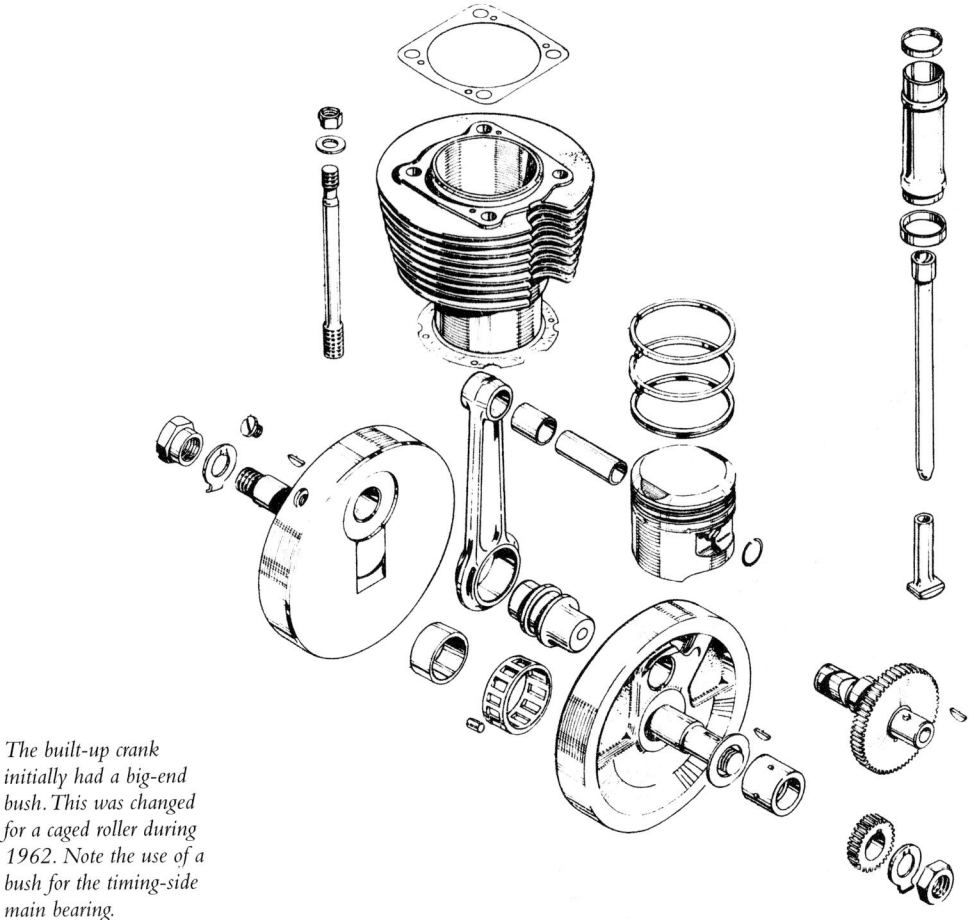

The built-up crank initially had a big-end bush. This was changed for a caged roller during 1962. Note the use of a bush for the timing-side main bearing.

On the drive side the crank was supported by a relatively large Hoffmann RL325L ball bearing. An external seal prevented engine oil from leaking into the primary chain case.

In appearance, the engine proclaimed its membership of the BSA marque by having a vertical cylinder and head, while the Tiger Cub's cylinder was inclined forwards by 15 degrees. The distributor, which was vertical on the Cub, leaned backwards by about 15 degrees on the C15, further evidence of its Cub ancestry and the C15's dependence on the layout of that engine, despite the differences in the placing of the cylinder barrel.

The bottom end of the engine comprised three main castings and two outer cases. The drive-side casing incorporated the inner primary chain case and the drive-side main bearing housing. The timing side carried the drive-side main, the cam followers, the inner camshaft bearing and the inner gearbox shell, as well as the gearbox main and layshaft drive-side bearings. The inner timing case carried the outer camshaft bush, the gearbox main and layshaft timing-side bearings, as well as the gear change, clutch-operating and kick-start mechanisms. While this gave a compact and light unit, a major disadvantage of the layout, which would remain

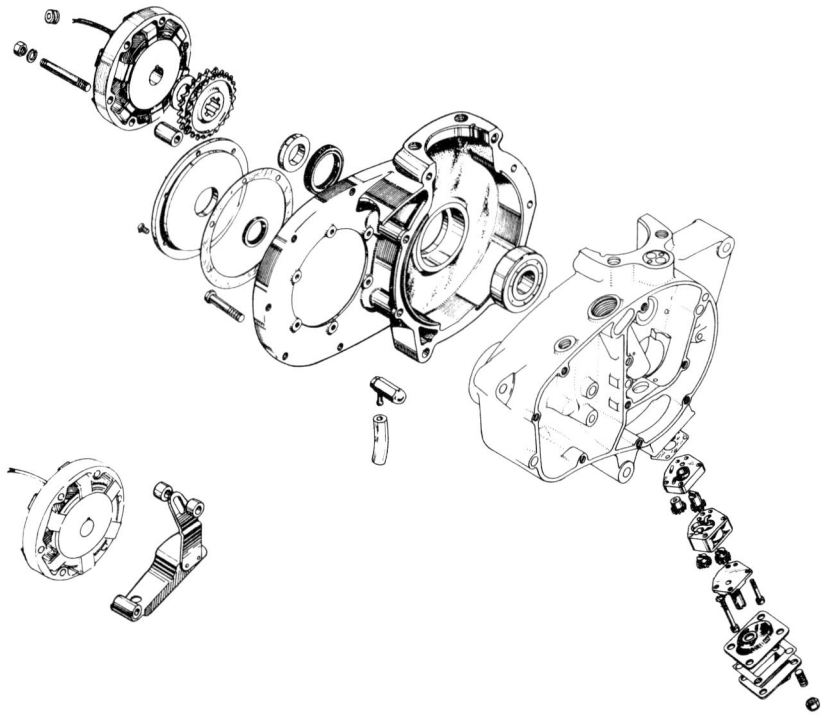

The C15 crankcases were similar in layout to the Cub. The oil pump was a gear type, which was screwed into the web by the crank and was driven by a shaft.

with the engine throughout its life, was that the removal of the inner timing cover was needed for any engine or gearbox work, which entailed dismantling the clutch (see Chapter 6 for a modification to avoid this problem). On later engines, with the ignition points driven directly from the camshaft, it also meant disturbing the ignition timing. The crankcases were fixed into the frame using three lugs, at the front, rear and centrally at the bottom of the castings.

The built-up crankshaft comprised two cast-iron flywheels, the right-hand side one incorporating a sludge trap that is accessible for cleaning through a slotted screw-in plug on the periphery of the flywheel. The crank pin was made from nickel chrome steel and was an interference fit in the two flywheels. The big end was a plain bearing, comprising a steel-backed lead bronze sleeve that was pressed into the steel connecting rod and bore on the crank pin. The drive-side crankpin carried the primary drive sprocket and the alternator rotor. The top end of the engine comprised a cast-iron barrel with, following Triumph practice, a separate chromed pushrod tube which introduced two joints that could leak oil. Bore and stroke were relatively under-square (that is, bore is longer than the stroke) at 67mm × 70mm – much less square in proportion than the Tiger Cub bore and stroke of 63mm × 64mm. Note that the claimed capacity of the C15 unit was 249cc, but in fact the measurements give a capacity of 247cc. This error was perpetuated in the official factory specifications until the 1969 model year, when the correct capacity of 247cc was listed!

The cylinder head was an all-alloy item, which carried two valves. The head and barrel were fixed onto the crankcases using four long through studs that screwed into the crankcases and were secured using nuts and bolts. The nuts on the drive side were easily accessible for a socket set and torque wrench. However, the two nuts on the timing side were buried under the platform for the rocker box, which did not have enough room to fit a socket. While this made it difficult to use a torque wrench on the head bolts, it must be remembered that in the 1950s torque wrenches were not in common use in the motorcycle industry. BSA service notes of the time merely instruct the mechanic to: 'Screw on the four cylinder head nuts and washers, and tighten down firmly and evenly.'

This could only be done with a cranked and thin-walled ring spanner, which made it difficult to tighten down all four nuts evenly. Later versions of the BSA workshop manual listed a short cranked spanner with a square socket drive to enable the use of a torque wrench, along with the calculations required to take into account the increased leverage as a result of the length of the crank. The valves were carried in iron valve guides with a conservative 76-degree angle between the two, with the inlet valve of 1.317in and exhaust also 1.317in in diameter. The valve seats were close-grained iron inserts that were cast in place during the manufacture of the cylinder head.

The valve rocker gear was carried in a separate alloy rocker box, again following Triumph practice, but perhaps surprisingly not as practised in the Cub engine, which carried

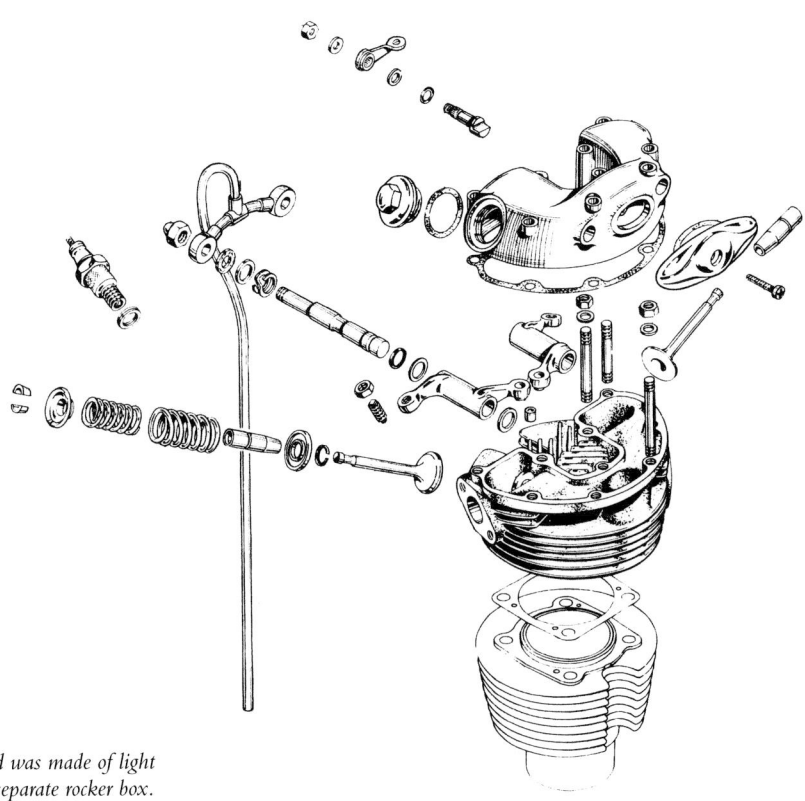

The cylinder head was made of light alloy, as was the separate rocker box.

its rockers in cast-in bearers in the head itself. The C15 design had the disadvantage of placing the whole rocker box under load as the valve gear operated and hence promoted oil leaks between the rocker box and the head. This weakness was acknowledged in later models by BSA upgrading the diameter of the nine holding studs from ¼in to ⁵⁄₁₆in. The centre two studs were used to carry a triangular plate, which had the head steady-bolted to it and a bracket fixed to the frame's top tube to cut down on vibration. There were two rocker shafts for the inlet and exhaust valves, which were lubricated from the return side of the oil system. The rockers had individual screw and locknut adjusters for valve clearance adjustment, accessible (or rather just about accessible) from round Triumph twin style caps with X-shaped slots on them for tightening. Again, this did not follow the Cub's example, which had large bolt-on covers that allowed easy

access to the valve adjusters. These valve caps joined in with the honourable Triumph tradition of distributing themselves over the local countryside as they were difficult to tighten adequately, until fairly quickly into the production cycle the slots were replaced with a hexagon that allowed the caps to be properly tightened down using a spanner. They still made it awkward to adjust, as there was little room to get a feeler gauge into the gap between the tappet and the valve.

The exhaust valve had a hard stellite tip at the top of its stem and the top of the inlet valve's stem was hardened to minimize wear. Pushrods were made of alloy with steel top caps to keep the weight of the valve train down to a minimum. Cam followers ran directly in the right-hand side crankcase and were case-hardened and ramp-formed to provide quiet operation. The cylinder head with the rocker box attached could just be removed from the

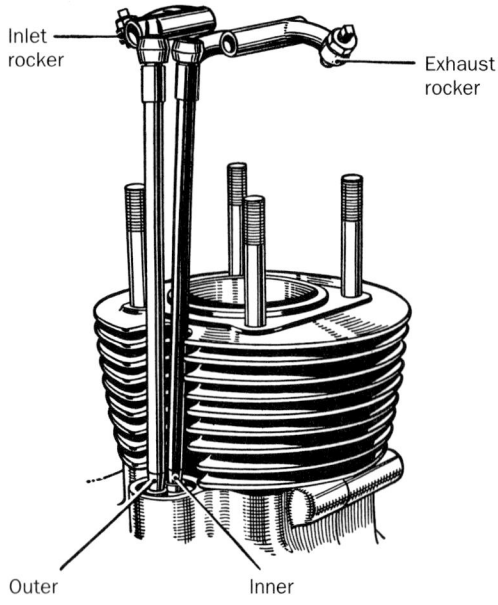

The valve gear was operated by pushrods driven from cam followers running in the crankcase. Tappet adjustment was by screw and locknut.

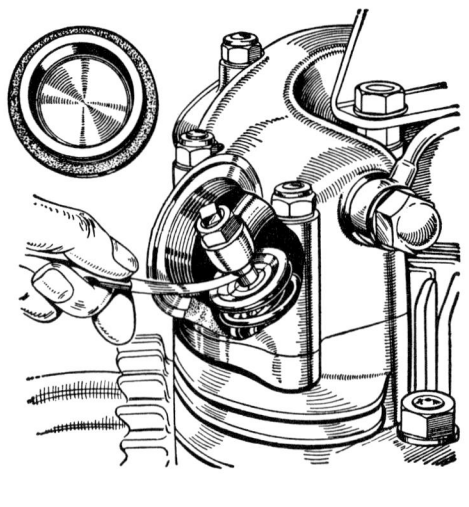

Valve clearances were relatively accessible for adjustment.

engine while it was still in the frame, although a certain amount of fiddling was needed!

The engine breather was a mechanically timed affair, driven from the end of the camshaft. It allowed crankcase pressure to be vented into the space between the inner and outer timing cases. The camshaft was hollow and had a radial drilling that was brought into line with a drilled port in the inner timing cover when the piston was at the appropriate position. This allowed pressure from the crankcase to be vented, hopefully reducing the likelihood of oil leaks being caused by excessive pressure. The piston was a truncated cone, light alloy unit and gave a compression ratio of around 7.25:1 (although some sources quote 7.3:1). It carried three rings, the top two being solid compression rings and the third an oil scraper. The gudgeon pin was located by wire circlips. BSA claimed that this first version of the C15 engine gave 15bhp, hence the designation.

The B40 engine followed the same layout of the C15 and the only external differentiator was the B40 barrel with a cast-in pushrod tunnel as opposed to the C15's chromed separate tube – the B40 reflecting BSA's practice with the A7/A10 twins while the C15 reflected Triumph practice with its engines. The B40's increase in capacity over the C15 was achieved by boring, with dimensions of 79mm × 70mm giving an over-square unit with a capacity of 343cc. However, the apparent similarity of the B40 unit concealed the fact that a number of internal changes had been made, both to strengthen the engine and promote efficiency. The crankcases were beefed up, both to accommodate the larger bore and hence a larger crankcase mouth, but also around the main bearing at the bottom end, to increase stiffness. The cylinder head was also altered, with a valve angle of 70 degrees, as opposed to the C15's 76 degrees. The B40 did retain the C15 type main bearings, with a plain copper lead timing-side bush. The drive-side main bearing was a 2⅜in diameter roller.

Primary drive was by duplex chain from the engine sprocket to the clutch basket. Initially there was no chain tensioner.

Interestingly, unlike the C15, the 350cc model's designation of B40 did not represent the power produced by the motor – a 40bhp B40 would have been some achievement and would have been a pretty good performer!

Primary Drive and Gearbox

The C15 and the B40 shared the same primary drive and gearbox. The primary drive was on the left-hand side of the engine and comprised the duplex chain drive from the crankshaft end to the clutch. A Lucas alternator was positioned concentric to the crankshaft, with the stator bolted to the crankcase and the rotor fixed to the main shaft outboard of the primary drive sprocket. This was in contrast to the Tiger Cub, where the stator was bolted to the inner face of the chain case, which made it difficult to measure the air gap required between the rotor and the stator. No chain tensioner was fitted for the ⅜in pitch duplex primary chain. The clutch was of conventional design, with four springs, four friction plates and five plain plates, with a built-in rubber shock absorber and a centre adjuster screw accessible through a screw-in cover in the polished chain case. The chain case also showed Edward Turner's influence with a stylized scallop running from front to back, which, while not as obvious as Triumph's styling cues, was in

93

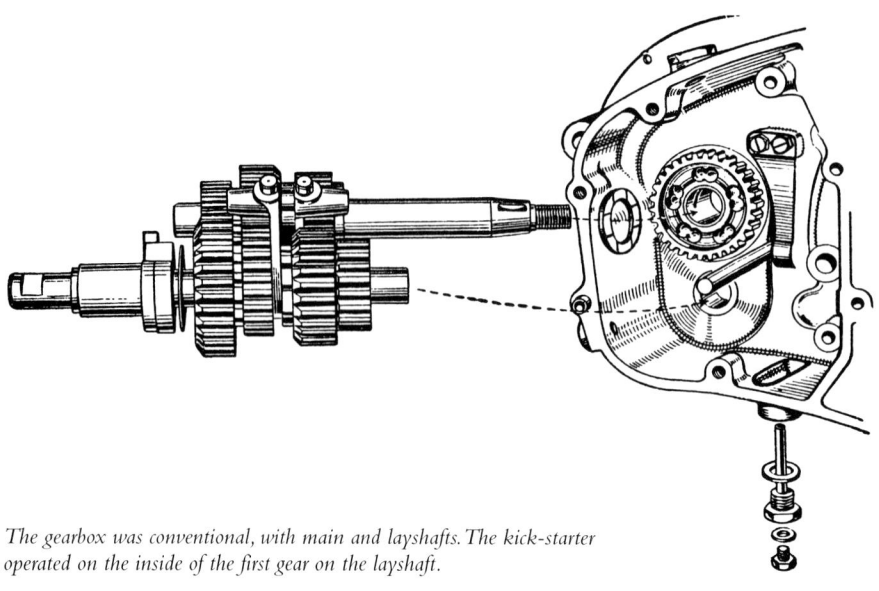

The gearbox was conventional, with main and layshafts. The kick-starter operated on the inside of the first gear on the layshaft.

The Lucas Energy Transfer Ignition System

Off-road competition machines in the 1950s were often powered by big four-stroke singles (and some twins) and they almost all were equipped with magnetos to provide ignition. During the late 1940s and 1950s the quest for lighter and cheaper ignition systems led to the introduction of battery and coil systems. In addition, lightweight two strokes were beginning to appear in off-road competition and their lightness and consequent manoeuvrability, improved reliability and good power to weight ratios was enabling them to become increasingly competitive. On production models for day to day use, the days of the magneto were waning and new engines such as that in the C15 were designed from the onset to be battery and coil ignition rather than use an expensive and complex magneto. This type of coil ignition required direct current (DC) to power the ignition coil and the DC current was supplied from a battery that was charged from the alternator via a rectifier that converted the alternating current (AC) to DC. However, in the off-road competition field, a battery was looked on as unacceptably heavy and was potentially unreliable as it was vulnerable to vibration damage and would not be too happy if the bike was dropped. In

addition, it required regular maintenance and needed to be either charged with the consequent complex charging circuits, or run as a total loss system and hence need recharging off the bike.

The Lucas Energy Transfer Ignition system was designed to provide a battery-less ignition system for these types of competition machines that were fitted with the newly introduced alternator systems. The system was described as incorporating 'certain characteristics of both magneto and coil ignition'. Essentially, the system provides a burst of current to an ignition coil at (or about!) the time it is needed to produce a spark – so it can be seen that the position of the rotor and stator is very important to ensure that maximum power was supplied to a coil just before the contact breakers open to trigger the collapse of the magnetic field in the coil that produces the spark. The system utilizes the basic six-coil stator and six-magnet rotor, with four of the six stator coils being used to power the ignition. The remaining two coils provide some additional power for lighting, if needed.

The four ignition coils are connected in series with each other and with the primary windings of a separately mounted ignition coil.

marked contrast to BSA's earlier plain chain cases.

The kick-start mechanism was fitted in the outer timing cover and comprised a ratchet and pawl rather than the more common quadrant and pinion normally seen on British bikes. The kick-starter spindle carried a sprung pawl, which engaged in the first gear on the layshaft. The right-hand face of the gear was hollowed out and machined to accept the pawl. When the kick-starter was operated, the pawl engaged with the first gear layshaft pinion, which then turned the engine over. The advantages of the system were its compact nature, minimal number of parts and that its design was based on that used on the Tiger Cub. The main disadvantage was that it was not particularly robust and wore quickly. The first

batch of bikes revealed parts of the mechanism had been wrongly heat-treated, resulting in a spate of failures and a large number of bikes requiring rectification before they could be shipped to the dealers.

The four-speed gearbox was a developed Tiger Cub item and followed standard industry practice, with a hollow main shaft connected to the clutch, with the clutch-operating pushrod running through it from the operating mechanism on the timing side. The layshaft sat below the main shaft, making for a compact unit. The main shaft was carried on a bronze bush in the timing side and a roller bearing on the drive side. The main shaft was connected to the clutch to allow power to be transmitted into the box, while power was output to the gearbox sprocket via a

At the time the contact breaker points are closed, the ignition coil primary winding is short-circuited and the four ignition coils are energized by the magnetic field of the rotating magnets in the stator. While the contact breakers are closed, the AC current generated in the stator coils is lost to earth via the easiest route through the contact breakers. When the contact breaker points are opened, a pulse of energy (that is, a sudden burst of electricity) is discharged to earth through the primary winding of the ignition coil, which induces a high voltage in the ignition coil secondary winding that is sent to the spark plug.

So it can be seen that as accurate timing is essential to get the motor to start and run, the accurate setting up of the rotor, stator and ignition timing is vital. If it is not set up correctly, the bike will either start and not run (ignition too retarded), or will not start easily but will run after a bump start (ignition too advanced). As set at the factory, the contact breaker is set to open when the AC supplied to the coil is at a peak, to ensure that the strongest spark is produced. The efficiency of the system can be adversely affected by inaccurate placing of the rotor on the crank, use of an unsuitable rotor, misalignment of the stator in the primary chain case or inaccurate setting of the timing. The system was used on other bikes in the range, especially the Triumph

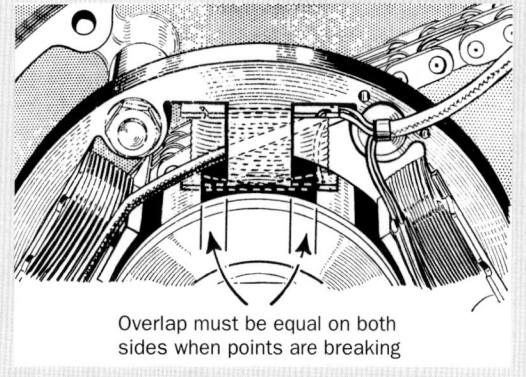

Overlap must be equal on both sides when points are breaking

The Lucas energy transfer ignition relied on the exact positioning of the alternator relevant to the timing in order to work.

Tiger Cub, where it gained a poor reputation, but I have been unable to find any criticism of the system as fitted on the C15S or C15T models. So the conclusion has to be that the system ran reasonably well on the BSA unit singles – or that riders chucked it away at the first opportunity and fitted a standard ignition system using a capacitor rather than a battery!

concentric pinion on the main shaft inboard of the clutch. The layshaft was supported on a bush on its drive side and by the kick-starter spindle, which was supported in the inner timing case on the timing side. One sliding and three fixed pinions were mounted on each shaft to give the four speeds. The two selector forks were moved using tracks in a cam plate which sat vertically ahead of the two shafts and moved up and down through a ratchet system operated from the foot pedal. Each selector fork engaged with the single sliding gear on both lay and main shafts to change between the four speeds and neutral. The cam plate pivoted about a shaft in the inner timing side and a positive stop mechanism for each gear position was implemented using five notches in the end of the plate that engaged in a leaf spring bolted to the clutch side of the gearbox casting. The foot-operated positive stop mechanism provided a Triumph style one-down, three-up change pattern.

The gearbox had its own oil supply, separate from the engine, with a filler on the top of the casing and a drain plug that incorporated a level tube on the underside. Output to the rear chain went out of the gearbox behind the clutch through a concentric sleeve to which the final drive sprocket was splined and fixed in place with a large, thin nut and locking washer. The inside of the sprocket had a specially ground flat surface that fitted into the oil seal for the main shaft, while the outer edge of the sprocket had a felt washer to prevent leakage from the primary chain case. A round screwed-on alloy plate was provided in the inner chain-case casting, behind the clutch, to enable the final drive sprocket to be replaced – however, this operation did require the dismantling of the clutch and primary drive so was not an easy or quick task. Luckily, British machines of the era used high-quality steel in the manufacture of the sprockets, so when a chain wore out the sprocket would not usually be too badly worn, so did not need to be replaced too often. This was in stark contrast to the Oriental machines of the 1960s and 1970s, in which the poor-quality sprockets wore along with the chain and needed to be replaced as a set – chain, front sprocket and rear sprocket.

In conclusion, the engine and gearbox design of the C15 did not break any new ground – which was probably a good thing bearing in mind the limited time that BSA had for developing a completely 'new' model. The Tiger Cub ancestry was initially well hidden, simply by using a vertical cylinder barrel rather than the Cub's inclined design. While this was in tune with the BSA corporate appearance at the time, it did not make for a particularly good-looking unit. The design as a whole had a number of weak spots -- the big end, timing-side bush, kick-start mechanism and overly complicated distributor to drive the points, but all of these would be overcome with design revisions throughout the life of the motor. The engine did meet the needs of the punter when it was first introduced as a softly tuned commuter and touring bike. Competition and the higher performance roadsters exposed the weaknesses and generated the fixes, which led to extensive revisions to the engine unit throughout its eight-year life.

Engine and Gearbox Development

There were three main changes to the C15 and B40 engines, all of them driven by the development work of the competition shop. The first was the introduction of the roller big-end bearing, first seen in the SS80 of 1961; the second was the relocation of the contact breaker points to the timing cover; and the third was the replacement of the timing-side bush with a roller bearing and new oil pump during 1967.

The introduction of a roller big-end bearing came in 1961 and initially was only used on the SS80, B40 and SS90. This involved a completely new crankpin and con rod,

ABOVE: This 1960 C15 Star is a nicely restored and original-looking example. (Mick Walker)

BELOW: The 1971 Triumph Blazer contrasts with the 1960 C15T – but there is a definite family resemblance.

ABOVE LEFT: The C15T featured in this book is lacking the chromed tank. The bike is set up as an on-/off-road trail bike.

ABOVE RIGHT: The author aboard his restored 1960 C15T.

ABOVE: The timing side of the restored C15T shows the high-level exhaust system as fitted to the Trials model. The C15S had an open exhaust and so was not suitable for road use.

LEFT: The drive side of the C15T shows the purposeful styling of the model.

RIGHT: The 1970 Triumph TR25W Trophy was an on-/off-road bike. Its dominant feature was the upswept exhaust with its silver fibreglass heat shield.

BELOW: The last Starfire of 1970 was a handsome bike, with its modern styling and full size proportions. (Mick Walker)

ABOVE: The 1971 machines had new switches on the handlebars for the indicators and lights. This 1971 T25SS has the optional tachometer fitted.

For the 1971 range the BSA publicity machine produced a range of excellent publicity shots. This shows the famous Triumph development rider and road racer, Percy Tait, on a B50T.

the most popular motor cycle in the world **BSA**

XON940

ABOVE: Another 1959 publicity shot showing a C15 in the Cotswolds.

ABOVE: For the September 1959 brochure BSA put an artist's impression of the then new C15 on the cover of its brochure.

RIGHT: The B40 was never a great sales success, mainly due to the decline of the 350cc market. This is a 1963 model.

BELOW: The B40 SS90 was marketed at home and in export markets. This is the US version, with high bars, a passenger grab rail and rubber gaiters on the forks.

New **BSA** super-sports lightweight

High-compression piston, competition camshaft, large-bore carburetor.

Metallic Blue tank with chrome panels, chrome fenders, lots of other parts in brilliant chrome.

BSA SS-90 Sportsman 350cc

ABOVE: The B25/T25 engine unit was a clean and attractive unit. It was light, compact and powerful, if somewhat fragile.

ABOVE: BSA used the local area to find locations for publicity shots. Here in September 1960 the Shakespeare theatre at Stratford-upon-Avon forms the backdrop for an early C15, a 650cc A10 and a BSA scooter.

The 1971 T25T Trail Blazer was a competent off-road bike. Differences from the roadster (T25SS) were limited, but included braced handlebars and high-level front mudguard.

The 1971 B25SS Gold Star's name was controversial, raising the hackles of die-hard BSA fans.

ABOVE: *The park at Shirley, near Birmingham, was the venue for this 1959 publicity shot. It features a C15 and a 175cc D7 Bantam Super.*

LEFT: *BSAs were exported and promoted all over the world. Here is a 1960 model C15 in Cape Town, South Africa.*

BELOW: *The US version of the C15 differed little from the UK market model. This 1960 model shows the high 'Western' handlebars.*

A *brand new* BSA! . . . a brightly finished, snappy performing 250 c.c. overhead valve lightweight of clean, ultra-modern design. The new Star engine is built in-unit with clutch, primary drive and four speed gearbox, and features easy starting, dependable idling, and cool running, with quick acceleration to top highway speeds.

Full width hubs, powerful brakes, hydraulically controlled suspension and comfortable dualseat are designed to increase comfort, safety, and riding pleasure. Finish is bright red baked enamel with white striping on fenders, black frame and lots of brilliant chrome and polished alloy. You'll be proud to own and ride this brand new BSA Star!

Complete specifications on pages 14-15.

BSA
"250 STAR"
250 c.c. O.H.V. Single

Get *Star* Performance with this New BSA 250 O.H.V.!

ABOVE: In the USA BSA pushed the Victor Enduro model as a trail bike. Here a 1968 model is in the woods.

RIGHT: The US B44 Shooting Star was the roadster version of the 441cc unit single. Glamour came as standard!

The Victor Grand Prix was only produced for a couple of years. It was the competition version of the Victor Special and roadster. With a close relationship to the works bikes, it was a competitive mount for the clubman. (Simon Cheney)

The 1970 TR25W had its exhaust moved to the drive side. Still high-level, it sported a large silver metal-flake fibreglass heat shield.

ABOVE: The author's 1971 T25SS Blazer, showing the timing side and the large lozenge-shaped silencer with its stainless-steel head shield.

BELOW: The drive side of the T25SS is a neat and clean design, with typical 1970s styling.

Gearbox Level Plug

The first C15s had a relatively complex arrangement to manage the gearbox oil level. There was a conventional filler plug on the top of the casing and a drain plug on the underside. The drain plug was of a relatively large diameter and had a concentric hole in it, sealed at the bottom with a small secondary bolt and washer, and had an open tube projecting up into the gearbox. The length of this tube was set to be at the correct level of the gearbox level. The objective was to fill the gearbox with the drain plug in place, but with the small secondary plug left out. Once oil started to dribble out of the centre hole, the oil level was correct and the centre secondary plug could be replaced. This was all very well, but there was a problem. While many owners would not bother with the gearbox oil level, a diligent owner who checked the gearbox oil regularly could end up inadvertently draining the gearbox oil.

Each time the level was checked, oil in the tube would dribble out – indicating to the diligent owner

that the oil level was slightly over level. However, what was happening was that the oil was flung into the tube by the action of the gears whizzing around. So there was always oil in the tube, which the diligent owner was draining off each time the level was checked. The end result would be low gearbox oil, but with the indicator showing that the level was correct (or slightly over). This overcomplicated system was replaced by a simple one-piece 'normal' drain plug and a plastic filler plug with a built-in dipstick on the B25, reducing the number of parts needed and making for an almost foolproof oil checking system!

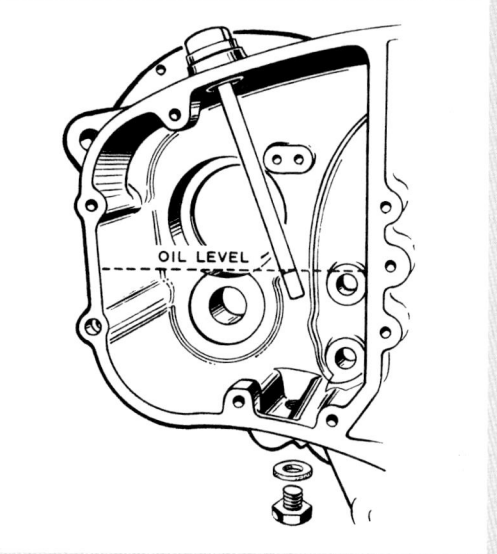

The C15 hollow tube and plug used to check and drain the gearbox oil level.

The B25 used a more convenient dipstick and solid plug – cheaper to produce and easier to use.

replacing the steel backed bronze bush with a caged roller bearing. The C15 Star model eventually gained the better bottom end in 1964.

To counter instances of teeth breaking off the layshaft's top gear, a new tooth form, usually referred to as a 'stub' tooth, was introduced for the top gear pair. The pitch of the teeth on

the 'stub' pinions was the same as the previous type, but the teeth were slightly smaller in height than the old type.

The first set of changes that altered the outside appearance of the engine came in 1966, with the 'points inside' engine, designated C15F and B40F. The changes were substantial – along with the deletion of the distributor, the

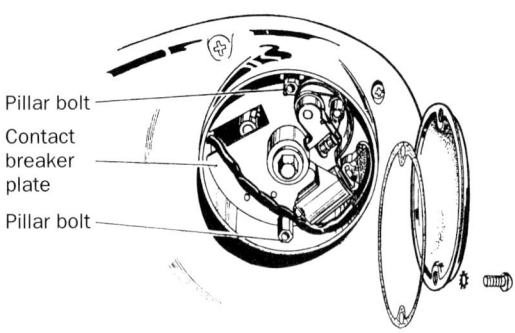

Pillar bolt

Contact
breaker
plate

Pillar bolt

The distributor was replaced with the points in the side of the engine driven directly from the camshaft.

clutch-operating mechanism and the kick-start mechanism were both redesigned.

The points were relocated to the timing side and were driven directly from the end of the camshaft. The advance/retard unit was fitted on a taper in the end of the camshaft and located with a bolt and the points were mounted on a plate fixed to the outer timing case. The points were covered by a round chrome cover. This gave the engine a more modern look, as well as making the points more easily accessible for maintenance. In conjunction with these changes, the kick-start mechanism was also redesigned. A quadrant replaced the pinion mechanism inside first gear on the layshaft and operated on a ratchet fixed to the end of the main shaft. This meant new main and layshafts in the gearbox, new first-gear pinions and a modified inner timing casing. The clutch mechanism was also updated to a rack and pinion mechanism within the inner timing case, driven by a lever on the top of the casing. This made changing the clutch cable a lot easier than before.

The final development of the C15 and B40 engine units was the C15G and B40G. Building on the F series changes, this development took all of the experience gained from the competition models and resulted in what was probably the best 250cc engine BSA ever put

into production. This engine at last lost the timing-side main bush, having timing-side ball and drive-side roller-bearing mains. Oil for the roller big end was fed through oil ways drilled in the timing-side inner cover into the end of the crankshaft. Hand in hand with this development came a new oil pump, albeit still with two sets of gears for feed and scavenge. The pump bolted onto the side of the crankcase and was driven directly from the screw drive on the crank, enabling the distributor drive shaft to be dispensed with. This was probably the most rugged and reliable engine of the C15/C25/B25 family and is identifiable by the prefix C15SG for the Sportsman models. Its ancestry can be traced directly back to the works competition units, with the improvements making it into an engine that could be driven hard with few, if any, ill effects. Unfortunately, the engine was short-lived, as it was replaced by the C25/B25 unit, which, although cheaper to produce, was nowhere near as strong or reliable.

Frame and Swinging Arm

At the introduction of the C15 range, the bike was hailed by BSA and the contemporary press as being up to date. However, the frame, as well as being heavily based on that fitted to Triumph's Tiger Cub, owed much of its design to BSA's earlier offerings and earlier ways of manufacturing. Firstly, the main loop of the frame was made up of twenty carbon steel tubes, brazed into malleable iron lugs. The head lug was dip-brazed to impart more strength. This method of construction was somewhat surprising as BSA had already moved across to all-welded construction frames for most of its models – examples being the swinging-arm frames used for the A series twins (A7 and A10), the B series singles (B33) and the Bantam – and indeed the C12 frame was of mainly welded construction.

Secondly, the C15 frame was formed of two parts that were bolted together – the brazed up front loop and the rear subframe, which was of part-welded and part-brazed lug construction. Again, this method of construction was based on past practice and did not reflect the current methods in use on BSA's own A and B series ranges. However, the new C15 frame did mirror the Triumph Tiger Cub's frame to a great extent in layout and construction. Both shared the brazed lug construction method and the lightweight rear subframe bolted onto a substantial main loop. Even the 'swan neck' cast-iron head lug of the Tiger Cub (a known weak point on the Cub that was countered by incorporating two bracing strips within the fuel tank) was retained on the BSA frame. Note that on the BSA frame, the head-steady was bolted to a circular bracket bolted to the top tube of the main loop, rather than to a rigid, welded-on bracket.

The frame had single top, down and seat tubes, plus a duplex cradle supporting the engine. The swinging arm was supported on a thick pin, which fitted tightly into the main frame lug, and the swinging arm pivoted on phosphor bronze bushes. These bushes had to be line-reamed to ensure an accurate fit and hence alignment of the swinging arm. The rear section of the frame bolted onto each end of the swinging-arm pin and to a lug at the back of the main loop. This helped to brace the swinging-arm pivot. Rear shock absorbers bolted onto the rear loop. The steering head was formed from a single 'swan-neck' casting, which, like the Triumph Tiger Cub and the C series 350/500 twins, resulted in the top of the steering head being unbraced. This did not seem to affect the steering of the bike in standard tune and meant that the fuel tank could sit on top of the top tube and not need to have a large tunnel that would restrict capacity. The steering head angle was 65 degrees and the steering lock was 50 degrees.

The basic roadster frame was used with some modifications on the trials and scrambles models that were introduced in 1959, with some success. However, the brazed lug construction was heavier than an equivalent all-welded frame and, combined with the bolt-up construction, was potentially less rigid than a one-piece frame.

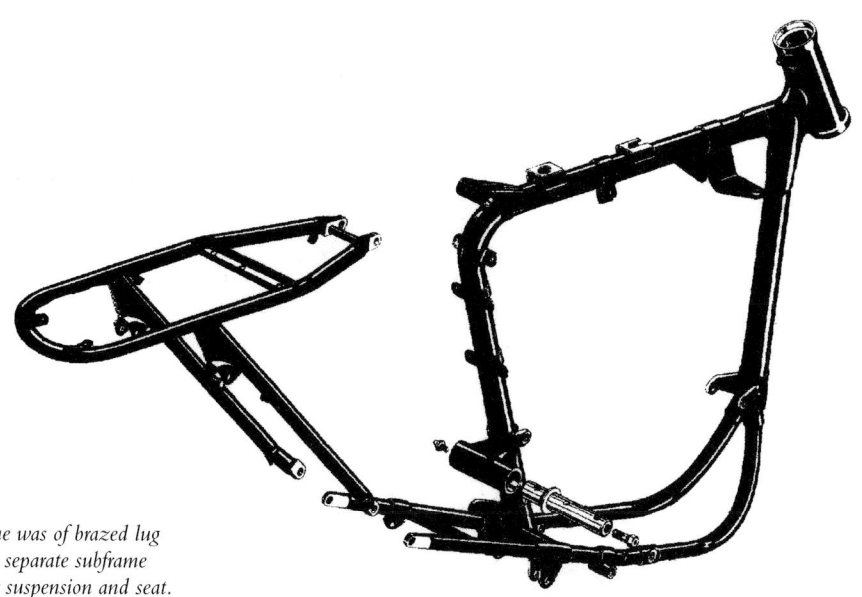

The C15 frame was of brazed lug construction. A separate subframe carried the rear suspension and seat.

This led to the development of an all-welded one-piece frame during the early 1960s for the works competition models, which was introduced on the production competition models for the 1965 model year – keeping the works machines ahead of the production models! The new frame featured on both the competition-oriented range in the UK (the C15T Trials and C15S Scrambles) and the trail bikes such as the US Market 250cc Starfire 250cc competition models (the Scrambles, Trials Cat and roadster) and the 350cc B40 Enduro Star. The roadsters continued with the original frame until they were discontinued in 1967.

The B40 frame was almost identical to the C15 roadster's original unit, being strengthened to handle the extra capacity. It followed the developments of the C15 frame.

The C15 remained in production with the

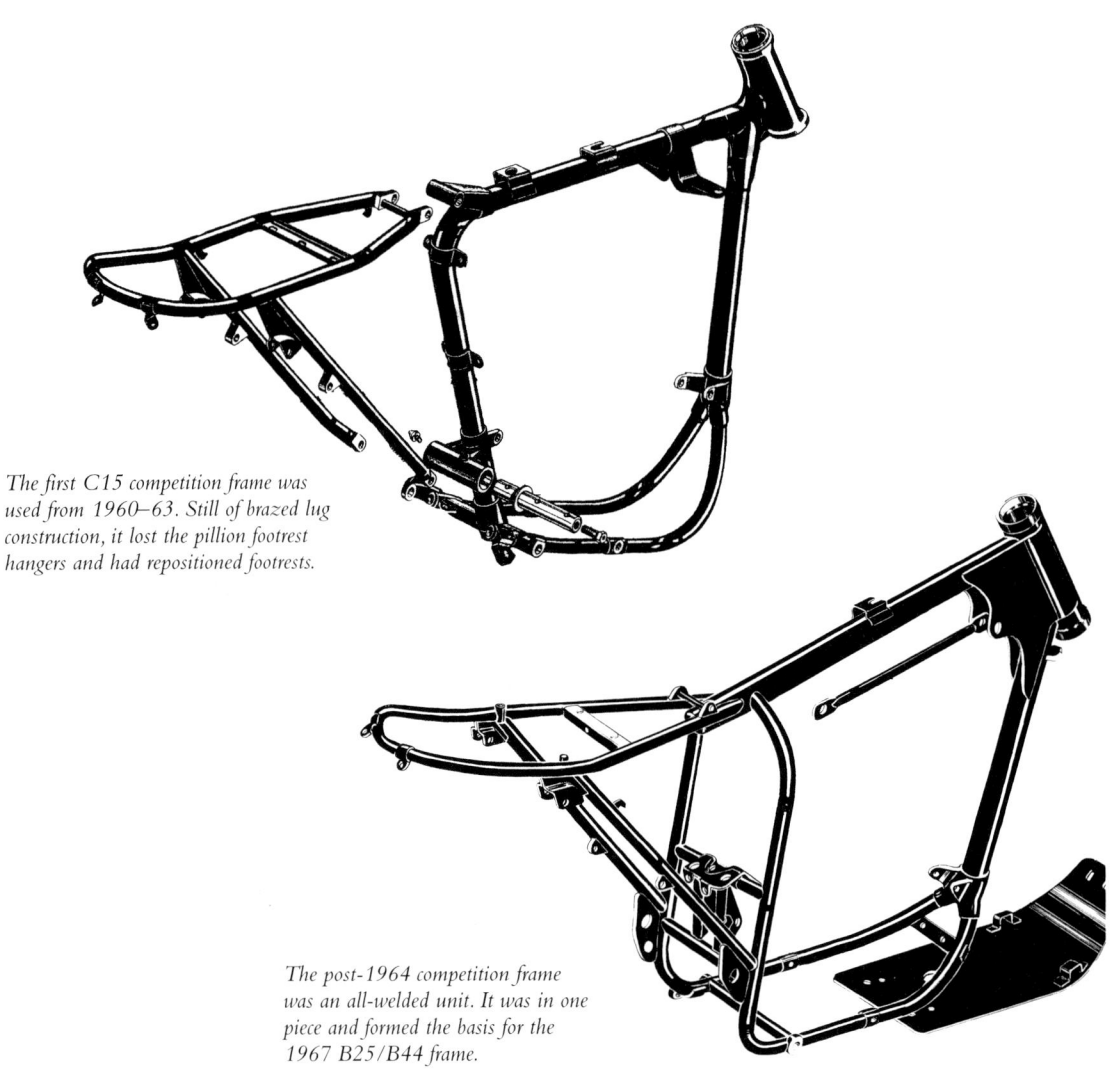

The first C15 competition frame was used from 1960–63. Still of brazed lug construction, it lost the pillion footrest hangers and had repositioned footrests.

The post-1964 competition frame was an all-welded unit. It was in one piece and formed the basis for the 1967 B25/B44 frame.

original type of frame during the 1967 model year, but had disappeared from the catalogue for 1968.

Front and Rear Suspension

The standard forks fitted to the C15 were one-way damped, internal spring units. They were fitted with metal shrouds to protect the sliding portions of the legs and extended upwards to encase the yokes. They also carried the headlamp cowl. A metal shroud covered the top yoke.

The forks were relatively lightweight, in line with the Edward Turner philosophy of drawing with a sharp pencil and using the minimum amount of metal needed to get the job done. Despite this, the forks gave satisfactory service and remained in use on the C15 throughout the life of the model.

However, the competition models soon dispensed with the standard item, replacing them with the heavyweight forks fitted to the larger bikes in the range. These units sported external springs, initially covered with rubber gaiters on both the trials and scrambles. Later models of the scrambler with the 7in brake single-sided front hub sported steel shrouds.

The stanchions used were considerably thicker than those used on the roadster models. This gave greater strength and rigidity than for the roadster units, which was needed in the heat of competition. The competition model forks boasted external springs covered with rubber gaiters, but still initially had no rebound damping. The yokes were the same width as the early forks, allowing the standard full-width hub to be retained, with the bolt-on front axle. However, the competition range offered the 7in half-width hub with push-in spindle as an option during 1960 and used the larger brake as standard from 1961. The B40 had heavy duty forks, with external springs, different oil seal holders and thicker stanchions like those fitted to the competition models,

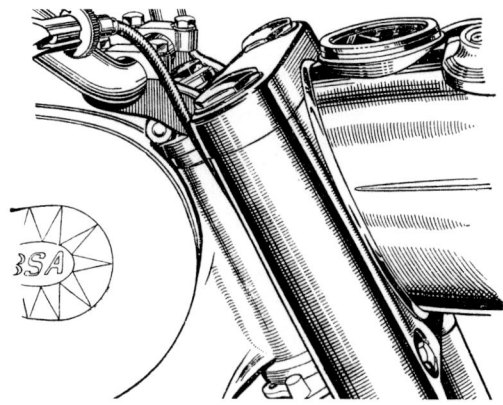

The C15 forks had internal springs and carried the headlamp in a cowl. The top yoke was covered with a pressed-steel cover.

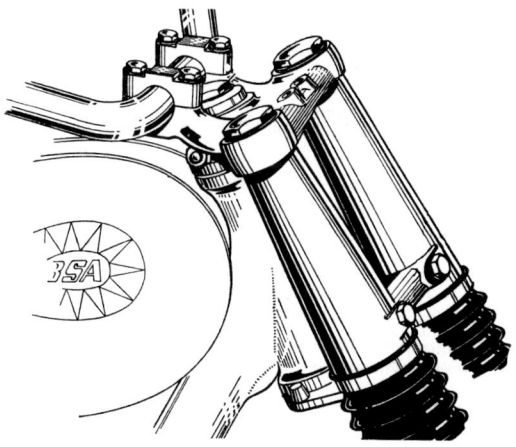

The competition models had heavyweight forks with external springs.

although the B40 retained the bolt-on front wheel throughout its life. The heavy duty forks were not immediately apparent, as the B40 had a similar headlamp cowl and close-fitting steel covers over the springs, so looked very similar to those fitted to the C15.

Brakes and Wheels

Wheels were all new and carried 17in

The C15 had full-width cast-iron hubs. The wheel was fixed to the fork by caps.

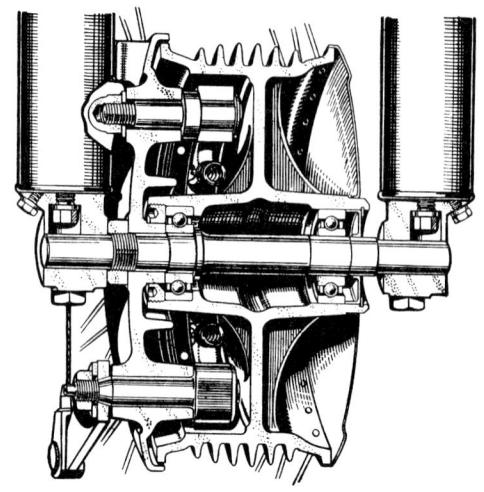

A cross section through the front hub shows its construction. The design allowed for the use of straight spokes.

chromed steel rims. The hubs were made of cast iron and were both 6in diameter full-width jobs, with cooling fins cast into their circumference. The hubs were designed to allow the use of straight spokes, which made for a strong and rigid assembly, but were pretty heavy.

The front hub had the brake drum incorporated in the casting. The rear brake drum, which also incorporated the rear sprocket, was a separate casting that bolted to the rear hub. The speedometer drive was bolted onto the right-hand side of the hub. Brake shoes were only ⅞in in width, giving a total braking area of about 16½ square in (110 square cm). They were considered adequate at the time of introduction – so read inadequate for today's traffic and that they would fade if subjected to heavy use. Brake back plates were made of alloy and were reasonably rigid, with a raised, polished outer rim and a black painted, rough finished inner. They were matched on the other side of the hub by a push-on chromed trim, again with a polished outer rim and a black painted inner.

Both the front and rear hubs were obviously designed with strength and rigidity in mind, rather than weight-saving, in stark contrast to other parts of the model. The front hub weighed around 6lb (2.7kg), while the rear, with its bolt-on cast-iron brake drum and sprocket, came in at about 10lb (4.5kg). These were pretty heavy, even by the standards of the day, especially as the weight was unsprung (that is, not isolated from the road by the suspension). This added significantly to the inertia of the suspension system. It is little wonder that any works bikes and the later competition models used the lighter pressed-steel single-sided hubs for the front, although all of the competition models made do with the same rear hub.

The rear hub has the added weight penalty of a separate brake drum and sprocket carrier to get a correct chain line with the engine – with a separate sprocket (either fifty-two, fifty-six or sixty teeth) for the competition models, or a cast-in one sprocket for the road models.

The standard C15 came with 17in rims front and rear, while the competition model had a 20in front and an 18in rear on the trials model and a 19in rear on the scrambler. The brakes, while considered adequate in their day, were only 6in diameter drums with ⅞in width lining. At the time, great play was made of the full-width hubs and good brakes, but the actual braking area was not much more than the C12's half-width brakes. Later models had substantially larger brakes.

The B40 was provided with 18in wheels front and rear and heavyweight forks with external springs from the word go, giving it a larger appearance and feel than the C15, helping to differentiate it from its small sibling. While it shared a rear hub and 6in diameter rear brake with the C15, in acknowledgement of the B40's greater performance and weight, it had a 7in diameter front brake. This was fitted in a cast-iron full-width hub, a scaled-up version of that fitted to the C15, which was identically styled and weighted even more. While the diameter of the brake was larger than that fitted to the C15, the shoes were still only ⅞in in width and so braking performance was adequate rather than outstanding.

Tinware

The C15 moved away from the then current BSA look, with an all-painted 2½gal (11.4ltr) capacity steel fuel tank, which had a stylized flash incorporated into the tank pressing above a plastic 'BSA in a star' pear-shaped badge rather than having the chromed sides typical of the range. The tank sported triangular grey rubber knee grips behind the badges and two chromed trim strips running over the central two ribs on its top. The tank was mounted in the standard BSA way, with a single through bolt fixing it to the top tube of the frame and rubber bushes insulating the tank from the frame. Mudguards were painted the same colour as the fuel tank and incorporated deep valances to keep road dirt off the bike and

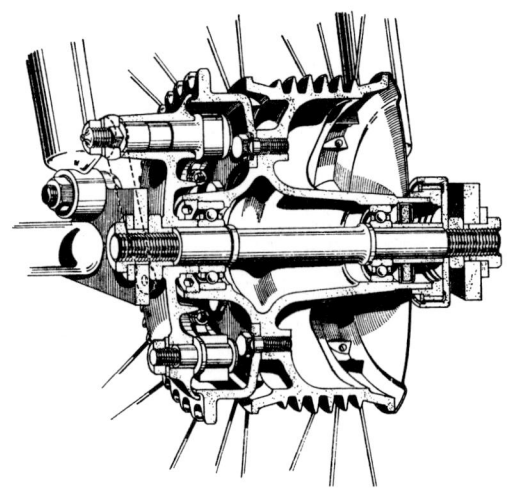

The rear hub was similar to the front, but carried its brake drum and sprocket in a separate bolted-on casting.

rider. Much play was made at the time about their cantilever design, which basically meant that the front of the front guard and the rear of the rear guard had no stays to support them. This worked well at the front, but if the rear was loaded, for example by fitting a luggage rack to it, then it could suffer from fatigue cracks at the edges.

The model had a rounded-off triangular oil tank on the right-hand side and a matching detachable cover on the left. This cover was held on to a backing plate with two pillar screws, which were difficult to locate. The tool kit was carried in a tool roll, which was located in the side panel with a spring clip. The backing plate had a large hole in it to give access to the battery. The space between the side panel and oil tank under the nose of the dual seat was filled by a flat, colour-matched metal fairing, which also carried the ignition switch and air cleaner. The toolbox, oil tank and central fairing were painted the same colour as the fuel tank and mudguards.

Two solid (that is, not metallic) colours were offered in the first year of production,

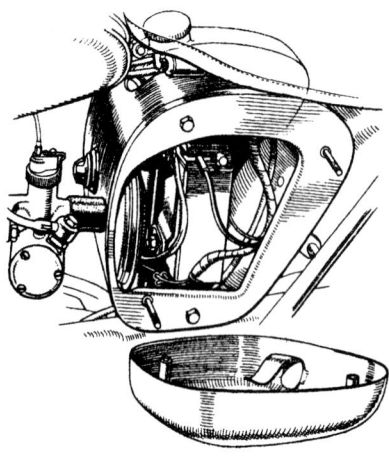

The air cleaner and battery were covered by the left-hand side panel. The tool roll would be secured by the sprung clip on the inside of the panel.

either Fuchsia Red or Turquoise (a light green shade). The rest of the cycle parts were predominantly black, highlighted with chrome wheel rims and seal holders on the front forks. The oil tank and side panel carried a transfer of the BSA piled arms trademark, while the oil tank had an additional 'Minimum Oil Level' transfer in gold. The springs in the front forks and rear suspension units were fully shrouded with black steel covers. The headlamp was carried in a neat nacelle or cowl as BSA described it, which also contained the speedometer, an ammeter and the light switch. Rider comfort had been thought about, as the footrests were adjustable, being mounted to the frame on tapered fittings. However, the BSA standard 'W' bend handlebars had welded-on lever pivots and so although the bars could be adjusted by rotating them in the clamp-on fitting on the top yoke, the lever positions remained fixed, which was not ideal. The dual seat was initially offered in a light grey finish on its edges, with a darker grey top and white piping separating the two colours.

Electrics and Instrumentation

The 6V battery hid under the seat in a carrier bolted to the rear tube of the main frame loop, nestling between the toolbox cover on the left-hand side and the oil tank on the right. The headlamp was mounted in a cowl on the front forks and was a 6in diameter Lucas MCF575P item, equipped with a 30/35W bulb. The rear tail and brake light was a standard Lucas 564 type mounted on the number plate carrier and incorporated a reflector to meet the legal requirements of the time. The brake light was a BSA rotary action unit, mounted on the frame and operated from the rear brake lever. The lights were operated via a three-position (off, pilot, main) switch in the nacelle or cowl and were dipped from a handlebar-mounted Wipac Ducon switch which also operated the horn. The horn was mounted close to the battery behind the fairing between the oil tank and toolbox, which was possibly not the most sensible position if it needed to be heard! Road tests of the time made this point, but the position was not changed until the advent of the C25/B25 range.

The ignition switch, again located on the front of the fairing alongside the horn, was inconvenient to use and initially was not key-operated – those days were more trustworthy than today. It had three positions: off, on and emergency. Emergency switched the whole output of the alternator through to the coil and was used if the battery was flat. Instrumentation was basic and would remain so throughout the range's life, with the headlamp cowl carrying an ammeter and a 3in diameter, black-faced Smith's magnetic speedometer, with milometer. No trip meter or warning lights of any description were fitted.

The use of coil ignition meant that the condition of the battery was crucial if the bike were to start. The bike had two ignition switch positions – normal and emergency. The worst aspect of the electrical system was the crude control of the alternator output, with no automatic regulation. The output from the alternator was split into two parts, with one part operating on the output of two of the alternator coils and the second part working from the output of four of the alternator coils. With just the ignition on, the output from two coils from the alternator were 'switched in', providing an adequate charge into the battery to balance the ignition's demand for power. This setting also provided just enough power to service the pilot (or parking) lights. When the main lights were switched on, the output from the remaining four alternator coils were switched in. So there were two charging rates, neither of which was really correct!

If the battery was flat, there was an emergency setting on the ignition switch. When used, it operated as a form of energy transfer ignition, directing the full output of the alternator to the ignition circuit at about the time it was needed to energize the coil. Once the engine was running, it was advisable to switch over to normal, when the battery would be recharged reasonably quickly.

While the system did work reasonably well, the overall result of this was permanent over- or undercharging of the battery, which would not be overcome until the system was swapped to 12V, with Zener diode charge control at the introduction of the C/B25 and B44 ranges.

Stage 2: C25/B25 and B44 1967–70

Engine Layout and Design
The B25 and B44 range departed from the previous C15 and B40 family by having significant differences in the crankshaft design, as well as the different capacities. The B25

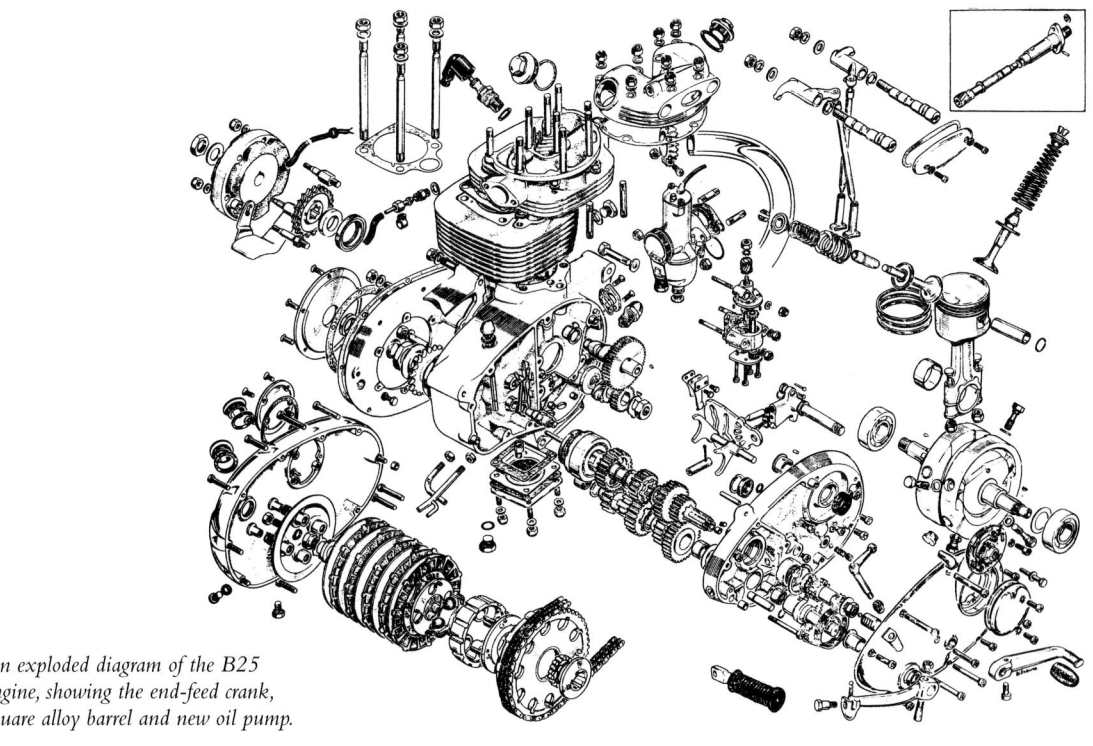

An exploded diagram of the B25 engine, showing the end-feed crank, square alloy barrel and new oil pump.

bottom end has a plain bearing big end, while the B44 has a roller-bearing big end. This meant two completely different crankshafts being used, as well as the usual different barrel and piston.

The B25 engine followed the basic layout of the C15, but was in fact completely new. While it maintained a similar appearance to the C15, the crankcases, barrel, piston and head were all different. Internally, the final strong C15 built-up crank with its roller big end was replaced with a one-piece forged steel crank, with two full-diameter bolt-on flywheels. The flywheel bolts (four for each flywheel, two long, two short) were waisted and stretched when torqued up. It was vital not to reuse these bolts, as they were weakened when used and could fail, with catastrophic consequences for the engine. This crank followed the practice used on the BSA/Triumph twins and borrowed its connecting rod from Triumph's C series 500cc engine, with its split two-piece white metal plain bearing. The theory behind using this

The 'square' B25 barrel was alloy with a steel liner and cast-in pushrod tunnel. Note the two additional studs to seal the pushrod tunnel.

type of crank was sound – it was a strong one-piece unit and was likely to be cheaper to produce than the pressed-up C15 design. Its white metal big-end bearing was the same as that used in the Triumph 500 and was well tried and tested in that application. In comparison to the most highly tuned Triumph, the T100 Daytona, the BSA produced 96bhp per litre (24bhp from 250cc) at 8,500rpm, while the Daytona produced 76bhp per litre (38bhp from 500cc) at 7,500rpm – a substantial difference, reflecting the BSA single's high state of tune, which impacted on reliability.

Two aspects of the design further mitigated against its survival in the competitive learner market of the mid to late 1960s – the B25's ability to rev above its 8,500 red line in the lower gears (which, with no tachometer as standard and a very willing engine, was an easy thing for a learner to do) and the lack of decent oil filtration. Throw in the usual learner rider's bodgery, lack of maintenance and the likelihood of 'teenager tuning' by over advancing the ignition, and it was no surprise that the big end quickly gained a reputation for failure. BSA did have the good sense to keep the ball and roller main bearings and a decent oil pump. The oil supply to the big end was fed to the end of the crank through oil ways drilled in the crankcase and the inner timing case. The oil way runs through a join between the crankcase and the inner timing cover, where it is sealed with a small 'O' ring and from there it passes into the end of the crankshaft, where the join between the timing cover and the crank is sealed by a garter oil seal. Both of these seals are critical, and should be changed if disturbed.

Otherwise, the rest of the layout of the bottom half of the engine followed that of the final C15, with points in the side, a very similar primary drive and a four-speed gearbox.

The connecting rod was based on that used on the drive side of the late 500cc C series

Triumph twin and the relevant Triumph part serves as a direct replacement. The rod was made from forged alloy with a steel end cap to hold the plain metal big end. The end cap was held on with two captive bolts. Like the fly-wheel bolts, these were waisted to stretch when torqued down and fixed with self-locking nuts. The rod had a small hole drilled in it at an angle of about 45 degrees from the centre of the bearing surface out to the primary drive side, to assist with oil flow. The cylinder barrel was an attractive alloy casting with a steel liner. The original liners had location problems that could lead to the liner dropping in the barrel, but this was fixed early on in the production cycle.

The barrel was located to the crankcases using four through studs that were firmly screwed into the crankcases and these were also used to fix the head to the barrel. The pushrod tunnel was incorporated into the barrel, thereby loosing the leak-prone pushrod tunnel, and the barrel featured two additional studs to the right-hand side front and rear of the pushrod tunnel to assist with oil tightness. These additional studs made it even harder to get to the head nuts on the timing side. As mentioned earlier, BSA workshop manuals of the time gave details of how to cut down a ring spanner and weld a hexagon to it to allow the use of a torque wrench to tighten these nuts.

The piston was a conventional domed design, with two compression and one oil control ring. Compression ratio was a heady 10 to 1 and the engine produced a claimed 25bhp – hence the new designation of C25/B25.

The cylinder head also differed substantially from the C15 item, but retained the C15 layout of an alloy head casting holding the valves and springs, with the rockers carried in an alloy rocker box that was bolted on using nine studs.

The rockers were carried on eccentric shafts, which meant that tappet adjustment

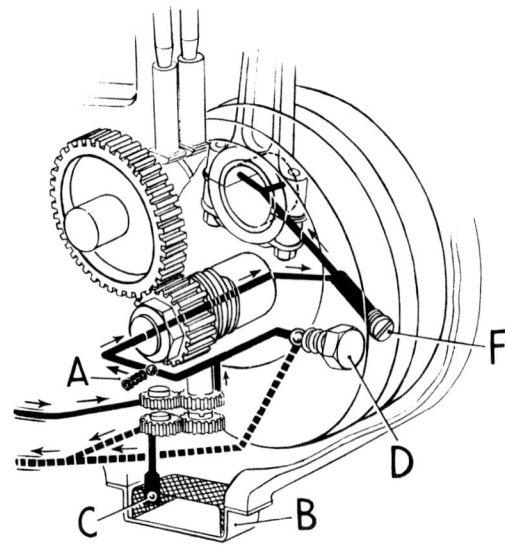

The B25 oil system fed the oil to the plain big end through the end of the crank.

was carried out by rotating the shafts to get the correct clearance. This system had the advantage of lowering the weight of the rockers, as it removed the need for individual tappets and locknuts on the end of each

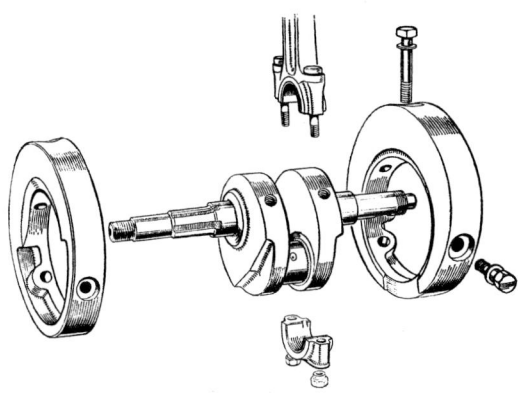

The B25 crank and con rod assembly with its plain big end could cause problems, especially if the oil was not changed regularly.

107

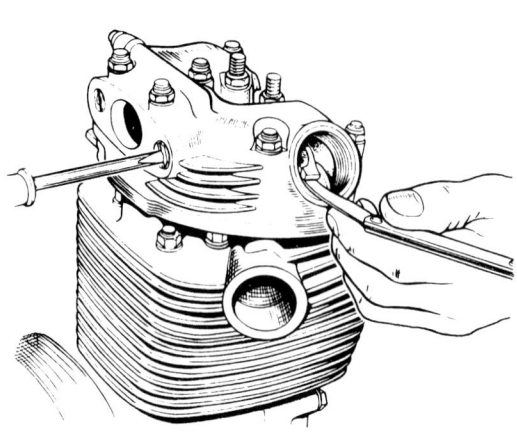

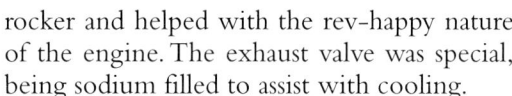

ABOVE: The rockers on the B25 were mounted on eccentric shafts. To adjust the valve clearance the shafts were rotated.

RIGHT: The B44 engine had a roller big end and a built-up crank. As on the B25, oil was fed to the big end through the end of the crank.

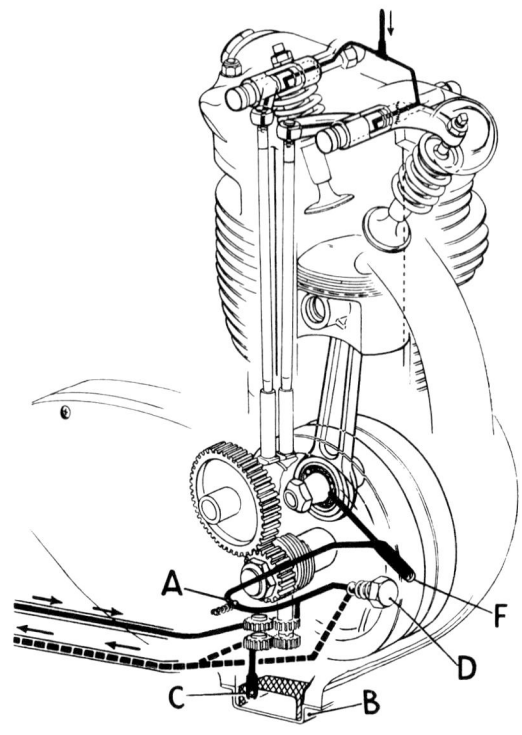

rocker and helped with the rev-happy nature of the engine. The exhaust valve was special, being sodium filled to assist with cooling.

The primary drive was much the same as the C15 in design and layout. A Lucas RM19 alternator, rated at 60W, gave ample power for the 12V electrical system.

The B44 engine was much closer in design to the last of the C15Gs, with a built-up crank, roller big end and conventional tappet adjusters. It retained the end feed for oil to the crank and the square barrel, and appeared almost identical to the B25 unit. The engine was in a lower state of tune than the B25, with a compression ratio of 9.4 to 1, and produced a claimed 29hp at 5,750rpm.

The light alloy cylinder head retained the C15 type of valve operation, with the valve clearances being set at the ends of the rocker arms using tappet and locknuts.

Frame and Swinging Arm

BSA introduced a new frame for the 250cc C25 Barracuda and the 441cc B44 range. Identical for both models, the new frame was based heavily on that used for the C15T and C15S production models and was a one-piece design of all-welded construction, with the rear subframe an integral part of the structure rather than being a separate, bolt-on affair. It was both lighter and more rigid than the previous C15 roadster brazed lug type frame.

The steering head was properly supported, with the top tube running to the top of the steering tube and a second bracing tube running below the main top tube. It was additionally braced through the use of steel plates on either side. The swinging arm was suspended on a single long shaft that pivoted on rubber and metal silent-bloc bushes. Each end of the swinging arm was located by bolting it to side plates on the twin seat tubes. The silent-bloc bushes were very long-lasting and were maintenance-free, but could be difficult to remove and replace when they eventually wore out. They also gave slightly less precise location of the swinging arm than solid bushes would have, though this did not seem to affect the handling. The seat was supported on a loop running from the seat nose, which also carried the top mounts for the rear shock absorbers. Overall, the dimensions of the new frame were slightly larger than the C15 frame, giving more of a big bike feel to the range, and the roadholding and handling were praised in the contemporary road tests. The frame did impart a much more modern feel and look to the range and was presumably cheaper and easier to make than the outgoing C15 brazed lug, bolt-up frame.

In the meantime, the works bikes were moving forwards with the oil-in-frame concept, first seen in the early 1960s, which meant that the works models were still further advanced than the production models.

Front Forks and Rear Suspension

The introduction of the C25/B25 saw the disappearance of the lightweight internal spring front forks from the BSA four-stroke single range. The new range used the heavyweight forks, as on the competition models, and featured external springs, two-way damping and thicker stanchions. The roadsters had metal shrouds covering the springs for 1967 and the 120mph Smith's magnetic speedometer was carried in a large rubber cup mounted on a bracket on the top yoke. The end of the headlamp cowl was signified by a separate, chromed 7in headlamp, which was carried on 'ears' fixed between both yokes. For 1968, the width of the fork yokes was increased to cater for the reintroduction of full-width hubs. Rubber gaiters gave a more up to date look and probably saved some money in parts and paint.

The forks saw little change after that, apart from details to allow the fitting of the TLS front brake for 1969. A chromed headlamp with an ammeter and light switch was fixed to ears set between the top and bottom yokes and

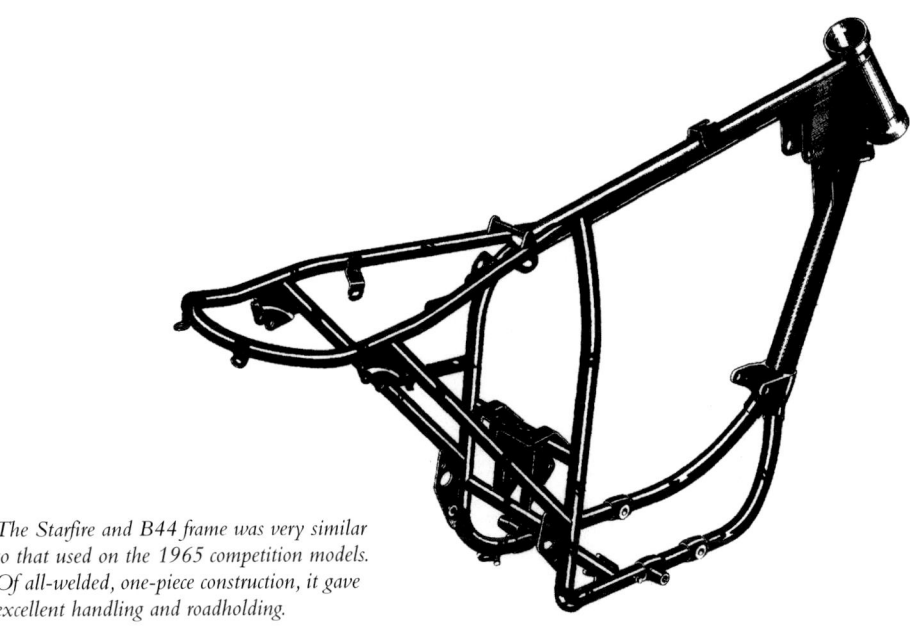

The Starfire and B44 frame was very similar to that used on the 1965 competition models. Of all-welded, one-piece construction, it gave excellent handling and roadholding.

the heat sink for the Zener diode was fitted in the air stream under the bottom yoke.

Brakes and Wheels

The B25 and B44 road bikes were introduced to the world with a single-sided 7in front brake in a single-sided hub, much as had been used on the trials and scrambles models previously. Front and rear wheels were 18in in diameter. The rear brake was a 7in half-width unit, fitted in conjunction with BSA's quickly detachable rear wheel. This wheel design had been used on BSA (and Triumph) models for many years and was genuinely quick and easy to use.

The wheel hub had a splined fitting that mated with a separate axle that was incorporated into the rear brake drum, which was itself bolted to the left-hand side of the swinging arm. The drive sprocket was mounted on this brake drum. Removal of the wheel spindle, a spacer and the speedometer cable from the left-hand side of the bike allowed the wheel to be moved sideways and out of the splined fitting and hence be removed from the bike without disturbing the rear chain or brake. All in all, this was an excellent design and was a real boon to serious riders, enabling the quick and easy repair of punctures. Interestingly, the design had been used on the larger bikes in the range and its use on the unit singles indicated a move towards commonality in components across the various model ranges. The design stayed with the models throughout their life.

The front wheel was changed in 1968, with the B25 gaining a full-width 7in hub with an SLS brake, while the B44 gained an 8in diameter SLS brake in a full-width hub with a flange carrying the spokes on the brake side, giving an increased drum width. The brake was the same as fitted to the 650 twins the previous year.

The front wheel hub changed again in 1969, to a full-width design to which was fitted a 7in diameter version of the BSA/Triumph TLS brake.

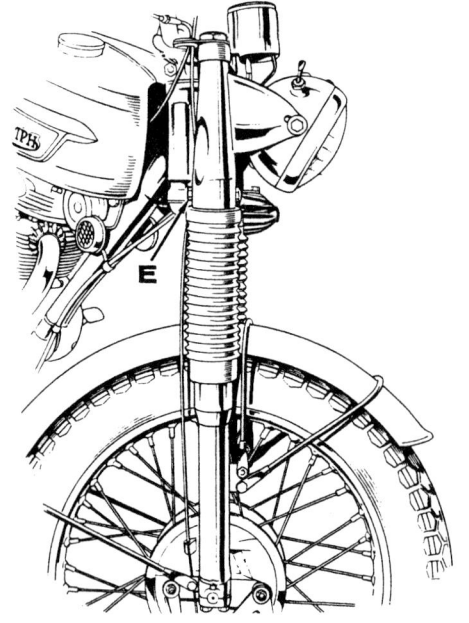

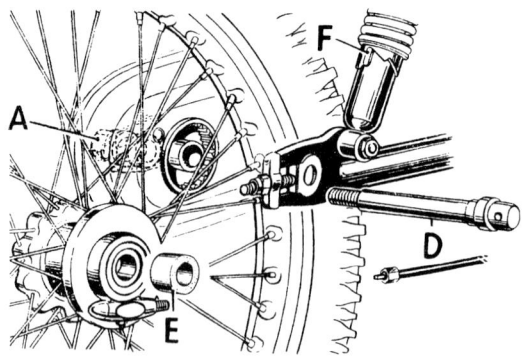

ABOVE: The B25 and B44 used the famous BSA quickly detachable rear wheel. The wheel could be removed without disturbing the rear brake or chain.

LEFT: B25, TR25W and B44 front forks were heavyweight units that coped well with the bike's performance. This illustration is of a 1970 Triumph TR25W.

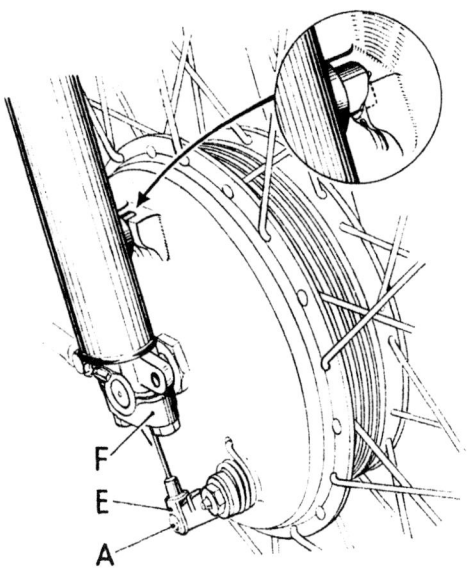

ABOVE: *The 1968 B25 and B44 had a new full-width hub, with a spoke flange on the brake side allowing for a wider drum.*

RIGHT: *The 7in TLS front brake as fitted to the 1969 and 1970 250cc models.*

The new hub provided a larger braking area than the previous design by incorporating a spoke flange on the brake side, enabling the braking area to be extended to the edge of the hub. This was the first year that the brake design was seen in this size and it was a development of the 8in unit introduced on the larger bikes for the 1968 model year. It was similar in appearance to the larger version fitted to the BSA and Triumph 650cc twins in 1969. This new version featured the 'bell crank' operation, with the cable following the line of the fork leg. This operating system replaced the 1967 8in unit's problematic 'long cable' operation, in which the operating cable entered the brake plate from the rear. This system could result in the cable being trapped by the front mudguard, with dangerous results for the rider, but was never used on the 7in brake. The B25 and B44 roadster model's brakes and

wheels remained unchanged for the 1970 model year.

The 1967 B44 Victor was equipped with the same half-width hub and 7in front brake as the Starfire and roadster B44, but retained the original C15 style rear wheel with its 6in diameter brake. Wheels were 19in diameter front and 18in diameter rear.

Tinware

The most striking element of the B25/B44's styling was the fuel tank. It moved away from the BSA corporate style of the rounded tank with chrome panels to a much more sculpted shape, with well-defined scallops for the rider's knee recesses and badge positions. The overall style was similar to the large capacity tank first seen in alloy on some Gold Stars and adopted (in fibreglass) in 5gal (22.7ltr) form for the BSA A65 Spitfire Mk2 of 1966, but slimmed

111

right down to give a 2gal (9ltr) capacity. The tank was made of fibreglass and some versions had contrasting off-white (called Ivory in the brochure) colouring for the knee recesses. The oil tank and battery were covered by large, similarly styled fibreglass covers which were the same colour as the main tank and carried transfers to denote the model.

The B44 Victor was styled practically for its intended off-road use. The fuel tank was an alloy 2gal (9ltr) unit with a flip-up fuel cap. The front half was painted yellow and the rear half left in polished alloy. The oil tank was uncovered, with a matching triangular side panel on the left, both finished in black.

Chrome blade type mudguards were fitted to the B25 and both B44 models front and rear. Black painted tubular stays and a black painted frame stayed with the models from start to finish.

Electrics and Instrumentation

The electrics fitted to the range were the 'Standard British' fitted throughout the BSA and Triumph ranges of the time and saw no significant changes. A Lucas alternator fitted on the drive side of the crank provided 12V of alternating current (AC). The AC was converted into direct current (DC) by a Lucas rectifier, where it was used to charge a 12V battery and thus provide power for the lights and ignition system. A Zener diode was used to regulate the current supplied to the battery, which, when the battery was fully charged, would 'dump' the excess output of the alternator as heat – hence the large alloy heat sink fitted under the bottom yoke. All in all, the 12V system was much simpler and more reliable than the 6V systems that preceded it and gave much better lights as well.

The 8in chromed headlamp shell carried an ammeter and three-position light switch, initially a rotary type, but for 1968 it changed to a flip type. A headlamp main beam warning light was fitted to the left of the ammeter from

the model's introduction and, at long last, in 1969 an oil pressure warning light was fitted, balancing the main beam warning light in the headlamp shell. The ignition switch was slightly awkwardly positioned at the nose of the seat on the left-hand side, but was at long last operated by a proper key. The horn sat under the fuel tank, where it had half a chance of being heard in contrast to the C15's effort, while the tail light was an attractive alloy casting with the Lucas type 679 'tit' rear lens.

Stage 3: B25SS to B50SS 1971–2

Introduction

The final phase in the history of the BSA unit singles was played out in the dying embers of the once great marque. BSA was recovering somewhat from the disastrous 1969 season, when the company failed to get enough bikes across to its American dealers to capitalize on the US's limited 'sales window' and a major part of the recovery was a completely revamped range of models. Unfortunately, when this new range was planned, the decision was taken to replace all the frames and running gear, but to leave the engines largely unchanged. This somewhat bizarre decision has been debated for many years, but no clear reason for the decision has ever been given. The redesign of the running gear was comprehensive, with the unit singles and the 'A' Series 650cc twins getting completely new frames, forks and wheels. The Rocket 3 got new forks and wheels, but the Bantam received none of the new gear, being quietly dropped during the model year.

Engine, Primary Drive and Gearbox

The 250cc engine used this year was relatively unchanged from the previous year's Starfire. The crankcases had a revised rear engine mounting lug which was substantially wider than the previous year's, to suit the new frame with its separate rear engine plates. The new rear engine plates carried an external paper cartridge type oil filter similar to that found on the WD B40. This addition probably was one of the most significant factors in increasing the engine's reliability, helping to ensure that only clean oil got to the plain big-end bearing, rather than the coarsely strained oil as in previous years. Internally, the crank was slightly revised to allow the fitment of a slightly stronger con rod. The effect of these revisions was minimal, although it made it impossible to fit a 1971 engine into an earlier frame. BSA did produce a batch of 1971 crankcases with the rear mounting narrowed to fit earlier frames as spare parts.

The B50 unit was a more significant revision of the 441cc unit. The increase in capacity was gained by increasing the 441cc unit's 79mm bore to 84mm, giving the B50 a bore

and stroke measurement of 84mm × 90mm. The bike featured an additional main bearing on the drive side, on the outside a ball race and on the inside a roller. In the light of corporate experiences with the 650cc Triumph twin engine the previous year, the B50 breathing system was substantially revised, which made the engine less prone to oil leaks. Rather than relying on the timed breather on the camshaft of the B25 and B44, the B50 employed a static system with no moving parts, which was both simpler and more efficient. The seal between the drive-side main bearings was omitted, which allowed the crankcase to 'breathe' through the two main bearings into the relatively large volume primary chain case. The case was then vented to the outside through a large diameter pipe fixed to the top of the casing. This arrangement also had the advantage of keeping the primary chain case

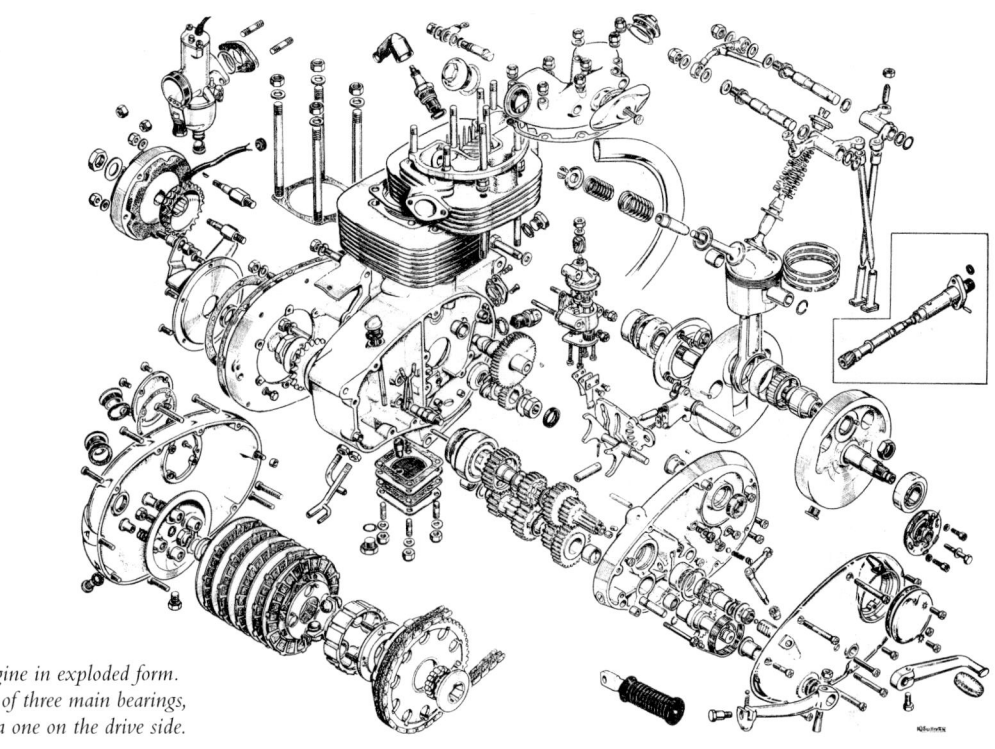

The B50 engine in exploded form. Note the use of three main bearings, with the extra one on the drive side.

oil shared with the engine oil. The level was automatically maintained as the oil was able to flow back into the crankcases to be scavenged back to the oil tank via a weir formed by drillings in the crankcase when it reached the required level. The B50 unit shared the 250cc unit's wide rear mount, but did not have the cartridge oil filter fitted. Presumably, the works decided that the lack of plain bearings in the engine meant that the increased level of filtration was unnecessary – a stance taken with the previous B44, but not taken on the WD B40, which was an all ball and roller engine.

Frame and Swinging Arm
The oil-in-frame production models finally saw the light of day in 1971, just as the BSA competition shop was being run down because of the company's financial problems.

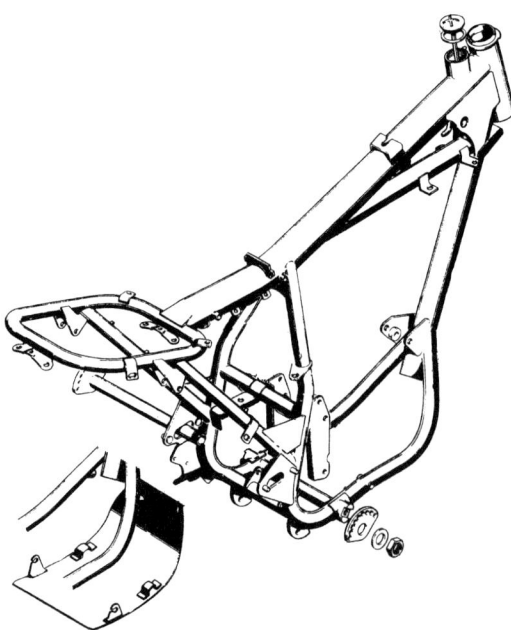

The new 1971 frame was based on the oil-in-frame competition frame, but retained the single down tube and cradle for the engine. The oil bearing top tube extends backwards under the seat.

The new production range comprised 250cc and 500cc road and trail bikes and the B50MX competition machine. All of these bikes used a similar frame, which was taller than the C25/B25 frame and, like the works machines, carried its oil in the frame. However, the overall layout of the frame was not the same as that seen on the works machines and the production Victor GP. Unlike the oil-in-frame competition models, there was no oil header tank under the air cleaner and the oil-bearing top tube was longer, running back under the seat rather than terminating at the seat nose.

The frame comprised a large diameter (approximately 2¼in) top tube, which carried the bulk of the oil. The oil ran from the headstock back under the seat to about halfway to the rear shock absorber top mountings. Oil capacity was a reasonable 4pt (2.3ltr). The main oil drain plug was situated at the rear of this tube, accessible from behind the air cleaner assembly or battery carrier. A supplementary tube ran horizontally from the lower end of the headstock back to the main tube to act as a brace. The oil filler was positioned at the front of the top tube and protruded up in front of the petrol tank, just behind the headstock.

The oil filler cap looked from the outside to be identical to a Triumph rocker cover cap, but was modified to carry a dipstick. The oil return feed was routed to this area, so that an owner could see if oil was flowing properly. From the well-braced headstock ran a smaller diameter (1½in) down tube, also oil-carrying, with the main feed to the engine coming out of the bottom of the tube. A wire mesh oil filter was incorporated in the main oil feed at this point and sat inside the down tube. Two tubes spayed out from this down tube, curving out and backwards to form a cradle that supported the engine, and then continuing up behind the engine to connect to the top tube at the seat nose. Flat plate gussets were fixed to the rear of the cradle to carry the swinging arm and (on the left-hand side) the side stand.

*The 1971 frame had its oil filler ahead of the slim fuel tank.
Note the rare tachometer fitted to this particular T25SS.*

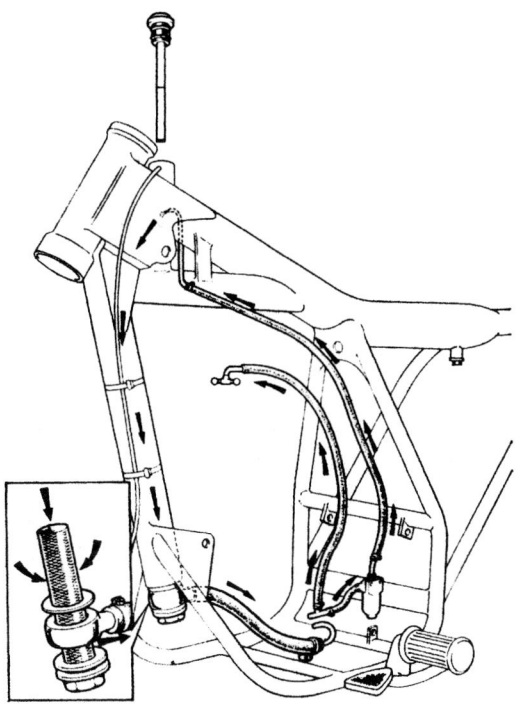

*The oil circulated from the bottom of the front tube and was
fed back to the headstock. This caused poor circulation of oil
within the large top tube.*

Three bracing tubes ran between these two
cradle tubes, one between the footrest
mounts, one at the bottom rear which carried
the centre stand lugs and a final one just above
the swinging-arm gussets. These last two carried the fixings for the rear engine plates and
the lower one also carried lugs for the optional centre stand. Unlike the previous frame
design, the seat loop ran from the end of the
main top tube, which was about 12in (30cm)
behind the nose of the seat. The rear shock
absorber top mounts and the rear of the seat
were carried on this loop. The rear of the seat
also bolted onto this loop and slotted into a
forked fixing at the nose, while the rear mudguard was bolted onto the end of the loop. A
bracing tube ran from the shock absorber top
mount on each side down to the swinging-

arm pivot. The frame provided a large surface
area to assist in cooling.

One problem with the frame is the circulation of the oil. As the feed is at the bottom of
the front down tube and the return line is to
the top of the headstock area, circulation tends
to occur in the front half of the frame only. The
poor circulation is demonstrated by checking
the temperature of the frame tubes after a run
– the oil in the rear of the main tube is usually cooler than that in the down tube. Some
riders have plumbed a second oil return into a
modified drain plug at the rear of the main
tube, to ensure that all of the oil is in use.

The swinging arm was carried on needle
roller bearings and was fixed in position
between the two gusset plates by a large
diameter spindle. The spindle fitted into an

115

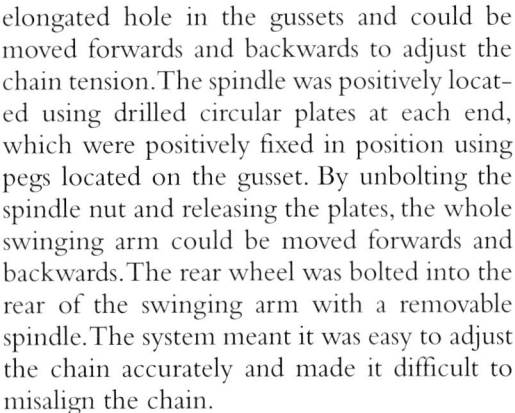

ABOVE: *Most, if not all, of the 1971–2 frames for the B50 had extra gussets just above the swinging-arm pivot. This is a B50T with just such a gusset Note the 'cam' type chain adjuster plate, which fixes the swinging arm in position.*

RIGHT: *The front forks on the 1971 range were high-quality Ceriani type, with internal springs. This particular T25SS has fork gaiters fitted to protect the stanchions from road dirt.*

elongated hole in the gussets and could be moved forwards and backwards to adjust the chain tension. The spindle was positively located using drilled circular plates at each end, which were positively fixed in position using pegs located on the gusset. By unbolting the spindle nut and releasing the plates, the whole swinging arm could be moved forwards and backwards. The rear wheel was bolted into the rear of the swinging arm with a removable spindle. The system meant it was easy to adjust the chain accurately and made it difficult to misalign the chain.

Frames for 1972 had an additional bracing plate fitted just above the swinging-arm spindle, joining the seat support tube and the rear shock support tube. It is unclear when this modification was first made and whether it was introduced during the 1971 model year.

Inspection of physical bikes has shown frames with 1971 model year numbers with the plates and 1972 model year frames without!

Forks and Suspension
For the 1971 range it was all change, with completely new forks. These were developed from those used on the motocross bikes and were described by the factory as being: 'Proven on the road and off by John Banks, champion British motocross rider.' The forks had lightweight alloy sliders and chromed steel stanchions.

There were no fork bushes as such, the stanchions running directly on the sliders. While this seems like a recipe for expensive replacement, in reality the system works very well and few cases of worn-out sliders seem to occur. The front wheel had a fixed axle, which was attached to bottom of the slider using an alloy block, located on four studs. This fixing was claimed to give the forks such good rigidity that a brace at the top of the sliders was not needed. However, the forks could and did twist under pressure. The first-year fork sliders (1971) had a rough cast finish with a raised styling strip (approximately 4mm wide) that was cast in and ran from the drain plug at the bottom up to the rubber dust protector at its top, with its face polished. This feature was discarded for 1972, with the sliders gaining a smooth polished finish all over.

The stanchions were exposed to the elements, with a tough rubber 'wiper' or dust excluder being fitted to the top of the slider to prevent the ingress of abrasive grime and water. Oil seals were fitted below the dust excluders. The forks performed well, with dual damping, soft springing and around 5½in to 6in (depending on which specification you read) of travel. Their modern looks and excellent performance led to them being described as the 'Ceriani' type, but they were developed in house with no external influence. These forks were used on all of BSA's 1971 models from 250cc to 750cc. The sliders were left in their natural aluminium finish. The head bearings were taper rollers as standard, a superior fitment to the ball races of the previous frame.

Rear suspension was catered for using the ubiquitous Girling rear dampers, with three spring preload positions. These units were good performers with excellent springing and damping characteristics. The only jarring note was the use of Dove Grey paint on the road and trail rear units to match the frame. The 1971 brochure shows the B50MX as having its rear units finished in black, however, possibly indicating the use of uprated units for this competition variant.

Brakes and Wheels

The road versions of new range, the UK specification B25SS and T25SS, and the B50SS shared the same wheels as the rest of the BSA 1971 range, while the trail versions, the B25T, B50T and B50MX, shared the corporate rear wheel, but had a unique front wheel and brake.

The front brake fitted to the roadsters featured an all-new 8in diameter TLS front brake, cable-operated and fitted into a new conical hub. The brake was designed to use Austin Mini brake shoes and had ratchet cam adjusters built in, which could be accessed via a small hole in the body of the hub. The brake's operation was simplified from the previous unit, and used the cable to pull the front arm in and the cable outer to push the rear arm. This, in theory, should make the brake self-compensating as the forces on the outer and inner cable should balance out, giving even pressure on each shoe and eliminating the possibility of errors in adjustment.

In practice, the brake works well, although it does rely on the use of the proper heavy duty cable and the concept behind the operation does not allow for the compression of the cable outer, which can lead to heavy operating pressures. The brake had a large air scoop projecting forwards to direct cooling air into the brake and two large apertures cast into the

The 8in TLS brake fitted to the 1971 'Street Scramblers' was equipped with a large air scoop to assist cooling.

back plate to let the heated air out. The inner drum was a shrunk-in steel affair and the brake shoes were also made of steel. This gave rise to the erroneous assumption that the shoes would expand slower than the drum (which the ill-informed assumed to be alloy), leading to a loss of efficiency. The brake came in for some criticism; certainly on the larger and heavier 650 twins and the 750cc Triple it could overheat and fade. Despite the theoretical faults, though, on the relatively light unit singles the brake was more than adequate. All the 'SS' bikes had 18in diameter front and rear wheels and were equipped with Dunlop K70 tyres.

The trail bikes (and the B25SS in the US brochure) had a smaller, cable-operated 6in diameter front brake, in acknowledgement of the off-road aspirations. The brake was an SLS affair on an alloy back plate. A torque arm ran

from the front of the back plate to a large cast-in bracket on the rear of the slider. The trail bikes and the B50MX were equipped with a 20in diameter front rim and an 18in rear, and had Dunlop Trials (trail bikes) or Dunlop Sports (B50MX) specified.

The rear wheel had an alloy conical hub that carried a 7in diameter SLS brake on its left-hand side, which was rod-operated. It had an alloy back plate and a short operating lever. The rear sprocket was bolted to the hub outside of the brake drum.

Tinware

The 1971 models were styled radically differently to the previous year. BSA wanted to promote a 'Street Scrambler' look, giving a hint of off-road capability to all the models, and they certainly succeeded. The brochure describes the new range as displaying: 'The Power of

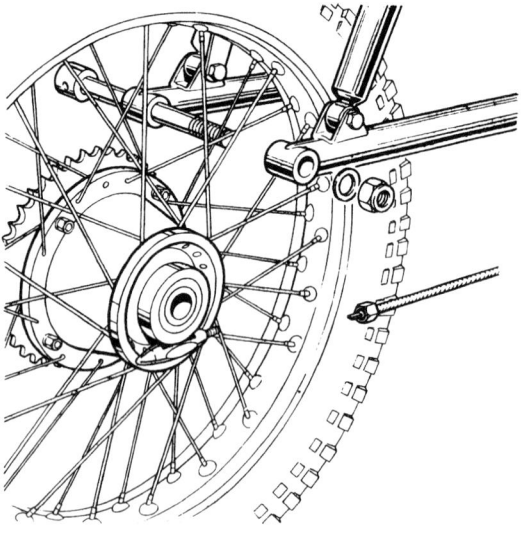

ABOVE: *The bikes lost the QD rear wheel in 1971 with the introduction of the conical hubs. Removal of the rear wheel meant disconnecting the rear brake and chain.*

LEFT: *The off-roaders for 1971 were equipped with a 6in SLS front brake.*

The author as a young man carrying out running repairs on his 1971 B25SS. Note the Dove Grey frame and extravagant exhaust!

British Engineering. The Glory of American Styling.'

All the bikes had high and wide Western style handlebars and sleek side panels, plus a small, slim fuel tank that gave them a real 'get up and go' look. There were two controversial styling features – the Dove Grey frame and the silencer (or muffler). The Dove Grey finish to the frame was supposed to make the frame look as it was nickel plated, like some of the more exotic off-road racing bikes, but only succeeded in looking grubby very quickly. The frame was black for 1972. The black painted exhaust pipe exited the head in the usual unit single manner, sweeping above the points cover and the top of the crankcases, before diving behind the frame tubes to emerge just above the swinging-arm spindle. At this point, it was all change, as the pipe entered what was probably at the time the world's largest motorcycle exhaust – a lozenge-shaped black box that sat above the swinging arm, with its exit pipe at the same height as the top of the rear

mudguard and with a stainless steel heat shield covered in five rows of three large holes to protect the passenger's leg. It was pure 1970s kitsch and the punters either loved it or hated it. The rationale behind it was to meet the emerging noise standards that were emasculating the rich exhaust notes of motorcycles, and by having a large volume to dissipate the noise the impact on performance was lessened. It did set a style trend followed by many of the Japanese trail bikes after the mid 1970s, as it gave good ground clearance and the volume needed to reduce the noise. The B50MX was spared the unit, making do with a short 'silencer' that didn't really live up to the name.

Fuel tanks came in two capacities initially – small and smaller! The road SS bikes had a steel 2½ US gal (7.9ltr) version, while the trail bikes (T) got an alloy version, of the same capacity. The B50MX got an alloy tank of 1¼ US gal (4ltr) capacity, which was similarly styled.

For the UK market in 1971, the Fleetstar got a larger capacity steel tank, with a

119

ABOVE: *The later B25s had an oil pressure warning light. It was driven by a pressure switch mounted on the front timing side of the crankcases, next to the lozenge-shaped tachometer drive cover plate.*

LEFT: *The MX models had an even slimmer alloy tank than the road models. This is Chris Burrell's 1971 B50MX with the original paintwork cross over the alloy.*

pronounced hump at its rear and a 3 UK gal (13.6ltr) capacity, which also went on the 1972 B50SS for the UK.

Mudguards were in steel on the road and trail bikes and in alloy for the B50MX. The front guard on the SS models was rubber mounted to the fork sliders using wire brackets that had to be modified early on to prevent breakage. The trail models and the B50MX had the front guard mounted high above the wheel on the bottom yoke to give adequate clearance and the trail-bike look.

The side panels obviously caused BSA some problems. The brochure shots show a Dzus type fastener at the top front of the cover in a deep indentation. When production started, the side covers were difficult to manufacture without them cracking around the indentation. A new version, with no indentation, the Dzus fastener set at an angle and a revised fitting on the frame, was made up 'on the fly' by

BSA factory engineers to allow production to commence.

Electrics and Instrumentation

The road and trail bikes were equipped with a full set of electrics, including lights and indicators. Ignition was by coil and a 10 amp hour battery was carried behind the right-hand side panel. The headlight was supported on wire stays that were rubber mounted on the top and bottom yokes. It was a small 6in chromed item with a rotary light switch (pilot or main lights) and three warning lights for main beam (blue/green), indicators (amber) and oil pressure (red).

The wiring harness from the headlamp was led into an alloy electrical box that sat beneath the front of the fuel tank, where a nine-pin connector allowed the whole headlamp assembly to be quickly detachable for off-road use.

The electrical box (as its name suggested) was an alloy box with a bolted-on lid, containing all of the major electrical components. These consisted of the ignition coil, condenser, rectifier, Zener diode, capacitor (for battery-less ignition), flasher unit and the four-position ignition switch (parking lights, off, ignition, ignition and lights). The capacitor, condenser and flasher unit were rubber-mounted in a purpose-made moulding; the other components were bolted to the box. The box itself was rubber-mounted onto the frame using various brackets. The back of the box was open to the elements and carried the nine-pin socket for the quickly detachable headlamp's wiring plug.

The coil faced backwards and the HT lead came out of the open back of the box, giving a short distance to the plug. The rest of the wires came out of the top of the box through two holes protected with rubber grommets, to meet with the cables from the handlebar switch gear in a rat's nest of wiring below the fuel tank. The box itself was used as a heat sink for the Zener diode. The combined ignition and light switch was positioned on the left-hand side at the front of the box and was operated with the usual FS series ignition key. This was reasonably convenient, although it was a bit of a stretch to turn the lights on while moving. While the box seems like a good idea, it severely limits accessibility to the electrics. The box also came in at least two types, with detail differences between them, such as the use of round or oblong yellow reflectors on the side. The brackets used to mount the box to the frame also came in at least two types, with the front bracket having an extension to carry the horn that could either be on the left-hand side or the right! This lack of standardization was just plain mad – and a reflection of the state of BSA at the time.

The rear light was the corporate standard type for 1971, a long pressing bolted to the rear mudguard which carried a Lucas 'tit' type 679

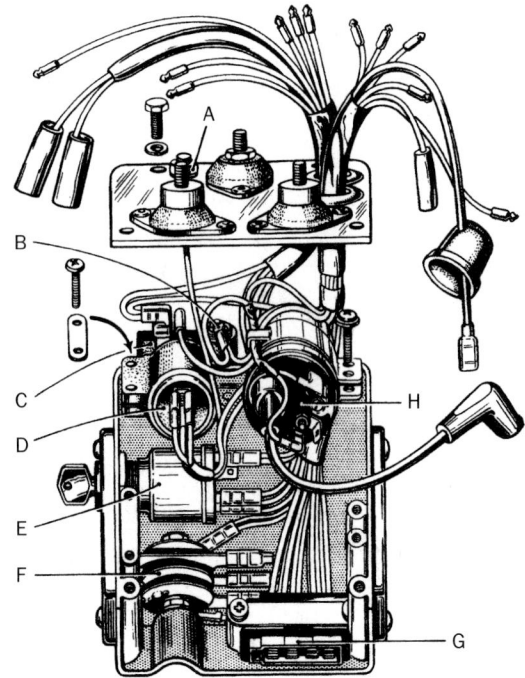

A: Zener diode
B: Condenser
C: Flasher unit
D: Capacitor
E: Ignition master switch
F: Rectifier
G: Headlamp harness socket
H: Ignition coil

The 1971 models carried all major electrical components in an alloy box under the front of the fuel tank. Some components were rubber-mounted and the Zener diode used the box itself as a heat sink. The nine-pin plug provides the connection to the QD headlamp.

lens, with the indicators bolted onto each side. This design was generally considered to be unattractive and was nicknamed the 'gargoyle' type.

A speedometer was fitted as standard to all models except the B50MX, with a tachometer as an optional extra. The B25SS had a 3in, black-faced Smith's 80mph unit, while the B50SS and all of the trail versions had a larger 3½in Smith's unit. The speedometer was mounted in a rubber cup that was fixed to the right-hand side fork leg top nut using a figure

The optional tachometer matched the 3in black-faced speedometer on the B25SS and T25SS.

Handlebar switches for 1971 were integrated with the lever pivots and while they were a long reach for some thumbs were considerably better than what was used in earlier years.

of eight shaped chromed bracket. If fitted, the tachometer was placed in an identical way on the opposite side.

The road models had new Lucas electrical switches that incorporated two press switches and one toggle switch. The left-hand side operated the horn, headlamp flasher and dip/main beam; the right was engine kill and indicators. The switches incorporated the lever pivots and had good-quality alloy levers with integral cable adjusters. While the switches

came in for some criticism due to the long reach needed to get to them, they were a quantum leap forward from the low-quality pressed-tin units used before.

Electrics for the B50MX were basic, comprising energy transfer alternator and coil, with the contact breakers in the normal position on the timing side. The electrical box under the tank was deleted on this model; there were no lights or horn and no handlebar switches to operate them.

4 Competition History

Introduction

The BSA unit single range has a long and illustrious competition history, especially in the off-road scene where they were winning trials and scrambles competitions from almost as soon as the range was introduced. For the unit singles range, competition formed a vital part and input into the development of the model range, both in the introduction of production competition machines, from the C15T to the B50MX, and in the introduction of modifications and new models based on the experiences of the BSA competition shop. The job of the competition shop should not be underestimated, in taking a simple, cheap roadster and developing it to the point that it was able to compete and win in the world arena. This culminated in the BSA unit single, with Jeff Smith riding, winning the 1964 and 1965 World 500cc Motocross Championship. When you consider that the bike ridden started off as a 250cc stretched version of the Tiger Cub, itself stretched from the 150cc Terrier, the achievement of the BSA competition shop was even more spectacular. The feeding in of modifications to the production range based on the experience of the competition use of the model was a major factor in increasing the reliability of the overall range and helping it to remain as competitive as possible against the ever increasing opposition.

This chapter describes the initial design and subsequent development of the trials and scrambles models used by many to compete at a local, national and international level. While this was the main thrust of the BSA competition shop, there were various outside agents such as Eric Cheney and the Rickman brothers producing their own frames for the range and others like the dealers Mead and Tompkinson, who produced successful road racers. Where possible, their exploits are briefly described.

At the peak of the unit single's success, BSA made good use of its race wins in advertising – here from 1967 giving an impressive list of wins during 1966.

Eric Cheney – Intermoto

Eric Cheney was a well-known and skilled scramblers star during the 1950s who enjoyed considerable success. After a prolonged illness in during 1961, he decided to retire from racing to concentrate on frame building and preparing bikes for other riders. Starting off based in his home workshop, he was soon successful enough to move to bigger premises and employ several workers.

Eric started off building frames for the unit singles in the early 1960s for the 250cc engines and as the works scramblers were developed kept in touch with the competition shop. This close contact paid off when Eric got a 'Black Bess' 420cc works engine in late 1965, which he equipped with a single down-tube frame. This machine was raced with success by Keith Hickman. In the mid 1960s Jerry Scott and Keith Hickman wanted a 'miniature Gold Star' using the unit single engine – and so Eric made a twin down-tube frame for the unit single.

Simon Cheney holds up one of his BSA unit single motocross frames.

Eric built frames for the BSA unit singles through the 1960s and early 1970s – although he did use various other engines for the scramblers and also built trials and road-racing frames. The 'standard' frames for the unit single were single down tube type, and had the oil contained in the frame from the word go. They were purpose-built to fit the unit single. This 'production' single down-tube frame was much easier to build than the twin down-tube version.

The Cheney frame building philosophy was to build on experience. Having ridden many works and production machines, Eric Cheney knew what could and did happen to the frames, and ensured that these faults were designed out in his frames, working on the principle that prevention was better than cure. His philosophy was to make the frames as strong and as light as possible. The unit singles works and production frames had several faults. They used to break at the bottom of the seat tube where it joined to the large diameter backbone and the 'swan neck' bends used in the lower frame introduced weaknesses that also led to breakage. The oiling system was also not ideal, with the pancake oil tank often breaking, leading to oil loss and disaster for the engine. The Cheney frames designed these weaknesses out and were built using the best materials around. During the 1960s and 1970s this meant using either Reynolds 531 or T45 steel tube. Nowadays, Cheney frames continue in this tradition, but use totally up to date materials such as top-grade 4130 steel tube.

The BSA 'Thumper' was a project between Cheney and Ken Heanes, a former ISDT rider and motorcycle dealer based in Fleet, Hants. The bike was produced in the early 1970s and was a Cheney framed, B50 engined scrambler. The deal was that Cheney would build the bikes and Ken Heanes would market them. Initially, Ken wanted Eric to build about 200, but had problems getting the parts from the factory. It is unclear how many of these bikes were eventually built but they were potent competition bikes which took over the four-stroke mantle from the BSA works B50s scrambles. The bike featured a Cheney frame, which used Reynolds 531 tubing.

The design followed Cheney's standard practice, with a large diameter top tube, single front down tube and with twin tubes forming the engine cradle. A square section swinging arm was used and the frame

This 1966 Cheney Victor shows how form can reflect function. The superb lines and simple styling complement the excellent handling and great performance.

and swinging arm were bright nickel-plated. The engine oil was carried in the top tube, giving an oil capacity of 3½pt (1.9ltr). Wheels were 20in front and 18in rear, the front mudguard was made from stainless steel while the rear was alloy and the brakes were both SLS, with a 6in diameter front and a 7in diameter rear both in alloy hubs. The front forks used aluminium sliders and had two-way damping and alloy fork crowns to reduce weight. The rear chain adjustment was by quadrant adjusters at the rear wheel spindle. All in all, the bikes were state of the art for the time and provided a competitive mount for many clubmen.

As the 1970s progressed, Cheney moved away from the four strokes that were becoming increasingly uncompetitive in the scrambles market and embraced the two stroke, building his frames to take engines from other manufacturers and maintaining his reputation for producing competitive bikes.

The firm restarted doing BSA engined bikes again in 1988 as the market for classic bikes and classic scramblers started to emerge. The market developed from people asking for their Cheney classic scramblers to be 'reverse modified' to make then eligible for classic events, to requests for batches of copies of works type frames. Cheney saw that demand for his classic frames was on the up and recommended building the scrambler frames, including those for the BSA unit singles.

Eric Cheney sadly passed away in 2001 and today the company is still family run by Eric's son, Simon. The firm still makes frames following the Cheney philosophy and offers frame kits, rolling chassis or complete frames, in scrambles, ISDT or road trim. Engines catered for include the BSA unit singles from 250cc to 500cc and unit and pre-unit Triumph 500cc and 650cc engines. Pre-unit singles from BSA, Ariel, AJS and many other makes are also catered for. Renovations of customer's bikes are offered, and they stock or can supply spares for all of the firm's products. Trading as Intermoto, Simon Cheney operates from Unit 3, Potters Industrial Park, Coxmoor Close, Aldershot Road, Church Crookham, Fleet, Hants GU52 6EU, and can be contacted on 01252 613680.

Prototype C15 Trials

In the 4 December issue of *The Motorcycle*, the week that saw the publication of the journal's first road test of the recently announced C15 Star, George Wilson recounts how he snatched a brief ride on Brian Martin's C15 based trials prototype. Brian had just completed the British Experts Trial at Ludlow, Shropshire, and reading between the lines of the brief article, Mr Wilson must have had a spin on the bike and gave it a detailed examination, pronouncing it a 'very, very businesslike picture'. Some interesting details emerge from this snippet, buried in the back of the magazine. Firstly, Mr Wilson praises the spread of power and the good power to weight ratio. He found that the bike would 'plonk' along at very low revs but had enough power to lift the front wheel when the throttle was whacked open. He compared the power favourably with that of a 350cc machine, describing it as 'a rugged he-man type of power that one expects from a three-fifty'. He was impressed with the engine's set up, giving smooth power all the way through the rev range, with no fluffing or hesitation encountered, and expressed admiration for the BSA competition shop and 'the impeccable way in which they [the BSA works bikes] have been prepared'.

He listed the differences from standard, including a new wider rear fork to accommodate the 4.00 × 18 rear tyre and this, combined with the larger 3.00 × 20 front tyre, led to the greater ground clearance. The front forks were from an 'older C type BSA', presumably the C12, and new one-off yokes were used to provide steeper rake and to increase the trail. Frame modifications were noted as being simply resited footrests, but examination of the photos that accompanied the article show that the frame was in fact missing both the 'standard' footrest mounts and the extension tubes that carried the pillion footrests. The other changes from the standard roadster included a high-level exhaust pipe, running down the right-hand side of the bike with a short Burgess type silencer; the looped kick-start lever to clear the rear set footrests; a short gear lever; an alloy fuel tank; and a single seat. Power was a claimed 15bhp and weight (with oil but without fuel) was claimed as 250lb (113kg). The bike seems to have been very close in specification to the soon to be announced competition models. The closing line in the report was: 'In fact, it is so businesslike that ere long sister models of Martin's will be ridden by the entire BSA team!'

Which really was a bit of an understatement, bearing in mind the winning performance of the various C15-derived models that dominated the off-road competition world over the next decade!

The competition history of the BSA singles, the riders, the bikes and the wins has been covered in a number of books (*see* Bibliography). Rather than present a dry list of riders, events, placing and models, the following sections give a view of the competition successes and failures of the unit singles, concentrating on the events that resulted in the development of improvements to the overall model range. They emphasize the importance of the works competition shop in the development of the model from its rather fragile beginnings to the world-beater that it became. If ever there is proof needed that racing improves the breed, then the unit singles development in the light of competition proves it.

It is impossible to collate a full list of the unit singles' successes. Looking in a single copy of the weekly magazine, *Motorcycle*, for 2 April 1964, we see Jeff Smith winning both the heats of the Hants Grand National Scramble on his 420cc BSA. In the same week, 420cc BSA's again won the three-cornered international scrambles between the UK, Sweden and Belgium at Brill, with Jeff Smith and Arthur Lampkin riding. Probably every week during the 1960s, a similar range of successes would be recorded at club, national and international levels for the BSA singles, showing its versatility and competitiveness over the whole decade. Indeed, the story of the BSA unit singles competition history is still being played out in classic motocross and pre-1965 trials events in the UK and abroad, where the basic strengths of the unit single of light weight, good power, low costs and (relative) reliability mean it is a still a favourite and competitive ride for many.

The competition heritage of BSA's unit singles did have a swansong, in the form of developments by Clews Competition Motorcycles (CCM), which was founded by Alan

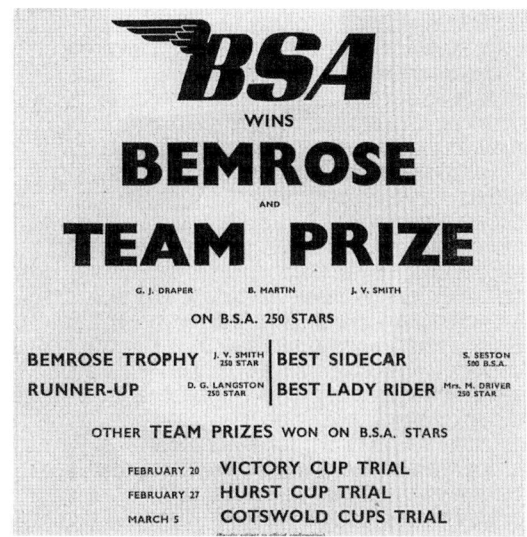

BSA
WINS
BEMROSE
AND
TEAM PRIZE
G. J. DRAPER
B. MARTIN
J. V. SMITH
ON B.S.A. 250 STARS
BEMROSE TROPHY
J. V. SMITH 250 STAR
RUNNER-UP
D. G. LANGSTON 250 STAR
BEST SIDECAR
S. SESTON 500 B.S.A.
BEST LADY RIDER
Mrs. M. DRIVER 250 STAR
OTHER TEAM PRIZES WON ON B.S.A. STARS
FEBRUARY 20
VICTORY CUP TRIAL
FEBRUARY 27
HURST CUP TRIAL
MARCH 5
COTSWOLD CUPS TRIAL

RIGHT: *In 1960 BSA works C15s won the Bemrose trial. Along with other victories, a special advert was placed in the press.*

BELOW: *An anonymous B50 being competed. Note the use of standard front forks and conical hub, with extra ventilation. (Mick Walker)*

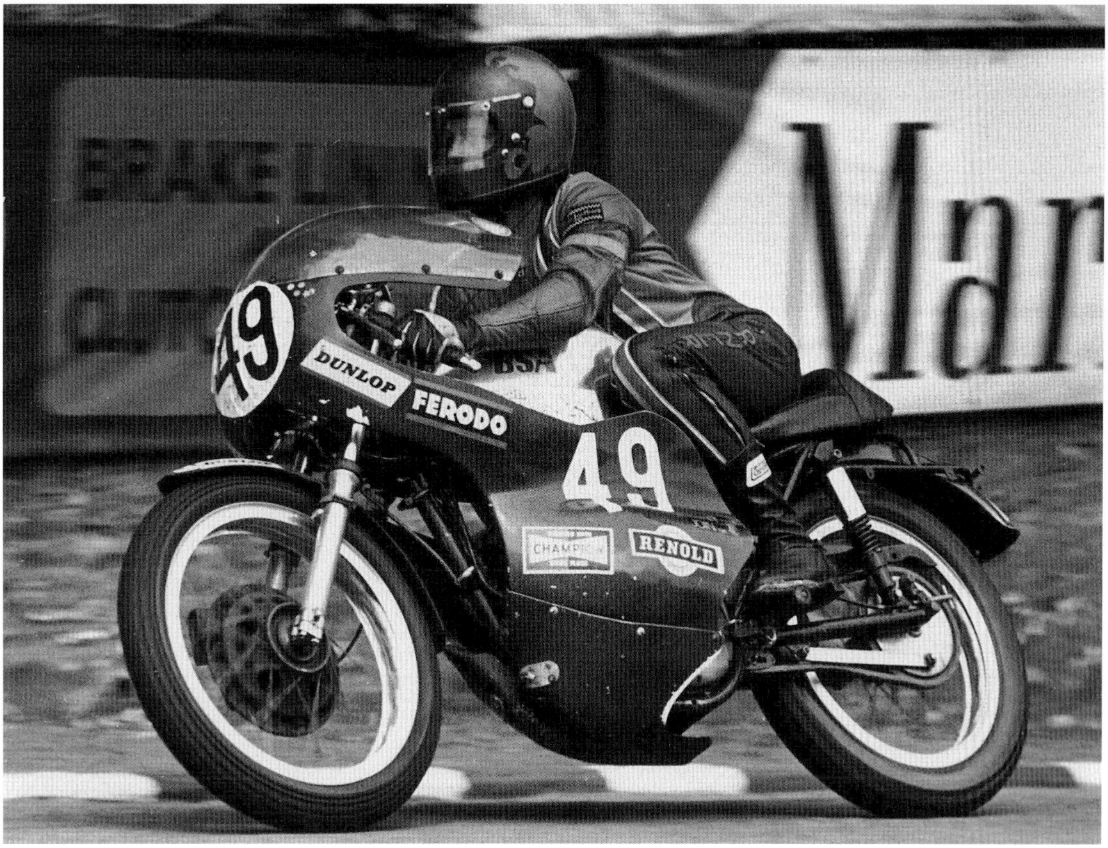
49
DUNLOP
FERODO
49
RENOLD

B50s and B44s are still competitive in classic scrambles. This highly modified B50 was seen in 2004.

Clews, an ex-BSA man. He set up CCM after effectively buying the contents of the BSA Competition Shop in the early 1970s and had some success in trials and motocross throughout the 1970s and early 1980s with competition bikes powered by developments of the basic unit single.

Trials

Brian Martin, a successful BSA works scrambles and trials rider, was appointed as BSA Competitions Manager in November 1960, taking over from Bert Perrigo. He was destined to play a vital role in the development of the BSA unit single line. Just prior to his appointment, the introduction of the C15 in 1959 gave the BSA competition shop some pause for thought. The bike was a cheap roadster, built down to a price and not particularly robust. In addition, the pre-unit Gold Star was incredibly successful in larger capacity (350cc and 500cc) scrambles classes; the 250cc scrambles series was considered to be pretty insignificant in comparison. The situation was different in the trials area – while there were

trials versions of the Gold Star, a smaller, lighter machine was needed to take on the new generation of small capacity singles, including Triumph's Tiger Cub, that were beginning to overcome the larger pre-unit bikes that had dominated the field all through the 1950s. BSA's competition shop designers at the time, Eric Webster and Bert Curry, were up to the challenge.

So the first 'works' unit single was a C15-based trials machine, which was arrived at relatively simply. The brazed lug frame with bolt-on subframe, based on the roadsters but subtly modified, was used initially, while a wider and longer swinging arm allowed the comp shop the use of a 4.00in section rear trials tyre. An 18in rear wheel and 20in front wheel were used to gain additional ground clearance. The engine was retuned to give the type of power needed for trials by installing a low compression piston along with a sports camshaft. The trials model was so good that it was still being used by the BSA trials team in the mid to late 1960s, albeit having benefited from extensive development, including a new all-welded one-piece frame for 1961. Notable

RIGHT: The C15T was a production version of the works trials bikes. This is the restored 1960 model featured elsewhere in the book.

BELOW: The C15T remained competitive through the early and mid-1960s. This advert celebrates a win in the 1966 Scottish trial.

BELOW RIGHT: The basic C15/B40/B44 engine could still be competitive during the 1970s. CCM produced this 350cc trial bike well into the 1970s.

BSA SCOOPS THE SCOTTISH

OUTRIGHT WINNER
A. R. C. LAMPKIN
(250 c.c. B.S.A.)

250 c.c. AWARD
A. R. C. LAMPKIN

•

MANUFACTURERS' TEAM PRIZE
(A. R. C. LAMPKIN, A. J. LAMPKIN, SCOTT ELLIS,
ALL ON 250 c.c. B.S.A.s

B.S.A. MOTOR CYCLES LTD.,
ARMOURY ROAD, BIRMINGHAM, 11.

wins for the C15T included the Scott Trial three years running, 1959–61, the Vic Brittain Trial of 1961, the Perce Simon Trophy Trial, the Hoad Trophy and the British Experts Solo in 1963, and the Scottish Six Days Trial, the Bemrose Trophy Trial and West of England Trial of 1966.

The B40 was introduced to the public in November 1960 and the competition shop got in on the act, with a trials version being fielded in December 1960, gaining its first win at the St David's Trial in January 1961, ridden by Jeff Smith. The B40 went on to score a number of successes in its class at events and was ridden with considerable success by Tony Davies, with wins in 1962 in the Mitchell Trial and the West of England Trial, following up in 1963 with wins in the Cotwold Cup, Hoad Trophy, the Victory Trial and the Wye Valley Traders. Development continued with the 350cc unit by CCM, which introduced a trials model in the 1970s. The B40 is still very popular today in the trials scene, as demonstrated by Sammy Miller's Otter, a B40-based trials bike still produced in 2005 to cater for the pre-1965 trials competitor.

Scrambles

Alongside the trials model the competition shop was also looking at the scrambles scene. It recognized that the C15 could be adapted to the scrambles role even if the 250cc class was not that important. So the scrambles model was developed, differing mainly in engine tune from the trials model, with a higher compression piston, larger inlet valve, larger carburettor and modified exhaust system. All these modifications were aimed at getting increased power, which was produced further up the rev band than the trials model to suit the type of riding needed in competitive scrambles. The result was an outstanding success and the pair of machines were 'productionized' and introduced to the public as the C15T trials and C15S scrambles production models in 1960.

While the factory made the production models, Jeff Smith and Arthur Lampkin were entered for the 1960 European motocross championships on what were initially catalogue specification 250cc scrambles models. After a year of learning, Jeff Smith came second in the championship, behind the

This period shot of the Pirbright 100-mile scramble of 1962 shows a C15S taking on an incline. Note the wider than standard handlebars and full-width hub. (Mick Walker)

250cc Greeves of Dave Bickers, and a raft of improvements to the bikes were identified and implemented. This season marked the first in a series of years where the competition bikes were broken, fixed and improved, with the developments feeding into the production models as time progressed. The modifications that came out of this first serious year of competition included improved oil pump drive gears, steel flywheels rather than cast iron, tougher engine shafts and, probably most significant, an improved roller big-end bearing.

BSA continued to compete in the 250cc motocross championship for 1961, again with Jeff Smith and Arthur Lampkin doing the riding. While they used engines that incorporated the changes from 1960, the frame of the works machines was a lighter, all-welded affair that would later see production in the next batch of competition machines and would serve as a model for the frame used on the Starfire/Shooting Star road models of 1967. While the 1961 season was again considered to be successful, again BSA could only take the runners up spot behind Greeves, with Arthur Lampkin gaining the honours this time.

September 1961 saw the introduction of the 350cc B40, an event that was not missed by the competition shop. By now, the dominance of the pre-unit Gold Star was waning in the 350cc and 500cc motocross classes and the B40 was chosen to retain BSA's dominance in this area. Brian Martin took a hands-on approach to the B40 – to assess the engine's potential he converted a unit to run on dope, fitted it to a 250cc scramblers frame and took the bike to the 1961 Red Marley hill climb. The hybrid won both the 350cc and unlimited cc classes, with a performance that was very close to the hill record. This was seen as being promising, so the competition shop started to develop the B40, using its experience of the 250cc motor. Retaining the standard bore and

Vic Eastwood, BSA works rider and World Champion, is seen here on his BSA Victor during 1966. (Mick Walker)

stroke of 79mm × 70mm, the competition shop fitted bigger valves, a larger carburettor and a racing camshaft. The bike was then entered into a 1961 Shrubland Park event, one of the major races of the British calendar. Ridden by Jeff Smith, the bike won the 350cc race, the 500cc race and the Grand National, all against strong competition. The bike was christened 'Black Bess', as the engine had been given a coat of black heat-dissipating paint to assist cooling, and made around 27bhp. While at this stage in its development the 350cc B40 did not make the same power as the Gold Stars, Brian Martin recognized that its light weight and manoeuvrability gave it a major advantage that a rider of Jeff Smith's calibre could exploit.

However, as the Americans like to say, 'there's no substitute for cubes' and the competition shop started to see if there was any potential to increase the size of the B40 with-

This close-up of the BSA 441cc motor clearly shows the energy transfer ignition coil just behind the petrol tap and the close-fitting upswept exhaust. (Mick Walker)

out making significant changes to the standard crankcases. Calculations showed that by using the standard B40 connecting rod and retaining the standard bore, the stroke could be increased from 70mm to 86mm, giving a capacity of 420cc. However, this led to problems with the standard connecting rod, as it was a bit too short to provide adequate clearance between the bottom of the piston skirt and flywheels, unless the flywheel diameter was reduced to an unacceptable size.

Salvation came with the discovery that BSA's experimental department had designed a connecting rod for a 79mm × 86mm motor that had never gone into production and this rod was longer than the standard B40 item. Luckily, the forging dies for the rod still existed. So, with the new connecting rod, the B40

engine could be safely stretched to 420cc and work proceeded apace to get the engine ready to race. Its first outing came in 1962 Hants Grand National held at Matchams Park, with Jeff Smith winning the heat easily. By now, BSA's design department was assisting the competition shop in the development process, and the decision had been taken to compete for the 500cc scrambles championship using the 420cc machine. However, on stripping down and inspecting the engine after the Hants Grand National severe wear of the gearbox was evident. On reflection, this should have been unexpected, as the gearbox internals were basically standard C15/B40 items. These were expected to be installed in gentle touring machines; they were not designed to handle twice as much power and the rough handling that the bike was subjected to on the track, with its rapid acceleration and deceleration, leaps, landings and fast clutchless gear changes. The teeth on the pinions were wearing excessively, despite being made of the highest grade materials. The BSA engineers set to work to sort out the problem, by redesigning the tooth form used to a stub-tooth form.

However, before the fix was done the BSA team riders had to use the suspect gearbox and would rebuild the box with new pinions after virtually every meeting, if not between races at a meeting. The 1962 World Championship season found BSA on a steep learning curve. Although the 420cc bike showed promise, with Jeff Smith winning the ACU (Auto-Cycle Union) Scramble Star, teething problems like the gearbox kept it off the winners' rostrum. However, BSA saw the bike's potential and built up a second machine for Arthur Lampkin to compete in the 1963 season. This season saw more problems, but finished with Jeff Smith gaining third place and Arthur Lampkin fifth in the 500cc Championship, so progress was being made.

BSA took the decision to make an all-out effort during the 1963–4 UK winter season to develop a world beater to win the 1964 500cc Championship. This was based on the potential demonstrated in the previous season's championship successes and the arrival of the BBC (British Broadcasting Corporation) featuring scrambles on the television, thereby reaching a wider audience and great advertising for the winners, and giving a great testing ground for the new works machines over the winter in domestic races before the world championship started. Much development work was carried out in the light of the previous two seasons, producing what was probably the definitive works machine, which had moved substantially away from its humble roadster roots and continued to do so through the 1964 season.

The all-welded one-piece frame was used and the B40-based crankcases flexed and lost power, so were replaced mid-season with a new design that was much stronger and more robust. The new cases also incorporated stronger main bearings, with the B40's drive-side ball race being replaced with a roller race, and the timing-side plain bush being replaced with a ball bearing, giving a much stronger bottom end that would tolerate the abuse hurled on the engine in racing conditions. The stub-toothed gearbox pinions were retained, having been proved reliable in the previous year. Upstairs, the B40 iron barrel was replaced with an alloy version with a chromed bore. This barrel had three advantages, being lighter, having better cooling properties and wearing slower than the iron one. The barrel was initially produced with 'round' fins like the B40, but was later modified to have 'square' fins, in which form it looked similar to that fitted to the B25/B44 roadsters.

The more efficient cooling that the alloy barrel gave enables the compression ratio of the motor to be raised from 10:1 to 11.4:1, boosting power. The running gear of the bike was not missed in this intensive phase of development. In the quest for lightness, a new frame

was designed. Although similar in layout to the existing all-welded item, it carried the engine oil in its tubes, enabling the elimination of the weighty separate oil tank and as a bonus allowing a larger, more efficient air cleaner to be fitted. Power output had risen to just under 30bhp at 6,000rpm and the bikes weighed around 228lb (103kg). The first outing of the new oil-in-frame 420cc bike was the Hants Grand National in 1964. With Jeff Smith riding the bike won, giving him his fifth successive win at the Hants event. The start of BSA's participation in the 1964 500cc Championship came in April 1964 in Switzerland, with Jeff Smith riding the 420cc works machine. It can fairly be said that BSA had a close run, with double world champion Rolf Tiblin of Sweden leading the series initially. As the series progressed, Jeff Smith slowly gained on him, taking first position in seven meetings, second in six meetings and third (due to a flat tyre) in one meeting, until the second to last round in East Germany left Smith and Tiblin level-pegging. The final round was played out in Spain on 13 September 1964, when Jeff won both heats, giving him and BSA their first 500cc Championship.

Taken in 1967, this Victor sports a custom twin down-tube frame made by Walwin, one of a number of frame makers who were using the Victor motor. (Mick Walker)

The BSA team did not rest on their laurels and development of the bike continued for the 1965 season. The new crankcases introduced in 1964 enabled the stroke to be increased again to 90mm, giving an extra 21cc in capacity and a power boost to just under 32bhp at 6,000rpm. The bike had the famous 441cc capacity used in the Victor Grand Prix of 1965, the 1966 US spec Victor Enduro and the 1967-onwards home market Victor and Shooting Star roadster. The 1965 season was an outstanding success for BSA, with Jeff Smith building up an unassailable lead by the end of July by winning the first six of the eleven events. By the end of the season, he had won the title with a significant lead over the runner-up, CZ-mounted Paul Friedrichs of East Germany.

With two world championships now under its belt, BSA continued development of the works machines for the 1966 season. Brian Martin recognized that the bikes would need to have increased power and so decreased the weight to remain competitive against the rapidly developing large capacity two strokes from CZ and Husqvarna. The BSA board concurred and substantially increased the budget for the competition shop to finance the next year's racing. This finance enabled a comprehensive and fast development programme, which with hindsight probably meant too many changes too quickly to the basic machine, which lead to unreliability.

The 441cc Victor engine had a capacity boost to a 494cc by increasing the bore and stroke to 82mm × 93mm, which gave a slight rise in power to 33.4bhp at 6,000rpm. Weight saving was seen as the way forwards and so the engine cases were cast from magnesium alloy, titanium was used for a number of engine components such as the con rod, engine sprocket and rockers, and, most radically of all, this material was used to make the frame.

This weight-saving effort worked, with the bike weighing just 212lb (96kg), but had dramatic effects on the reliability of the machine. The magnesium alloy engine cases had to be abandoned mid-season, as it was impossible to stop the main bearings working loose. The titanium frame gave rise to many problems, as it was prone to flex much more than its steel predecessor. This 'feature' affected the handling adversely and resulted in the frame cracking. The frame cracking caused major problems. When heated, titanium absorbs oxygen

The Rickman brothers also made use of the Victor engine in their Metisse frame. (Mick Walker)

SCRAMBLERS!

Twice a world championship winner-for you!

BSA also offered its own works-based scrambler for 1966. The Victor GP was closely based on Jeff Smith's own racer.

Eric Cheney, the frame maker, and Ken Heanes, BSA dealer and works rider, teamed up in the early 1970s to offer the 'Thumper'. This was a Cheney framed, B50-powered scrambler. (Mick Walker)

and hydrogen from the atmosphere and gets brittle. Hence it needs to be welded in an inert atmosphere when being made and repaired. This made it impossible to repair the frames properly when out in the field. In an interview in the January 1984 edition of *Classic Bike*, Brian Martin saw that the team just did not know enough about the material to recognize both its properties (giving the flex problems) and the difficulties they would have in repairing it in the field. To address the flexing, the titanium swinging arm was quickly replaced with a steel item and the titanium frame was dropped part-way through the season, with the team going back to frames made from Reynolds 531 steel tube. While this imposed a 20lb (9kg) weight penalty, the team got a better-handling bike that did not break so often and could be repaired easily if it did.

The 1966 season was a disappointment for BSA, with reliability problems dogging the team, and they only won one of the rounds outright. This was on 22 May at Helsinki in Finland, when Jeff Smith came second in the first leg and first in the second leg to win overall victory. Jeff came third in the 1966

championship and Brian Martin was to admit that it was a tactical error to start the racing season with an untried machine. However, at home the 441 Victor ridden by John Banks won the Experts Grand National and the British Championship, so the season was not the out and out disaster that it is sometimes portrayed.

The following year, 1967, showed a little improvement, with Smith gaining second place. A lesson learned was that a shorter stroke (82mm × 90mm) engine, while having a capacity of 475cc, gave slightly more power than the 494cc engine, paving the way for the development of a shorter stroke 499cc motor for the 1968 season.

The 1968 season saw the Victor engine being reworked, with an increase in the bore size and a decrease in the stroke to give 84mm × 90mm and a capacity of 499cc. With a compression ratio of 10:1 the engine produced just over 37bhp at 6,000rpm and was reliable. New long travel forks, with variable rate internal springs and magnesium alloy sliders, helped to update the suspension. By now, John Banks had replaced Vic Eastwood in the team and the

135

Cylinder Head, Barrel, Piston, Valves, Guides, Springs, Rockers, Push Rods, Cylinder Bolts and 32 mm. Concentric Carburettor... everything above the crankcase.

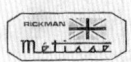
Rickman offered more than just frames – here is an advert for a 4-valve head produced for the B50 – engineered by Weslake. (Mick Walker)

team had a good season, with John Banks finishing just one point behind the winner, Paul Friedrichs in the world championship, and winning the British Championship. Jeff Smith finished in joint seventh place. However, BSA was finding it increasingly difficult to compete with the lighter and more powerful two strokes.

Because of this, the following years from 1969–71 saw BSA fall from its position as a contender to that of an also-ran. Keith Hickman was the highest placed BSA rider for the 1969 and 1970 seasons, finishing sixth in 1969 and then only making fourteenth in 1970. The 1971 season was worse, with injuries and increasingly uncompetitive machinery taking its toll. BSA took the decision to close down the competition shop after the British Motocross Grand Prix in July 1971. The works riders were offered the use of their machines and limited back-up. Dave Nicoll took up the offer and gave BSA a win in the December 1971 World of Sport televised meeting held at Cadwell Park – a fitting swansong for the BSA scrambles effort of the past decade.

International Six Days Trials

The International Six Days Trial (ISDT) was an event held yearly and was a severe test of both man and machine. The trial was just that – an extended test of the man and machine, featuring timed and observed rides both on- and off-road, and performance tests run over six days and nights. The rider had to do all of his own maintenance, using only tools and spares carried on the bike. Outside help could result in disqualification. The event was open to teams and individuals and BSA was a keen competitor as the tough regime was an ideal shop window for BSA's products. The C15T first appeared for BSA in 1961, while the team was usually mounted on Gold Star derived machines. The C15T and later the B40 and B44 possessed off-road ability, relative reliability and light weight, all of which were vital for success in the events, and slowly took over as the basis for the BSA presence in the event from 1961.

While the unit singles increased manoeuvrability over the heavier pre-unit models, there were some interesting problems encountered during the various competitions. One of the most successful BSA ISDT team members was Jim Sandiford, who gained four consecutive Gold Medals from 1961–4. However, other riders on the unit singles had less luck and ignition, gearbox and preparation problems all conspired to rob riders of gold medals. The final straw for the problem-prone singles came at the 1965 event, held on the Isle of Man. There were five works BSAs entered in the national team, three 350cc B40s and two further B40s with the large capacity 441cc engines. The works bikes were ridden by Arthur Lampkin (B44), Sammy Miller (B40), Alan Lampkin (B44), Jim Sandiford (B40) and Scott Ellis (B40). In addition, BSA employee Pat Slinn, riding a 350cc B40, was a private entry. All of the works BSAs retired with alternator failure. The British motorcycle press were scathing in their condemnation of what they perceived to be a slight on the UK's national pride, and demanded changes to the way the UK approached the event in the future.

Subsequent investigations showed that identical Lucas components were supplied to BSA and Triumph, but that all of the Triumph ones had run without a fault. The failure of the BSA alternators was put down to the different heat ranges experienced in the singles and was the justification for the BSA management sanctioning the building of all Triumph engined machines for the following year's

event. This set the scene for future British participation in the ISDT using purpose-built machines with 350cc or 500cc Triumph engines and BSA (or outside suppliers such as Cheney) frames and running gear.

Road Racing

The BSA unit singles were not campaigned on the tarmac racetracks of the world by BSA with any great enthusiasm, as the four-stroke single was not really the right configuration for international grand prix success during the 1960s. However, this did not deter the keen clubman, who recognized that the combination of light weight, relatively high power output, cheapness and motocross competition tuning components could be used to some effect in road racing. However, you can't keep a good competition shop down, and a 350cc road race machine was developed, ostensibly to assist in the development of the motocross machines! BSA did give some support to the riders, who included Bob Heath, but there was not a full road-racing programme.

BSA's 1973 offering to sporting riders was the B50MX, the last incarnation of the BSA unit singles. This year the MX featured a prop stand as standard; otherwise it was largely unchanged from the 1972 model.

Meade and Tomkinson were a successful dealership based in Hereford, England. They campaigned B44 and B50-based racers in endurance races such as the Thruxton 500 miles and the Barcelona 24-Hour Race at the Montjuich circuit.

Their Victor-based 441cc machine came second overall at Barcelona in 1968, ridden by Mick Andrews and Colin Dixon, and won the unlimited class – although the race was won at record speed by a Spanish Ossa. The dealership then moved over to the new B50 and in 1971, applying the experience gained with the Victor, proceeded to win the 500cc class in the Thruxton 500-mile race, the 500cc class at the Barcelona 24 Hours and won the Zolder 24-Hour Race outright. The fame of the dealership was such that it had a visit from *Motorcycle Mechanics* in 1971, to view the tuning work used to produce the successful endurance racers. The *Motorcycle Mechanics* journalist was surprised to find that there were no major changes made to the engine, just small improvements and careful assembly. Ports were smoothed and the inlet port opened out to take a 32mm carburettor (as on the B50 MX). The standard scrambles cam was used (again from the B50MX) and a standard big

end. The taper on the end of the pushrods was made gentler to avoid stress build-up and a later advance/retard unit was used. The primary drive was shimmed to ensure that the chain line was right, the cush drive hub cover was spot-welded on and a steel insert welded into the exhaust port to prevent the exhaust pipe coming loose. All in all, very few changes from the standard model were needed to produce a machine that won at Thruxton and came second in Barcelona.

Currently, the B44/B50 (and even some C15/B25s) are used in historic racing, with some success, reflecting the quality of the running gear, the tunability of the engine and the light weight of the basic machines.

The USA

The unit singles had a hard act to follow in the USA. BSA's Gold Star 350cc and 500cc pre-unit singles had a glorious history of success from the late 1940s and all through the 1950s in on- and off-road sports, including winning prestige events such as the Daytona 200.

In general, the unit singles were successful in competition in the US, but at a local rather than a national level. The Starfire 250cc

Pictured in 1988 at a Classic Racing Motorcycle Club (CRMC) event, this B50 Special featured a B50 engine with a grafted-on five speed gearbox, a one-off frame and a disc-braked front end. (Mick Walker)

A relatively standard B50 racer pictured in 1985 at Brands Hatch. Standard forks carry a non-standard front brake. (Mick Walker)

The BSA unit single's greatest successes came on the dirt. This 1966 B44 motocross bike of Doug Desborough sums up the spirit of those times. (Mick Walker)

competition models, the pure off-road Scrambles and the Trials Cat, were competed by private and dealer-supported riders in events across the US during the 1960s with success, for example Don Moreland of Peoria, who won the 250-mile Abe Lincoln Enduro in 1961, and who was featured in the BSA publicity of the day.

BSA unit singles continued to be popular with riders and were successful in trials, scrambles and short track racing. In 1965 BSA ran an advert featuring Jerry Underwood, who had accumulated an impressive array of wins and trophies on his C15-based short tracker. Interestingly, Jerry's bike has a rigid rear end grafted onto a stock-looking early BSA single frame – the 'swan neck' steering head is clearly visible in front of the stock C15T/C15S fuel tank.

The appearance of the 441cc Victor and Shooting Star gave riders a replacement for the by then obsolete Gold Star and BSA dealers offered 'Zip Kits' to convert the roadster into a racer, for scrambles and desert racing. Many 441cc road bikes were converted and the trend continued with the introduction of the B50.

BSA's competition success was advertised in the US press as well as in the UK. This 1965 advert says it all!

The B50MX was used in anger for many years on tracks and circuits; indeed, it still runs and wins in the classic events at the time of writing.

Triumph's Tiger Cub had acquitted itself well in the American Motorcyclist Association (AMA) Short Track Series during the 1960s. However, the Cub was discontinued in 1967,

being replaced in the national series by the BSA Starfire and Triumph TR25W when they were introduced in 1968. However, the bikes were heavy and underpowered in comparison with the opposition, typically the Spanish Ossa and Bultaco two-stroke 250cc singles. Even when equipped with purpose-built frames from companies such as Trackmaster and Red

BSA 'Zip Kits'

With the introduction of the Victor Shooting Star in 1967, BSA in the USA introduced a 'Zip Kit' that would convert the roadster into an off-road racer. To quote the brochure released by BSA Motorcycles – Western, the BSA distributors on the West Coast of the USA, the kit would: 'Convert your roadster to this trophy hunting beauty'. Whether the reference to a trophy was aimed at the Triumph Trophy or at the silverware awarded at the end of successful race is unclear!

The first kit included off-road modifications such as a bigger air cleaner, 2MC capacitor to replace the battery, rubber gaiters for the front forks and alloy valve collars and racing valve springs. A list of instructions gave details of other modifications, such as removing both mudguards, modifying the wiring harness, removal of extraneous electrical equipment such as the headlamp and tail light, the use of dirt tyres and the fitting of a straight-through exhaust pipe.

The Zip Kit was resurrected as the D/R Kit (for Dirt Racer) when the 1971 250cc or 500cc Victor Trail was introduced. It was pushed as 'Dick Mann's Favorite Dirt Racer' in the brochure issued by the BSA Motorcycle Corporation in 1971. This kit was a bit more comprehensive than the earlier one and revamped the electrics and exhaust to produce a bike suitable for off-road competition.

The electrics were modified with the loss of the electrical box, lights, turn signals, battery and wiring harness. The battery carrier was also removed. The electrical components that used to live in the electrical box, the 2MC capacitor, rectifier and Zener diode were relocated under the right-hand side panel. The capacitor and Zener diode were mounted on the alloy lid of the electrical box, which acted as a heat sink for the Zener. The speedometer was simply removed.

The cover of the brochure for the 1971 model Dirt Racer kit shows a converted B50T.

The coil and condenser were mounted under the left-hand side panel, and the kit supplied a longer HT lead. The switch boxes and control levers were replaced with steel Doherty (incorrectly spelt 'Dougherty' in the brochure) levers and a kill switch was also part of the kit. Dimensions were given to cut down the dual seat to MX dimensions and a new cover could be supplied from BSA as an extra. It was noted that the short MX

Line, they were uncompetitive and had little success. Engine tuning tended to be mild, but could include some reworking of the cylinder head, a 30mm carburettor and significantly the replacement of the BSA crank, rod and piston with stronger components from specialist tuning firms such as Sifton. The use of such components indicated that the fragility of the bottom end of the stock engine was recognized early on – probably from practical experience! Some successes were scored, with Gary Nixon winning the Daytona heat once and getting a win in the first event of the 1968 season, the Short Track at the Houston Astrodome in Texas, the TR25W's only National AMA victory.

DICK MANN'S FAVORITE ..... DIRT RACER

MX LOOK

ALL LIGHTS, TURN SIGNALS, WIRING HARNESS AND ELECTRIC BOX ARE REMOVED FOR CLEAN MX LOOK.
BATTERY AND BATTERY CARRIER ARE ELIMINATED TO REDUCE WEIGHT.

SEAT

THE DUAL SEAT CAN BE TRIMMED TO MX PROPORTIONS (DIMENSIONS INCLUDED IN INSTRUCTIONS). EXCHANGE COVER IS AVAILABLE. IF PREFERRED, MX SEAT #83-2746 WILL FIT RIGHT ON.

HIDDEN ELECTRICS

THE IGNITION ELECTRICS ARE RE-POSITIONED UNDER THE SIDE PANELS. USE ORIGINAL CAPACITOR, RECTIFIER, ZENER DIODE, COIL, CONDENSER AND HEAT SINK. SPECIAL WIRING HARNESS AND CAPACITOR FURNISHED WITH D/R KIT.

CONTROLS

HANDLE BAR CONSOLE SWITCHES REPLACED WITH DOUGHERTY CONTROLS.

D/R ADVANTAGE OVER MX: SIDE STAND 2½ GALLON TANK, SKID PLATE AND EASIER STARTING (24° IGN ADVANCE).

SPARKS

COIL AND CONDENSER ARE MOUNTED UNDER LEFT SIDE PANEL.
4" LONGER HIGH TENSION LEAD IS FURNISHED.

SPARK ARRESTER

MUFFLER IS REPLACED WITH APPROVED SPARK ARRESTER. Db LEVEL IS BELOW THAT RECOMMENDED FOR OFF ROAD VEHICLES.
SPARK ARRESTER, ADAPTER, CLAMPS AND BRACKET INCLUDED IN KIT.

The brochure referred to Dick Mann, a famous rider of the time. Modifications to the electrics removed the need for the separate alloy box, saving weight and aiding accessibility.

seat would fit straight on. The large box silencer was replaced with an approved spark arrester (this was a requirement of the US Forestry Service to prevent bikes from causing forest fires, which can be a major problem in the USA). This was specified as having a decibel level (noise level) below 'that recommended for off-road vehicles' – implying but not saying that it was not road legal.

The kit was advertised as having a number of advantages over the pure off-road MX model. The brochure actually states: 'D/R Advantage over MX: Side stand, 2½ Gallon Tank, Skid Plate and easier starting (24 Degree Ignition Advance)'

The cost of the kit for the Victor was a mere $42.50 and the instructions were free!

5   Owning and Riding Today

Introduction

For this section, I have broken the BSA unit singles range into two capacity classes – 250cc and over 250cc (that is, the 350cc, 441cc and 500cc engines) and three broad types of machine – pre-1967, 1967–70, and 1971–3 machines. These three types can be identified (with some notable exceptions), by the type of frame used. Prior to 1967, road bikes had the single loop, brazed lug construction double frame, with bolt-on subframe. Pre-1967 C15 road machines have got relatively low performance, dubious strength in the mechanicals, inadequate brakes, marginal spares availability and trouble-prone 6V electrics, although by the end of the line in 1967 most of these faults had been fixed. Handling and roadholding were considered good at the time, and are respectable today, although not in the Norton Featherbed class.

Post-1967 250cc bikes have the all-welded scrambler based frame. They all have 12V electrics with Zener diode regulation, a good robust and reliable system, sometimes let down by poor pattern parts. The frame is a good heavy duty design, with good handling and roadholding. The bike has a bigger feel to it than the previous 250. The brakes are good, with the front gaining a 7in diameter TLS design in 1969 that can cope with modern traffic conditions. The downsides of the post-1967 250cc bikes are the engine's life expectancy and a lack of low down torque necessitating the use of higher revs than the

C15 – which of course increases stress on the engine. As with the C15 unit, oil leaks can be difficult to trace and cure. However, regular oil changes, full flow oil filter and sensible use of the available rev range will help to prolong engine life.

The 350cc B40 engine is stronger than the 250cc, but the electrics, frame and running gear share the same problems as the early 250s. The 350cc WD B40 is a good all-rounder – with its well-developed and relatively under-stressed motor, standard oil filter and scrambles derived running gear it makes for a durable and pleasant machine, although performance, while adequate, is not up there with a decent 441 Victor or Shooting Star.

The only problem with the 441cc bikes is starting them. They do need to be in good mechanical condition and require a bit of a knack and some muscle to get going – but are nowhere near as bad as some elements of the classic motorcycle press imply once the knack is acquired. Once they are going, they offer sparkling performance with reliability and the excellent running gear gives good handling and roadholding.

The final models had a completely new frame, again based on the works scramblers. Oil was carried within the frame tubes, dispensing with a separate oil tank. The bikes adopted the suspension and running gear from the 650cc twins and 750cc triples. This meant new forks with alloy lower legs, internal springs and exposed chromed stanchions, an excellent 8in diameter TLS front brake for the on-road models and a less impressive 6in unit for the off-roaders that needs the rider to think ahead! Handling and roadholding are excellent and the bikes make great point and squirt townies or excellent green-laners. The 250cc engine was stronger than the Starfire unit but still had a weak bottom end, but the 500cc unit was considered to be excellent. The only question mark over the 500cc is the strength of the con rod. Like the 441cc models, there is a knack to starting them. Electrics are contained in an alloy box under the tank, which is a bit of a squeeze, and it can be difficult to find a place to fit an electronic ignition 'black box'.

Improvements that can be made to the bikes for use on today's roads are pretty much par for the course for 1960s British bikes. To describe those that can be applied to the BSA unit singles I have broken them down into three areas:

- electrics
- mechanicals
- running gear.

The following sections give specific guidance on each of these areas.

The Starfire 250cc -
New on the scene and hot on the track!

In no time at all, the Starfire, BSA's fastest ever production 250, has made its mark.

Already popular on the road as a light, easy to control machine with responsive steering and reliable performance, it's becoming an even greater success on the track. Under Jeff Smith's superb handling, it won the 250 class of the TV Grand Stand Trophy, and was never out of the first two places in all four rounds. All over the world, competition men are discovering the power and versatility of the Starfire. Developed from the champion 441cc. Victor Grand Prix, the Starfire 250cc. is fast becoming known as the most potent all-rounder in the motorcycle world today.

BSA Motor Cycles Ltd. Armoury Road Birmingham 11 **BSA**

The Starfire and B44 offered more performance than the outgoing C15 and B40. Reliability of the Starfire could be suspect.

Peter Isted's 1967 B25 Starfire

Peter Isted bought a B25 Starfire in 1974 in time for his seventeenth birthday. The bike in question was a 1968 model and cost the princely sum of £200 – which was about par for the course at that time. The bike was in standard trim and was bought by Peter to ride to school, for socializing and to go on holiday. It had the small 2gal (9ltr) fibreglass fuel tank, and matching fibreglass side panels. The condition of the gel-coat impregnated colour – which was solid Nutley Blue with Ivory pockets for the knee grips and an Ivory stripe across the top of the fuel tank – was very good indeed and was a good advert for the longevity of the fibreglass components.

continued overleaf

Pete Isted's B25 Starfire fully loaded and ready to go in Wales, summer 1975.

Peter Isted's 1967 B25 Starfire *continued*

Problems with the bike were limited to most of the usual areas, mechanical and electrical, while the frame and running gear were impressively reliable.

One fault that caused much head-scratching was electrical. When the fault first occurred the electrics died completely and the fuse was burnt out. Having identified this, it was thought to be the problem but in fact it was just the symptom! Replacing the fuse simply meant that the new fuse blew immediately. Eventually, it was worked out that the Zener diode had failed open-circuit, effectively connecting the live side of the battery straight to earth. Replacement of the (expensive) Zener diode cured the fault. However, the diode blew again quite quickly. It transpired that putting the Learner plate in its traditional position under the headlamp between the fork legs blanked off the flow of cooling air to the Zener's heat sink. An expensive lesson was learnt!

The 'Big Trip' that the bike achieved was a tour of Wales, from north to south, covering just under 1,000 miles over a couple of weeks. On the trip, the Starfire was accompanied by two Triumph 200cc Tiger Cubs, a Triumph TR25W 250cc unit single and a Matchless/AJS 250cc 'Lightweight' single. I rode pillion on the Starfire or the Cub and from that trip I can confirm that Pete's Starfire had the world's most uncomfortable pillion seat!

The trip ended with the usual Starfire problem, a blown big end, which happened only about 60 miles from home. The big-end shells were replaced but failed again very quickly – the crank was oval and needed regrinding and undersize shells fitted. Another step in the learning curve for us amateur mechanics!

Pete's impressions of the Starfire were generally good – albeit looking back over thirty years! He remembers having some initial problems mastering pulling away, with the combination of high gearing, peaky power delivery and a sharp clutch action. He still enthused about the bike's looks and performance, and pointed out that the bike could hold its own against the Japanese competition of the day. While it did not have indicators, the electrics were as good as anything the Japanese bikes had, while the lights were considerably better. At the end of the day, Pete could not think of any really bad points except the high compression and fragile bottom end – and this was only a problem if the bike was ridden hard all the time. Which in a nutshell sums up what a Starfire is all about!

Pete Isted's Starfire did make it to Wales from Hampshire in 1975 – two-up as well. Here it is with the rest of the crew at Llandegla, north Wales. Pete is second from right, with his face hidden by his mirror; author is second from left.

Upgrading the Electrics

In principle, the BSA unit single range has the basics that can provide a reliable electrical system as standard, but in practice the opposite is often the case. Age and general neglect would have taken their toll on the electrical system and will need to be rectified before reliability can be assured. There are a number of steps that the enthusiastic owner can take to improve the situation. The simplest and most important thing to do is to make sure that the electrical system is running at the highest level of efficiency possible. If originality is important then this is the only set of measures that is available. The main step in this approach, and indeed a step that should be carried out before any of the enhancements described below, is to clean up or renew the wiring harness. The old harness will have dirty or corroded joins and damaged wires, possibly with just a few of the strands of wire making a connection. Simply inspecting, cleaning (with contact cleaner), lubricating and where necessary renewing connections will make a difference. Bullet connectors between wires will benefit from cleaning with emery paper, as will spade connectors to components such as rectifiers and the multi-pin connectors used on the earlier light and ignition switches.

There have been instances of dodgy connections in old in-line fuse holders causing very obscure electrical problems – if in doubt change it for a new one. The complex switches used in the 6V systems, the late model handlebar switches and multi-function light switches will benefit from cleaning using WD40 or similar, or use of a proprietary switch cleaner. Once you have cleaned the contacts in the switches, make sure that they are protected against further corrosion and properly lubricated, for example with petroleum jelly.

Taking switches apart can be a risky business – there are usually a myriad small parts and

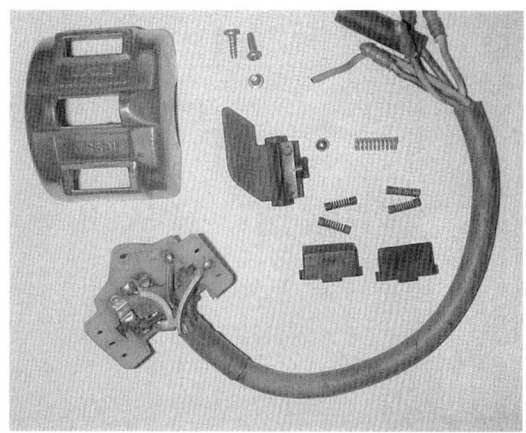

Switchgear is fiddly! This is a 1971 switch in a dismantled state – note the numerous small springs that are all too eager to escape when dismantling.

springs waiting to make a bid for freedom in the darker recesses of the workshop. Therefore dismantle only if really necessary, for example if cleaning with WD40 or equivalent did not work, or if something is jammed or broken. Carry out the operation with the switch and your hands in a clear plastic bag – then at least when it does explode all the parts will be in the bag! Whether you ever get it back together and working again is another matter. New parts for most switches are hard to find and it may be prudent to buy a cheap second-hand non-operational switch to use as a source of spares. However, Murphy's Law will make sure that the bit that's bust in your switch will be bust in the spare!

The next stage in uprating the electrics is to change from 6V electrics to 12V. The standard 6V alternator fitted to the earlier models in the range will happily provide 12V simply by joining two of its three output wires together. Which two will depend on the version of the alternator and expert advice should be sought to determine which is which! However, if the alternator is a non-encapsulated (pre-Lucas RM21), then I would advise buying a new

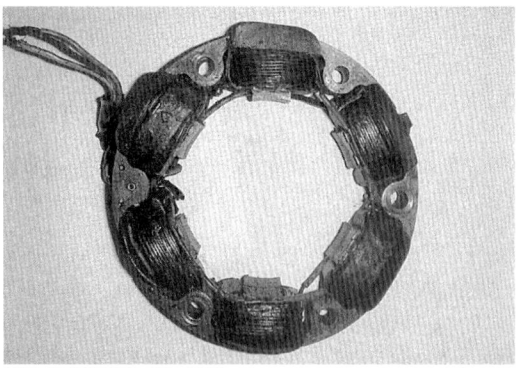

The earlier bikes had unencapsulated alternator rotors, where the coils were exposed to the hostile environment in the primary chain case. As many will be forty years old the insulation of the wires making up the coils will have suffered.

stator, either pattern or original, as the insulation and wiring will very likely be starting to break down.

Remember that such a stator could be over four decades old and will be tired. Converting is cheap and easy to do, only requiring a small amount of additional wiring, the addition of a Zener diode along with a suitable (and suitably positioned) heat sink and a new rectifier. Conversely, there are available proprietary 'black boxes', such as those produced by Boyer or Podtronics, which will rectify and regulate the alternator's output; they cost much the same as a new Zener diode, heat sink and rectifier. The advantages of 12V are easier availability of bulbs, lower resistance in the old joins of the wiring harness, which means brighter lights, and the possibility of upgrading to electronic ignition. One of the latest upgrades is the light emitting diode (LED) based rear brake/tail light bulbs. These are currently only available in 12V, but as they are solid-state devices should provide good resistance to vibration.

The C15 Star models are equipped with a 6in diameter headlamp and modern replacements are few and far between. The headlight reflector will have a bulb holder incorporated

The Author's 1971 B25SS Gold Star

Despite the trials and tribulations of my friends' Starfires and Trophys, once I finished my 'A' Levels in 1977 and had scraped up enough cash I bought a 1971 B25SS Gold Star from a local dealer, Monteagle Motors in Yateley, Hants. One of the main reasons I bought the bike was its looks. To my eye at the time the bike was incredibly stylish. While I was not 100 per cent convinced about the Dove Grey frame, the bike's long, lithe lines had really caught my eye, and still do.

The intention was to replace my 1968 BSA Bantam, which, while not a bad bike, had suffered from my amateur servicing regime and severe lack of funds for the year I had it on the road. The B25SS was a non-runner with a blown big end and as I was planning to use the bike to go on a camping holiday in Wales, an engine rebuild was the first job to complete.

The crank and barrel were entrusted to a local engineering firm for a big-end regrind and rebore, then the engine was rebuilt by me and my friend, Tony Sumner, with a fanatical attention to cleanliness and correct tolerances. At the time, we boasted that the engine was blueprinted, but on reflection it was subjected to a very careful rebuild, rather than a full blueprint. However, it did not leak (or burn) any oil and went like the clappers! The only problem in getting spares was with the gearbox sprocket – we could only find a sixteen-tooth one, rather than the proper roadster seventeen-tooth item.

Once on the road some minor foibles came to light – the battery was virtually dead, the fuel tank was split and the downdraft carburettor filled the sump with petrol if you didn't turn off the fuel taps when the engine stopped. The battery was not a problem, as the standard fit capacitor worked well, and the bike always started with no problems. Slightly more worrying was the state of the fuel tank. Closer inspection showed that it was split on the top seam behind the mounting hole. This had been 'repaired' by covering the split with epoxy filler. The filler was cleaned off and the split seam was properly welded up by a friend of a friend, once the tank had sat in the garden filled with water for a few days to exude any remaining fumes! The fuel leaking past the float needle and into the engine's sump was solved by turning the fuel taps off! If you forgot, then the petrol would be pumped into the oil tank, which would promptly overflow and spew a petrol/oil mix out of the overflow pipe on the filler cap. At this point, the only real choice was to drain the contaminated oil and replace it.

Despite these manifestations of character, the bike was ready for the holiday and did sterling service, taking me in company with Tony on his 1950s sprung hub Triumph Thunderbird from the sunny south-east to wet and wild west Wales fully loaded up for two weeks' camping, meeting up with other friends en route.

The trip was a success, the only problem being a complete failure to start after a lunch stop in Abergavenny on the way to Newgale. The problem was quickly traced to the electrics and was in fact the main power feed wire falling off the ignition switch. On a normal bike this would not have presented too much of a challenge, but on the B25SS the ignition switch is fitted into the alloy electrical box under the fuel tank. This makes it almost impossible to get at without dismantling a substantial amount of the bike's infrastructure! The problem was solved by hotwiring the bike, running a wire from the (still dead) battery to the power side of the coil. This worked for the remainder of the holiday and had additional anti-theft qualities as long as I remembered to disconnect the wire and hide it in the rat's nest of wires that lurked around the box!

The bike finally suffered a comprehensive blow-up, when I was trying to keep up with a Kawasaki Z1 900. The bike got up to an indicated 60mph in second before one of the flywheel bolts let go. The bolt did a trip round the engine, destroying the piston and liner before exiting out of the front of the crankcases. I heard a bang and saw something fly off the bike on the right-hand side and thought that the spark plug had come out. As I stopped I became aware of two things – the engine was still running and there was an awful lot of oil on the ground … A Starfire engine was procured and many of the new bits from the SS engine were built into it, but it was never quite the same again.

ABOVE RIGHT: The author's B25SS in the late 1970s – the prop stand was strong enough to cope with the pose!

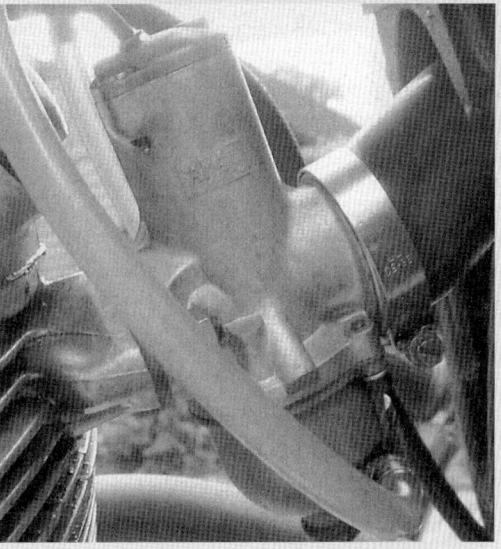

RIGHT: The relatively acute downdraft angle of the carburettor on the B25 can lead to problems with petrol flowing into the engine if the float needle is worn.

so this will dictate what type of bulb you can use even if you do uprate the electrics to 12V. Modern 6V halogen bulbs are available with fittings for original headlamps from specialist suppliers. These will provide appreciably more light than similarly rated standard bulbs. However, the reflector in the headlamp also needs to be in good condition to gain maximum benefit from these bulbs. Later bikes, the B25 Starfire and B44 with 7in diameter headlamps, are easily upgraded to a more modern design, such as the Wipac Quadoptic. These replacement units take modern 12V halogen bulbs available at any garage – so are a lot easier to replace than a 6V item. The final oil-in-frame bikes reverted to smaller headlamps and modern 5¾in diameter replacements that can take either normal or Quartz halogen bulbs in 'modern' fittings are available at the time of writing.

Once the bike has been converted to 12V it is cheap and easy to fit flashing direction indicators and decent handlebar switches.

The rear engine mounting lug of the last oil-in-frame B25s makes it impossible to fit into earlier frames.

Engine Modifications

A later Starfire engine will fit in the C15 frame (and vice versa). However, the final 1971 B25SS engines, with the improvements outlined previously that were fitted to the final oil-in-frame bikes, have a wider rear top lug on the engine. This makes it possible to fit earlier engines in the later frames with some judicious use of spacers, but fitting the last (wide lug) crankcases in earlier frames is tricky and requires either the cutting down of the crankcase lug, or cutting and welding a new frame lug. The early C15 frames have cast lugs so cannot be easily modified and the B25 frame pre-1971 has welded-on plates, again making it difficult to modify to accept the wider engine lug. However, BSA did produce some sets of 1971 specification crankcases with the narrow rear lug as spares for earlier bikes and these do emerge on the spares scene from time to time.

Firms are offering conversions of the early engine's timing-side bush to needle rollers. These comprise a new crankcase insert that replaces the traditional bush, a crankshaft hardened steel ring fitted over the crankshaft journal and a needle roller bearing. Two phosphor bronze rings are positioned at each side of the bearing to seal it and hence the oil feed to the big ends is maintained. The engineering of these conversions seems sound and was used on the restored C15T featured in this book. The conversion certainly makes sense, especially as it gets harder to find engineering firms who can accurately ream a new bush to size and the supply of good quality bushes dries up. The C15T that is the subject of the renovation covered in Chapter 6 has had just such a conversion fitted.

The C25 and B25 engines are very highly tuned and the condition of the engine components is vital for reliable operation – and to avoid expensive blow-ups. There are several known weak points in the engine's bottom

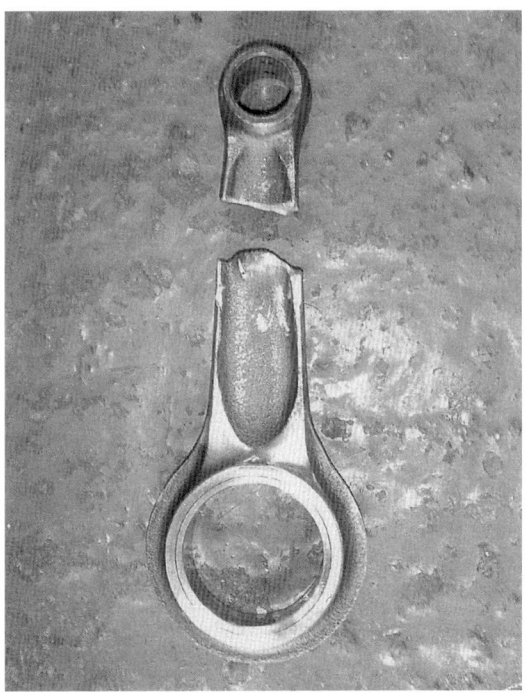

The B50 con rod can break. Bear in mind that a rod could be thirty-five years old and will have been subject to all sorts of stresses and strains in that time.

The B25SS/T25SS oil filter is a good unit and is a valuable retrofit to earlier Starfires. Mounted on the rear engine plates, it is relatively easy to access from below.

end, which require special attention when the engine is assembled. The connecting rod should be polished to remove any scratches or notches on its surface, and I would recommend that the con rod bolts (and their self-locking nuts) should not be reused. If the flywheel bolts are disturbed then they should not be reused. Both the connecting rod bolts and the flywheel bolts are waisted and are designed to stretch when torqued up. This weakens the bolts and while BSA recommended that the bolts be measured to see if they are within tolerance, I would not take the risk. The sludge trap must be cleaned out regularly, certainly whenever the crank is out of the bike!

B50 con rods – they can break! While ten or twenty years ago the perceived wisdom was that the B50 con rod could fail in competition,

there are more instances of the standard con rods failing in normal (that is, not racing) use. Bearing in mind that the rods are probably all more than thirty years old, and, because of the B50's robust bottom end probably are the originals in many engines, then it is perhaps not too surprising. The cure is a Carrillo rod from the USA.

Slightly less extreme, but just as valuable, is the fitting of a full flow oil filter. BSA did fit a neat unit as standard to the B40 WD that was bolted onto the left-hand frame tube above the crankcases, so it sat just behind the barrel – very convenient for access but not aesthetically pleasing. The 1971 oil-in-frame models featured a similar unit but this was out of the line of sight, bolted to the right-hand side rear engine plate. Both units took a paper cartridge

Chris Burrell's B50 Collection

Chris Burrell owns a number of B50s and has a deep interest in the model. His usual road machine is a B50T, which he uses for mild green-laning and has had on the road since the late 1990s. It had a low mileage engine, which Chris brought back from the US and rebuilt before he put the bike on the road. He replaced all the wearing items, pistons and rings, and all bearings but the con rod appeared to be in perfect condition. Riding the bike is a pleasure.

Unfortunately, the rod broke in two during normal use, basically wrecking the engine by punching a hole through the crankcases and destroying the barrel liner. Chris's cure for this has been to rebuild the engine using a Carrillo rod, sourced directly from the US.

The bike is a lot better than a B25 – with all its torque it gives a lot of low down grunt that makes it brilliant fun for green-laning. The B25 engine needs to have its neck wrung to get a comparable performance to that of the B50. The only downside to the bike is the ground clearance – while pretty good, it is necessary to go round rather than over really big obstacles. The bike is light, steers well and has comfortable suspension. Without gaiters, the oil seals can wear and the stanchions can also wear if the oil seals go. Chris runs the bike on 20/50 oil and it didn't burn or lose any oil before the blow-up. Wet sumping can occur if the bike is not used for a while. Chris runs a stock 20in wheel on the front, but is intending put a 21in unit when the bike is back on the road.

The bike has proved easy to start – but it did catch Chris once with a kickback, resulting in him not being able to walk properly for a week. But with proper use of the valve lifter and getting to know a bike's characteristics, starting is generally quite easy.

The lights are brilliant, as are the brakes despite having the 6in unit. Chris recommends cleaning out the brakes after a run, especially if they have been submerged in water, as the key for keeping them at full efficiency. In his runs off-road the electrics have been fine, even when well and truly soaked in water. The fundamental way to ensure electrical reliability is to use a good wiring loom and make sure that all terminals are clean, waterproof and tight. Chris still runs the standard points ignition, based on the assumption that if it does pack up, then it should be fixable out in the sticks. Chris has a passion for the oil-in-frame BSA singles, and his knowledge and expertise were a great help to the author in compiling this book and in rebuilding the author's T25SS.

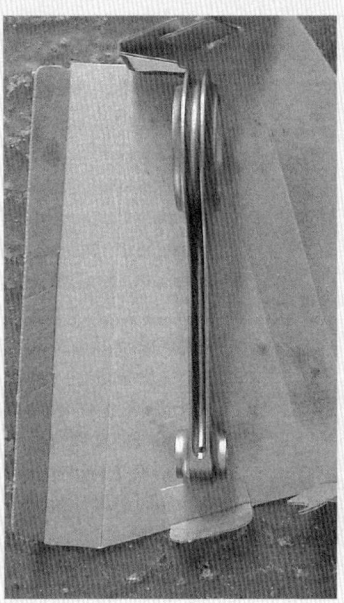

LEFT: *If a rod goes, the consequences are dire. On Chris Burrell's B50, the broken rod punches a hole in the cases just in front of the rear sprocket. It also destroyed the piston and barrel.*

RIGHT: *The cure for the B50 con rod is replacement with a Carrillo rod. This shows the deep 'I' section for the rod continuing round the big end, giving it great strength.*

filter, which was and still is cheap and easy to replace. These are a popular retro fit to many British bikes and this demand seems to have sparked a shortage of the relevant engine plate!

The condition of the advance/retard unit is very important. These Lucas units were built down to a price and were not particularly robust or reliable. The unit can fail in a number of ways: the springs can lose their tension; the central pivot can wear; and the bobweight mechanism can jam. All of these faults will result in inaccurate timing and hence difficult starting, poor running and possible damage to the engine. On the points in side motors, the fitment of a Boyer electronic ignition system replaces the advance retard unit, relying on the electronics for a suitable ignition advance curve and a 'one-piece' rotor unit bolted to the points drive in its place. A Boyer electronic ignition system will cost much the same as a new A/R unit, contact breaker points plate and new points.

On the B25, one of the most important issues is the oil feed to the big end. This follows a tortuous path from the oil pump, out into the inner timing case through a drilling and then into the end of the crank. The main points of leakage, and hence the possibility of low oil pressure, are between the crankcase and the inner timing-side case, which is sealed with an 'O' ring, and the feed into the end of the crank which utilizes a garter type seal. Both of these bushes should be replaced if disturbed and some users suggest regular replacement. The end of the crank should also be inspected

for wear where the garter seal fits it, as the crank end can be worn or damaged in use, especially if the oil is not changed regularly.

With C25 and B25 models do not leave the fuel tap on, or overfill the oil tank. The combination of a downdraft carburettor and float needle that is past its best can and will result in fuel leaking into the carburettor and then flowing into the engine and collecting in the crankcases. The first evidence of this is when the excess fuel is scavenged back to the oil tank, causing overflowing of an oil and petrol mixture – pretty unsavoury and messy. In addition, the fuel will have washed the oil from those vital parts such as the piston and barrel and the big end and main bearings, resulting in rapid wear.

Updating the Running Gear

In general, the running gear is pretty good on these bikes. The early model C15 brakes, while not bad, could stand some improvement. Unfortunately, as the early C15 forks were unique to the model, there are not a lot of 'slot-in' options. While a C15 front end can be modified to accept the larger B40 front brake or a complete front end with its heavy duty forks, it is probably a better option to replace the whole front end with the more robust B25/B44/B50 forks and wheel. The 7in TLS front brake fitted to the 1969–70 models is good, as is the 8in conical hub unit fitted to the oil-in-frame models, and both are up to modern-day traffic conditions.

6 Restoration of a 1960 BSA C15 Trials Model

Introduction

The subject of the restoration featured in this book was chosen for a number of reasons. I had completed the restoration of a 1971 Triumph T25SS a couple of years earlier and had access to a 1969 Fleetstar, the restoration of which my father-in-law had also just completed. These both feature heavily in the pictures in this book. As these two models represented the 'middle' and 'end' models of the 250cc range, I decided that I needed to restore an early model, with the brazed lug frame, to gain an all-round picture of the range. An early 'distributor' equipped engine would also be a challenge after the later B25 units.

One slight problem was that I could not gather much enthusiasm for the basic C15. While they are a good, honest machine, they were not the sportiest of machines and their late 1950s styling, with the rounded tank and heavily valanced mudguards, made them look staid and uninspired to my eyes – others will of course disagree, feeling that the look is classic BSA and echoes that of the larger machines in the range. Even the SS80 did not have that indefinable magic that makes a machine desirable to me.

However, I did find the competition models attractive, especially as they led the development of the model, going from the staid roadster through to winning the world motocross championships. The US versions of the competition models were even more attractive-looking to me, with their 'trail bike'

looks and road equipment as standard. So I decided to find a competition model and rebuild it to a US model specification for use as a trail bike. This was not without precedence, as the Trials model could be supplied with lights as an extra (costing £5 1s 6d in 1960!) and the US market did have the Starfire Scrambler in 1961, which had full road equipment – lights and a silencer! – attached to what was in effect a version of the competition model.

These models were not that common on the road in the UK when they were introduced, as the trail bike phenomenon did not really take off until the mid 1970s. However, such a bike should make a good basis for a nice classic green-laner, with a combination of period charm and looks, well-presented mechanics and a touch of competition 'street credibility'.

Sources of Information

The information sources for rebuilding and restoring bikes are many and various. For this model there a reasonable number of publications are available. The information can be divided into two types, original BSA documents and later aftermarket publications.

Original BSA handbooks for the C15 and B40 carried a great deal of information on the day to day and deeper maintenance of the models. The early ones are a lot more detailed than the ones from the late 1960s, and have a

The sources of information for the restoration of a bike are many. Amongst those used were service sheets, handbooks, workshop manuals, brochures and, probably most important, manufacturer's parts books.

lot more information in them on the mechanics of the machines. While BSA did not have workshop manuals per se for the C15 and B40, the company did publish *Service Sheets* for the C15 and B40 ranges. These separate sheets made up the 'workshop manual', comprising a series of information sheets that build up to cover the engine and running gear. By the time the later models, such as the B25/B44/B50 appeared, BSA was producing 'proper' workshop manuals.

One of the most important pieces of documentation for any restoration is the parts manual. These documents give exploded diagrams of every sub-assembly, showing where everything fits (and the order in which the parts are supposed to fit together), and giving the number for every part, which is vital when ordering spares.

All of these documents are available, either as reprints/reproductions of originals from specialist dealers, while originals are often available at autojumbles.

A final source of information is original factory sales brochures. A company like BSA issued at least one brochure per year showing the full range and often produced model-specific literature as well. A word of caution though – if you are doing a concours restoration the illustrations in the brochures often do not reflect what was actually produced. They are often heavily touched up versions of the previous year's model or artist's impressions of the proposed model. The treatment of the oil-in-frame model's side panels is a case in point, the brochure showing the pre-production type with the Dzus fastener set in a recess at the front of the panel. In addition, the same illustration was often used for a number of years and the printing technology available at the time did not accurately reproduce the colours. However, they are a good source of

The bike was completely dismantled when acquired – even the frame and rear subframe were separate. At least the front tyre looked almost new.

information on the basic specification of the machines and are often brilliantly produced, evoking strong images of the age!

Other sources of mechanical information and data include Rupert Ratio's *Unit Single Engine Manual* (Panther Publishing), which gives extensive details on the engine/gearbox unit of all the models, and the ubiquitous Haynes manual, which is a good source of rebuild information. While there are many books that feature the unit singles range, only Roy Bacon's *BSA Unit Singles* (Motorcycle

The engine was completely dismantled as well. This type of basket case can be a challenge!

Monograph No. 7 – Niton Publishing), Rupert Ratio's manual and the Haynes manual deal specifically with the unit singles. Titles that helped with the restoration included Roy Bacon's *BSA Singles Restoration* (Niton Publishing), which had detailed contemporary pictures of unit singles, and Roy Bacon's *BSA Singles* (Niton Publishing), which has a chapter on the singles and information on engine/frame numbers and detailed specifications.

As it Arrived

The bike I eventually found was a 1960 C15T, with a slightly later (1961) Trials engine, which was for sale on eBay, the online auction site. The bike was in bits – literally, as the engine was completely stripped down and the frame bare. Only the wheels were complete and in one piece – and even they were not as complete as first impressions gave. In many ways I prefer to buy bikes like this as they are usually cheap; with a 'complete' bike (a bike apparently in one piece), many of the parts on the bike will be either in need of total refurbishment or will be scrap anyway, while some will be missing. In addition, a bike in bits will usually fit into the car boot without any further on the spot dismantling! I saw several C15 competition models on eBay after the one I bought, but all were fully assembled and some even ran – and all were substantially non-standard and a lot more expensive!

This particular one had no tinware, apart from an oil tank, which gave me some concerns as to the availability of side panels and the tin shroud that sat between the two, but otherwise it was fine. I was expecting to buy a new period style alloy petrol tank, as the early C15T steel tank seemed to be rare, and expected to fit alloy mudguards. I also knew that there were aftermarket lightweight alloy oil tanks made for the UK pre-1965 trials movement, although as I had a standard oil tank this was not too much of an issue.

However, at the first autojumble I went to after getting the bike home there were at least two full sets of C15 tinware, which, while not C15T components, were very similar and formed the basis for modification to gain the slimmer C15T profile. At following jumbles, it was surprising how many stands had C15 tinware for sale – once you get your eye in, they turn up everywhere! This is obviously good news for anyone restoring a C15 who is worried about obtaining these usually hard to find parts, although I should warn that valanced mudguards did not seem to be so common. As the C15T had blade type guards in painted steel or chrome-plated this was not a concern, as I was planning to fit proprietary alloy guards anyway.

Wheels and Hubs

The front wheel that came with the bike had a 21in rim, of Italian extraction, which was in perfect condition, along with what appeared to be new spokes and nipples and a virtually unused trail tyre. So it appeared to be a recent (or at least unused) rebuild. However, the hub itself was showing signs of age. It was dirty and the paintwork had seen better days. In addition, the spindle and one bearing were missing, as were the fork caps, indicating that the wheel may have been robbed for spares. There was also 'C15 £70' written on the chrome trim plate, implying that the wheel may have been lurking on the autojumble rounds before being sold with the rest of the bike. The brake plate was all there, but the brake shoes were worn almost down to the rivets.

So the wheel would need to come to pieces to enable the hub to be renovated. The plan was, however, modified by buying a second-hand hub at a Kempton Park autojumble for £10, which had the spindle and good wheel bearings. As a bonus, it also had good brake shoes. So I decided to use this complete hub, rather than the original. There was therefore no need to buy a spindle, new brake shoes or a wheel bearing, which probably saved £10 and is a good illustration of how to save cash in this type of rebuild. The new hub was cleaned up using rotary wire brushes in the electric drill. In the 1960 model, the hubs (front and rear) were silver, so silver

The restored front wheel. The newly painted hub and brake plate complement the good condition spokes and rim that came originally.

The rear brake drum and sprocket carrier were in good condition. Black Smoothrite on the outside and a wire brushing of the surface rust were all that were required.

Smoothrite was sprayed on. A good hint is to put a hub horizontally in a vice, clamped on the spindle, and to spin it round to spray it in motion, to get an even layer of paint. The front brake plate was cleaned up and the inner part of the plate was painted to the 1960 factory specification in gloss black, with the outer rim left in polished alloy. The press-fit chrome trim from the other side was painted and polished to match. The hub was put in the lathe and the brake drum checked for ovality – it was okay. Had it not been I would have skimmed it in the lathe to ensure it was round. As the hub is pretty substantial, it is unlikely to be distorted when the wheel is rebuilt.

The rear wheel appeared to be as it left the factory, but it carried a 19in Jones rim which implied that the rim had either been changed or the wheel came from a Scrambles model. There were two tyre clamps present in the rim, which again appeared to be a standard fitment, although they were not illustrated in the 1959–62 parts manual. The rim was not in bad condition, but had several nicks and rust spots in

the chrome, so needed to be changed back to a standard 18in. The hub had the correct bolt-on sprocket carrier and a well-worn 4.00 × 19 Dunlop Trials Universal tyre. The hub and brake drum both needed refinishing but were in pretty good shape, while the wheel bearings were perfect. There was no rear chain sprocket.

The spokes and nipples were all pretty grotty, with dirt and rust marring their appearance, so they would be replaced. There were no outer wheel nuts. These are special sleeved items that fit into the chain adjusters, which were also missing. The brake plate was an alloy item, in good condition and just needing cleaning up, plus a lick of paint to match the front, as did the chrome trim on the other side. Luckily, there was a speedometer drive firmly bolted on the wheel. These are expensive items and it can be hard to find one with a suitable drive ratio. So the wheel had to come apart to allow cleaning of the hub and replacement of the spokes and nipples. A new rim and tyre (and by inference a new inner tube and rim tape) would be needed.

Removing the old tyre was the first hurdle. The two tyre clamps fitted in the rim always make the job of removal difficult, and when combined with the hardness of a well-worn Dunlop Trials Universal tyre it was quite a job to get the tyre off. Using rubber lubricant and long tyre levers helped.

With the rim off, the hub could be split from the brake drum by undoing the six bolts, which are locked in place with three locking plates. The drum was treated to a wire brushing and checked for ovality on the lathe. Again it was okay. With this type of bolt-on hub, there is no risk of it being pulled out of shape when the wheel is rebuilt as it is a separate component. The hub was cleaned up, again using wire brushes in the electric drill, and sprayed silver.

The front and rear wheel bearings were inspected, found to be fine and were repacked with clean grease. Rebuilding both wheels was

The rear wheel hub has six threaded holes where the rear hub is bolted on. Note the use of straight spokes, making it easy to re-spoke – one side of spokes is in position, ready to be attached to the rim.

straightforward, as the spokes are all the same length, have a straight pull and mount on the hub through holes in the flange that are about 4mm long, which directs them towards the rim. The spoke pattern is a simple two-crossover, with three holes on the rim between adjoining spokes at the hub. As long as the spokes are the right length, it is impossible to lace the rim on incorrectly! Before fitting the tyre it is important to make sure that none of the spokes are protruding through the nipples. If they are, they can fret through the rim tape and cause punctures. Also, if you are reusing an old rim make sure that the chrome is not lifting, as this too can cause punctures.

In the case of the C15, several spokes were proud of the nipple, so I removed them (one at a time) and ground them down to length using a bench grinder. This is possible on the BSA hub, as you can remove a single spoke easily – it is not possible on some other types of hubs and if that is the case the spoke ends need to be ground down in situ. The best tool to achieve this is a mini-grinding tool (generically known as a Dremel), with a grinding wheel attachment. Once the rim was on the hub, with the protruding spokes ground down and

refitted and the wheel trued, I fitted a new tyre, inner tube and rim tape.

After reassembling the wheel and fitting the tyre, the new fifty-six-tooth sprocket was bolted onto the drum, with eight bolts and self-locking nuts.

The rim is on and the brake drum has been bolted to the hub. The six bolts have been secured using the three locking tabs. The trials specification fifty-six-tooth sprocket is a tight fit on the drum and is fixed on with eight bolts.

157

The sprocket was a tight fit and had to be drawn onto the drum little by little by tightening the fixing bolts down a few turns each. The drum was then fixed to the hub using the six bolts and the three fixing 'washers'. Loctite was used on the bolts and the edges of the banana-shaped locking 'washers' were turned up to ensure that the drum would not work loose from the hub. The rear brake plate was fixed onto the drum with the left-hand side inner spindle nut. The refurbished and painted chrome trim was fitted to the other (non-drive) side and the speedometer gearbox was bolted in place with the right-hand side inner spindle nut.

Note that there are spacers on each side that fit between the inner spindle nuts and the hub. Both of these spacers fell out when fitting the new tyre, so check they are still there before fitting the brake plate and the speedometer drive gearbox. Once these items are bolted onto the wheel spindle the spacers cannot escape, so the problem should not arise when changing a tyre.

With the tyres fitted, the wheel rims were protected from damage and were ready to be fitted to the frame.

Front and rear brakes were the same size, 6in diameter with shoes a weedy ⅞in in width. Good for off-road use, not so good for the road with modern traffic conditions.

Frame

The frame of a 1960 C15T is similar in design to the standard roadster frame, with single seat tube, top tube and front tube, and a lower cradle to carry the engine comprising two tubes. The rear subframe bolts onto the top of the main loop and has a loop to carry the seat and rear shock absorber mounts, with two bracing tubes running down to the swinging-arm lug on the seat tube of the main frame. In addition, there is the swinging arm that pivots on a pin secured into a lug on the main frame loop seat tube. There are a few detail changes from the standard C15 roadster frame. The footrests are positioned further back than on the roadster frame, almost in-line with the seat tube, and both are secured onto lugs on the frame by a single through bolt. There are no rear footrest tubes sprouting backwards from the bottom of the engine cradle tubes and the steering head angle is different. The swinging arm is longer than the roadster item to give a longer wheelbase and provide clearance for a larger section rear tyre.

The two parts of the frame had already been stripped of 99 per cent of their attachments; it therefore appeared to be a quick and easy job to prepare the parts for sandblasting and powder-coating. The old steering head races were easily removed using a drift and the only other thing that I decided to change was the tube on the rear top frame lug that located the rear subframe. This is a simple steel tube that protrudes out each side of the lug to locate the subframe positively, which is then bolted up to the frame. The one on the frame was already butchered, with very little of it protruding to locate the rear subframe. This turned out to be problematical to remove, eventually requiring a lot of heat and hammering. Once this was off, the frame parts (and the swinging arm) were despatched for sandblasting and powder-coating.

Rebuilding of the frame once it returned

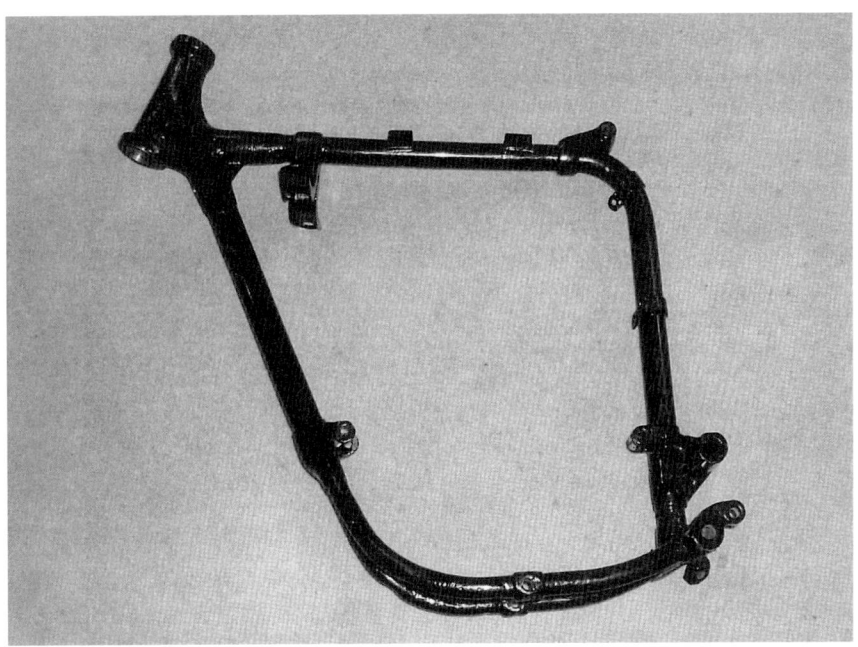

Back from the sandblasters and freshly powder-coated in gloss black, the frame is ready for the start of the rebuild.

from the powder-coaters was straightforward. A new tube was pushed in to locate the top mount of the rear subframe. The swinging-arm bushes were renewed and the new spindle was driven into place by using a brass drift in one of the locating bolt holes.

The new bushes did not need to be reamed for a good fit and the rear subframe was then bolted to the end of the swinging-arm spindle using new swinging-arm bolts, with their provision for greasing the bearings, and new grease nipples – the basic frame was thus completed.

Forks and Rear Shock Absorbers

The box of bits contained two assembled fork legs with good stanchions, new fork seals in good chromed holders, good bushes, springs and top headlamp shrouds. The only things missing were the yokes (or 'Triple Trees' as Americans like to call them) and the bottom caps that fix the axle in place.

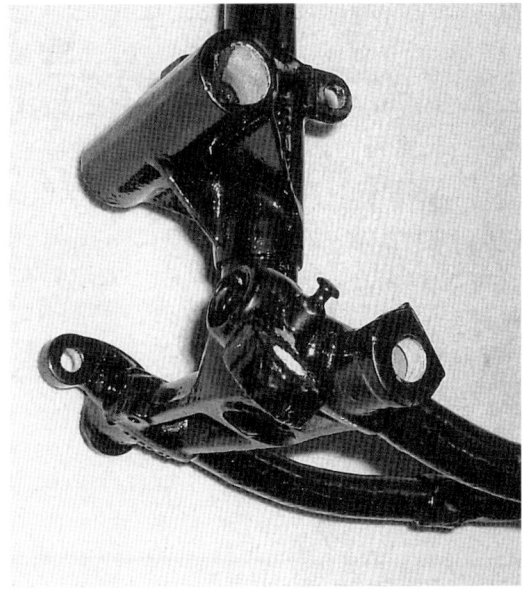

A detail shot of the competition frame showing the main differences between it and the road frame. The competition frame has rearwards footrest lugs, a right-hand side prop stand lug and no bottom cradle extensions for pillion footrests.

159

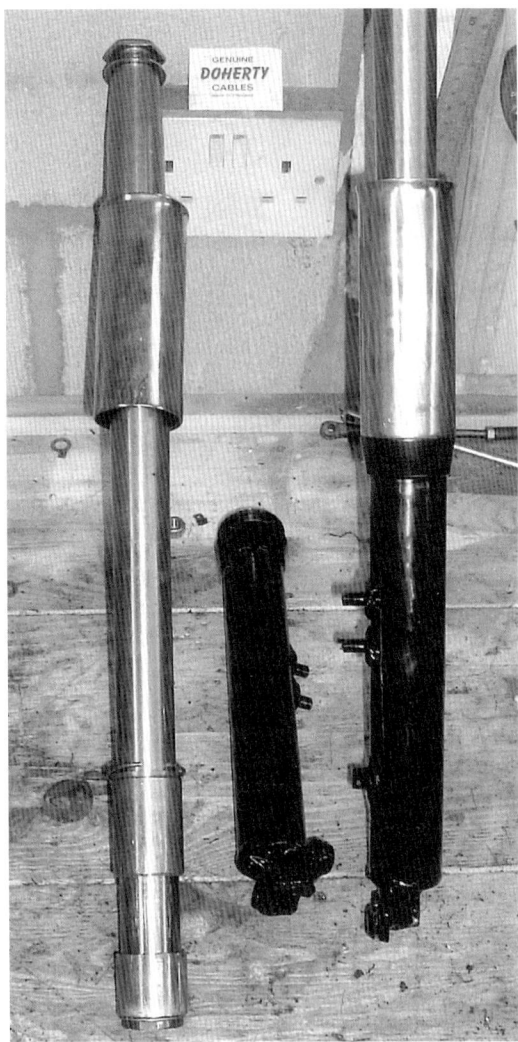

The fork legs that came with the bike were in good condition, just needing a respray. The stanchions are slightly thicker than the standard C15 internal spring units.

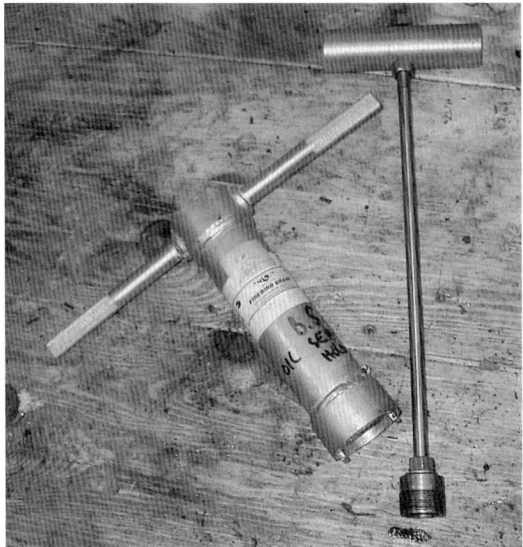

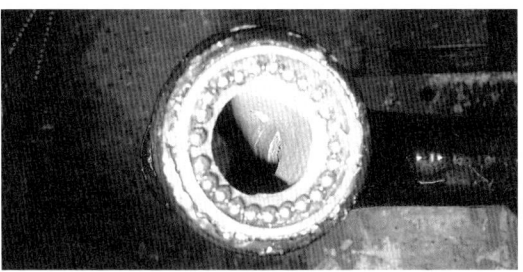

TOP: *Two essential tools for BSA forks. The seal holder spanner removes the chromed seal holders easily without damage. The homemade fork leg puller is an old top nut turned down so that it fits through the hole in the top yoke, attached to a long rod. Attached to the fork leg, it pulls the leg up into the yokes.*

ABOVE: *New head bearings and cups need to be well greased – both to lubricate the bearings and to hold the balls in place during fitment.*

Luckily, or so I thought, as a result of the restoration of my father-in-law's Fleetstar, I had a set of 1960s BSA fork yokes which were from a Starfire. The stanchions fitted in them, as did the headlamp carrier sleeves, so they were cleaned up, then painted and mounted on the frame using new steering head bearings. The bad news was that the yokes were too wide for the standard 1960 wheel. I should have measured them first! So it was onto eBay to source a set of standard C15 yokes; luckily there were a couple of sets available. I was hoping that these new yokes would also solve a second problem that I had with the Starfire yoke – namely the lack of lock stops.

Fitting the standard C15 yokes gave me two further problems. Firstly, there was no provision for fitting a speedometer bracket onto the yoke; the later Starfire yoke had two drilled and tapped holes in it. Secondly, and rather more importantly, the standard C15 used stanchions with a smaller diameter than the stanchions I had, so the holes in the yokes were too small! Further research indicated that I needed a set of yokes that were built from 1960–67, initially for the competition models and then for the first year of Starfire production. These had the requisite larger holes for the stronger stanchions but were of the right width to carry the C15 front hub.

The Starfire yokes were widened in 1968 and these were the ones that I had. This sort of issue is pretty common with British bikes. Often the incremental development of a model results in small changes, which affects parts commonality between years. Eventually, a suitable set of yokes was procured from Burton Bike Bits. New headrace cups were drifted into the headstock of the frame and

bottom yoke and new ball bearings were used when the correct yokes were finally fitted.

A Smith's light grey-faced 3in diameter speedometer was sourced from eBay. The speedometer was fitted into a 1971 speedometer rubber cup. These cups were made for the 1971 onwards oil-in-frame models and BSA must have produced huge numbers of them as they are very common and so easily available at UK autojumbles. The speedometer was fitted on the forks by making up an alloy plate, which was drilled with two holes to bolt it onto the top yoke and two holes to accept the speedometer mounting studs. The holes in the plate were drilled oversize, then rubber grommets were fitted in them to provide a degree of vibration resistance for the speedometer. Finally, the plate was bolted to the yoke. I found a speedometer light fitting in amongst my stock of old electrical components.

After a bit of a struggle the correct yokes were located. They are early (1967) Starfire units, which have the right width and accept the wider competition stanchions.

The speedometer was fitted into a 1971 B25SS rubber cup and fixed to the top yoke using a rubber-mounted alloy bracket.

Replica Amal alloy levers and a replica Wipac 'Tricon' handlebar switch (engine kill, dip/main and horn) completed the front end.

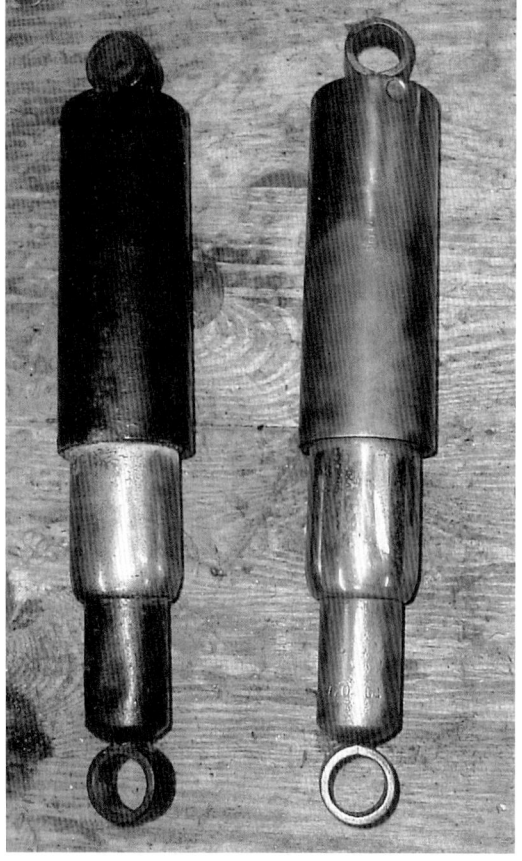

A set of C15 rear shock absorbers was resprayed. New rubber bushes were fitted top and bottom.

Handlebars were fitted to the top yoke using new chromed standard BSA clamps and bolts, and pattern Amal alloy levers, handgrips and pattern Wipac 'Tricon' dip/ main, horn and engine cut-out switch were fitted.

A new front brake cable was not available off the shelf (but a clutch cable was ...), so a suitable cable was made up from a Triumph 650 twin US spec front brake cable, with the inner cable cut down by 1½in. Suitable BSA adjusters were fitted, ready to attach to the front wheel.

The rear shock absorbers were missing, but I had a set of C15 rear shocks that had been fitted to the T25SS I restored a few years previously. They were in reasonable condition and still damped, although in need of a clean-up and respray. Once again, it was Smoothrite to the rescue and with new rubber bushes inserted in the mounting holes top and bottom they were as good as new.

With the front forks and rear suspension attached to the frame, the wheels were fitted, resulting in a rolling chassis that could be taken off the Workmate and wheeled around the workshop. This is always a significant event in a rebuild, as the collection of odd bits and pieces are starting to look like a bike!

Oil Tank, Side Panel and Mudguards

While the oil tank, centre shroud, side panel mounting pressing and side panel of the C15T are very close in appearance to the standard roadster items, they are listed as different in the parts manual. While the oil tank and side panel mounting pressing appear to be very similar, the centre shroud is substantially different. The shroud is narrower, to slim down the centre section that lies between the rider's legs, and does not have provision for the air filter or ignition switch. It features a circular hole in the middle, that either has a blanking plate or is where the horn is mounted for the road-legal models.

The frame, forks and swinging arms shown all together. Add the rear shocks and the wheels, and we'll have a rolling chassis.

On the C15T I had a roadster oil tank and side panel, which, combined with the standard C15 subframe, appeared to fit and be capable of being tucked in. The standard centre shroud was far too wide. The fittings on the frame also were not the same as the roadster's, and none of my contacts had any of the special brackets that would fix to these frame fittings. So the restoration would need some fitting and fettling, along with something to substitute for the missing centre shroud – which I needed, both for aesthetic reasons and as a place to mount the ignition switch.

A substitute for the centre shroud was found at a Kempton autojumble – I believe it to be a D10 Bantam centre shroud, in somewhat rusty condition. The profile of the pressing fitted the C15 oil tank and side panel, but the fittings did not match to the frame. I had to make up custom brackets from strip steel, both to mount the tank and side panel to the frame and to fit the shroud between the two. The end result, while not original, is neat, functional and in my opinion looks quite good. The oil tank, side panel and inner side panel were all sand-blasted and powder-coated gloss black.

The mudguards presented few problems.

The standard roadster side panel and oil tank were used. The tank had a thinner centre section, possibly coming from a D10 BSA Bantam. Custom brackets were made from mild steel strip to fit the assembly to the frame.

The front mudguard is from an indeterminate make. It was fitted using a standard BSA rear stay and a custom centre bridge piece.

The bike had originally been fitted with slim chromed-steel guards, which were relatively easy to match. I fitted a universal trials type alloy guard to the rear, which was bolted onto the rear subframe, and also a made-up bracket on the top of the swinging-arm lug on the main frame loop. The front consisted of a chromed-steel unit of indeterminate ancestry that came with a bike I had restored previously. This fitted nicely with a fabricated top mount and brackets, as well as a standard BSA rear stay.

Engine Work

The engine as bought was in pieces, so the first job was to try to sort out what was actually there. Examination showed that all of the main components, the crankcases, inner and outer timing covers and primary drive cover were all there, as were the barrel, distributor, head, piston and a complete crank. The crank's big end was good, with no discernible play. Apart from the main timing-side bush and the gearbox main and layshaft bushes, there were no bearings in the cases.

A good milestone in a restoration is the building up of the rolling chassis, as you are starting to get a bike rather than a set of boxes of bits.

164

All of the engine work was carried out with the excellent workshop manual, *The Rupert Ratio Unit Single Engine Manual* (*see* Bibliography), to hand for reassembly, good practice and tolerances.

The first job was to clean up the cases. This was done using degreaser in a parts washer to get rid of the oily muck and then putting the cases in the dishwasher (as long as the wife is out, plus it's a good idea to run the dishwasher empty through a cycle just to make sure any muck is flushed out!). This will clean them up to a pretty high standard – they will look almost as good as new and any casting finish will be maintained. The ultimate cleaning technique for alloy cases is vapour-blasting, which gives an as-new finish, but as this was not a concours restoration I decided not to bother.

One job that must be done is to clean out all of the screw holes and check the threads. To clean the holes, I used a standard casing screw with an edge ground down one side. When screwed into a hole this will clean all of the muck out of the threads and, more importantly, will push all of the old gasket cement, which will have collected in the base of the hole, up the side of the screw where it can be removed. A large quantity of red hermatite gasket cement was removed from most of the holes! This exercise also allows you to identify which holes have dodgy threads needing helicoiling. The holes in the front and rear engine mounting lugs were very oval on my cases, so needed to be welded up and then redrilled. This is not uncommon and is a result of running with loose engine bolts. I used the frame as a template to ensure that the new holes were redrilled in the right place by locating the case using the bottom mount and carefully marking their location on the welded case before drilling.

The crank was closely examined and by referencing the numbers on the connecting rod against those in the manual, the big end was

The crankcases cleaned up nicely. Note the fresh welding on the front and rear engine lugs – loose engine fixing bolts caused the holes to elongate, which increases vibration.

identified as an early bush type. However, it was apparent that the big end was in good condition, with very little sideways play and no discernible up and down play. The oil ways were checked by pumping oil through the feed holes in the main bearing side and ensuring the oil was clean when it came out of the big-end bearing. This will also ensure that there is some oil in the big end when the engine is first started.

At this point I cleaned out the sludge trap and replaced the sludge trap plug, using Loctite and punching it in place to ensure it didn't inadvertently come loose.

The crankshaft timing-side bush was present and examination indicated that there was some play in it, although the exact amount was hard to determine with the cases already split. The Rupert Ratio manual indicated that the tolerance between the bearing and the reinforced sleeve on the crank should be between 0.002–0.006in (2–6 thou), and that a feeler gauge can be used to measure this.

On the example, a 6-thou gauge could be slid between the bearing and crank, indicating that the bush was at the end of its life. I

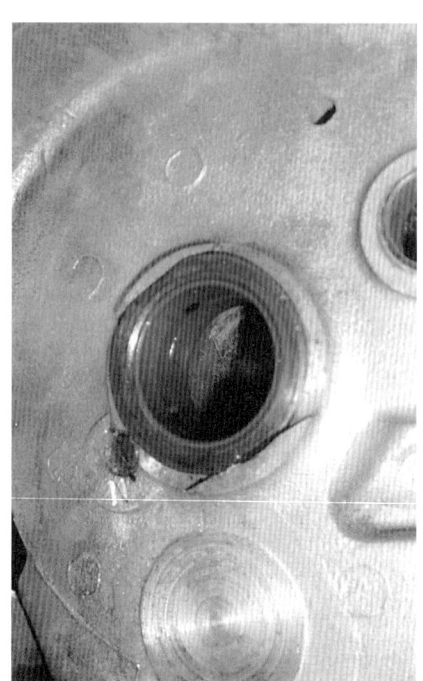

LEFT: *The sludge trap must be cleaned out. The trap centrifuges out impurities in the oil and the resultant muck will eventually block the oil feed to the big end if it is not cleaned out.*

RIGHT: *The old timing-side bush was worn, so needed replacing. Note the oil feed holes and the groove that carried the oil into the crank.*

took the decision to use a C&D Autos needle roller kit to replace the bush. Firstly, I have always been wary of bushes used as main bearings in any motorcycle engine – an irrational fear – and secondly the C&D unit claimed to be an exact replacement for the bush, with no machining necessary. At the time of writing, the cost of the C & D unit was £122, which was not that far from the cost of buying a new bush and getting it line-reamed to tolerance.

The first step to putting in the new bearing was the removal of the old bearing sleeve, which is (or should be) a tight fit on the crank. Rupert Ratio recommends that one grinds a groove along the bush then hits it in the direction of rotation! While this sounds drastic, it works. I ground down the bush with a grindstone in a high-speed hand-held mini-drill and with the bush cut about halfway through over three-quarters of its length, a sharp couple of blows at a tangent to the diameter of the

bush with a cold chisel cracked it along its length and it slid off the crank easily. Careful cleaning of the crank was needed to get rid of the grinding residue.

Fitting the new bearing was simple – the outer casing was fitted into the crankcases by heating the timing-side case up and dropping the outer into position, while the new sleeve for the crank was a push-fit and was driven home using an alloy drift, making sure to remember the inner oil sealing disc. The roller bearing was a push-fit on the crank and the outer sealing ring was positioned behind the distributor drive worm on the crank. A new gearbox main shaft roller bearing and layshaft bush were fitted at the same time.

A new main bearing was fitted into the drive-side crankcase, using heat to expand the casing after placing the bearing in the freezer beforehand to ensure an easy fit. With the new bearings fitted, the crank could be

ABOVE: The C&D Autos replacement roller bearing. The outer race goes into the crankcase, the inner race is a tight fit on the crank. The two discs go either side of the bearing to keep the oil in.

ABOVE RIGHT: Removal of the old bearing sleeve on the crank had to be quite brutal. By grinding it down, the sleeve could be cracked, making it possible to remove it.

RIGHT: The new bearing in place on the crank. Note the sealing ring trapped between the race and the flywheel.

fitted and the crankcases bolted up, with a thin smear of blue Hylomar gasket cement on the join.

With the crankcases together, it was a quick job to fit the barrel and piston. The barrel and piston were both on the first rebore, at +020 thou, and were relatively unworn. New rings were fitted, as none had come with the bike, and new circlips were attached to the piston as a precautionary measure. The piston was fitted to the existing small end, which showed no discernible wear, and the barrel was slipped on, using a ring compressor to avoid breaking the new rings. The engine was now beginning to look like an engine, rather than a collection of disparate parts.

The next job was to review the parts required for building up the rest of the engine. Careful study of the part book and the box of bits showed that quite a number of smaller parts were missing, such as woodruff keys, screws, the distributor clamp and a myriad

other bits. A list was made up and orders were placed with various suppliers on the 'diminishing returns' basis – no one supplier had all the parts, but in the end all the missing parts were sourced.

The gearbox was reassembled with all new bearings, sprocket oil seal and a set of standard roadster ratios. The gearbox was probably the most complicated part of the rebuild, as the box of bits that was the engine contained a fascinating assortment of C15 and B25 parts – which are fundamentally incompatible!

Even buying a C15 gear cluster on eBay resulted in another assortment of C15 and B25 bits. The good thing about this was that I was able to produce some pictures showing the difference between the tooth forms of the early and late boxes; the bad news was that making up a complete and compatible set involved a large amount of close inspection and counting of teeth!

Eventually, I had to buy a new main shaft, sliding pinions and new gearbox shims. The cam plate pivot pin is held in place with a split pin and a good hint is to replace the standard item with a late B25/B50 item. This has a threaded hole in its end, which enables it to be removed if required, which in turn means the inner timing cover can be removed without pulling the whole gearbox apart.

Once the gearbox was sorted the primary drive could be assembled. This was surprisingly straightforward, with new rollers, springs, shock absorber rubbers and plates being placed in the clutch, but reusing the clutch drum, primary chain and engine sprocket.

The alternator gave some problems. The original C15T had an energy transfer system, which I was not going to use. I fitted a second-hand rotor and an encapsulated stator from a

The timing side completed – the distributor shaft is in position and the camshaft is driven from the crank.

Trial fitting of the gears to check clearances. A new cam plate spring has been fitted; the gear teeth need the surface rust removed before final fitment.

This type of wear is typical on old gearboxes. If this pinion is not replaced, the gearbox will inevitably jump out of gear if any load is applied.

The primary drive was 'standard British' design and presented no real problems. New clutch plates, springs and shock absorber rubbers were fitted.

Triumph unit 650cc twin, which went straight in and should be reliable.

The cylinder head was reconditioned with new valves and guides. The head was heated up in the oven to enable the old guides to be driven out and the new guides, which had been put in the freezer overnight, to be driven in easily. The head nuts are particularly awkward to get at on the timing side as they sit under the rocker box platform and can only be accessed with a slim ring spanner.

The carburettor was in good condition and was refurbished with a new needle, jets and gaskets.

The head nuts are really inaccessible on the timing side, as they are tucked away under the rocker cover platform. Use of a slim ring spanner is recommended.

The Amal Monobloc carburettor was rebuilt with a new slide, needle and jets. Fitting was a bit tight between it and the position of the new ignition switch, but worked in practice.

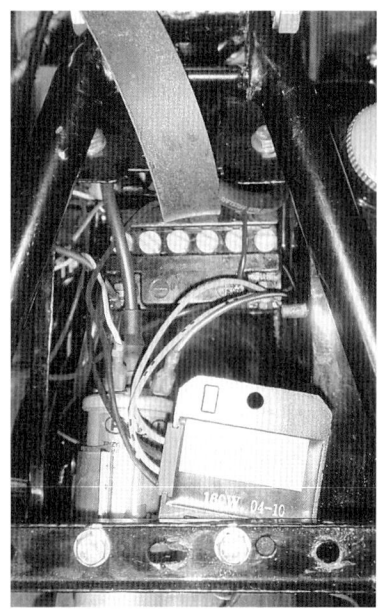

ABOVE: An original competition model fuel tank was sourced on eBay. It was in a bit of a state, with worn chrome and several dents.

LEFT: The majority of the electrics were fitted under the seat. The Podtronics rectifier/voltage regulator is visible next to the coil.

The electrics presented no real problems. Using the standard corporate BSA/Triumph wiring colours, I built up a wiring harness from scratch using the almost complete bike as a jig. All connectors (bullet and spade) were soldered. The use of a Podtronics combined rectifier and regulator enabled the wiring to be considerably simplified; the addition of a small 12V battery will hopefully give reliable starting. A new coil was fitted under the seat alongside the Podtronics box. The standard points ignition was retained, as no electronic ignition units were available for the distributor equipped bikes at the time of writing. The 6in headlight had a Bates type unit fitted that took halogen bulbs. The rear had provision for stop and tail, and a pattern Japanese stoplight switch was fitted to an alloy bracket that was pop-riveted to the chain guard.

The final part of the jigsaw was a fuel tank. While I could have bought a modern alloy tank from various pre-65 trials specialists, I eventually turned up a genuine C15T tank on eBay.

It was in pretty bad condition, with worn chrome and several dents. Rather than sending it away for a proper restoration and rechroming, which would have blown my budget, I used plastic filler to get rid of the worst of the dents and then sprayed it myself using aerosol car paint.

Wedgwood Blue (Colour Match Blue-33 CC YAF163), available from all good autofactors, was a good match for the original blue used and the results are, in my opinion, not too bad! Time will tell if the tank can handle the vibration without the filler coming out.

The end of the restoration was arrived at with the fitting of the tank – the bike was now ready to roll. It has only covered a few miles to date, but is shaping up well. The bike is quite small, much smaller than my T25SS, and is a bit dwarfed by me. It is, however, comfortable to ride and handles well on both the road and the rough. All in all, I am pleased with the bike, and its soft, docile engine, with plenty of low down torque, is in marked contrast to the T25SS.

ABOVE: *The finished project looks good. Noticeable is the slightly long roadster rear subframe and a prop stand that could do with being an inch longer.*

BELOW: *The side panel is held on by two chromed screws that can be difficult to refit. A BSA piled arms transfer provides a finishing touch.*

Finished at last – the author and his completed project.

171

Bibliography

Bacon, Roy, *BSA Buyer's Guide* (Niton Publishing, 1990, ISBN 0 9514204 1 0)

This contains a useful chapter on the unit singles. It also details engine and frame number prefixes and other range-specific details.

Bacon, Roy, *BSA Gold Star and Other Singles* (Niton Publishing, 1991, ISBN 1 85579 012 2)

An excellent history of all the BSA post-war singles, covering the pre-unit singles as well as the unit singles.

Bacon, Roy, *BSA Singles Restoration* (Niton Publishing, 2000, ISBN 1 85579 023 8)

This book contains many original works photos and illustrations, but is rather mixed up between the individual models in the pre-unit and unit singles, so it can be hard to concentrate on a single model.

Bacon, Roy, *BSA Unit Singles, C15 to B50, 1958–1973* (Niton Publishing, 1990, ISBN 0 9514204 8 8)

Apart from the Brooklands BSA Singles book, this is the only book solely dedicated to the BSA unit singles. One of the Motorcycle Monograph range, it is a good but short book on the unit singles.

Bacon, Roy, *Triumph Singles* (Niton Publishing, 1991, reprinted 1997, ISBN 1 85579 009 2)

An excellent history of all the Triumph post-war singles, covering the Tiger Cub, Tigress and Tina scooters as well as the BSA-derived unit singles.

Clarke, R. M., *BSA Singles Gold Portfolio 1945–1963* (Brooklands Books, ISBN 1 85520 441X) and *BSA Singles Gold Portfolio 1964–1974*, Brooklands Books, ISBN 1 85520 4428)

Compilations of contemporary road tests of BSA singles from the UK and US.

Holliday, Bob, *The Story of BSA Motor Cycles* (Patrick Stephens Ltd, 1978, ISBN 0 85059 277 1)

A good history of the BSA motorcycles. It tends to concentrate more on the models up to the 1950s.

Hopwood, Bert, *Whatever Happened to the British Motorcycle Industry* (Haynes Publishing, 1998, ISBN 1 85960 427 7)

This is the definitive account of the British motorcycle industry, based on the author's experiences of working for most of the major manufacturers, including BSA, from the 1930s through to the 1970s.

Ryderson, Barry, *The Giants of Small Heath* (Haynes Publishing Group, 1980, ISBN 0 85429 255 1)

A complete history of BSA from its formation to demise.

Vanhouse, Norman, *BSA Competition History* (Haynes Publishing Group, 1998, ISBN 1 85960 430 7)

The book provides a detailed account of BSA's competition success and failures, from the start of motorcycle production to the 1970s Triples.

Wilson, Steve, *BSA Motor Cycles since 1950* (Patrick Stephens Ltd, 1997, ISBN 1 85260 572 3)

This is a re-print of the BSA section of Steve Wilson's six-part 'British Motorcycles Since 1950', and is a valuable reference source, as well as being a good read.

Wright, Owen, *BSA – The Complete Story* (The Crowood Press Ltd, 1992, ISBN 1 86126 064 4)

This volume is a good, comprehensive history of BSA from its formation in 1855 to the end in the 1970s.

Sundry BSA literature, such as brochures and workshop manuals, is available through specialized booksellers and autojumble traders. Photocopies of parts books and workshop manuals are available from Bruce Main Smith & Company (BMS), and other vendors are also producing CDs containing scanned in copies of original BSA factory manuals.

Index